ELITES AND POWER IN BRITISH SOCIETY

Cambridge studies in sociology

Cambridge papers in sociology

ELITES AND POWER IN BRITISH SOCIETY

EDITED BY

PHILIP STANWORTH

Research Officer, Department of Applied Economics
University of Cambridge

ANTHONY GIDDENS

Fellow of King's College and Lecturer in Sociology
University of Cambridge

CAMBRIDGE UNIVERSITY PRESS

Published by the Syndics of the Cambridge University Press
Bentley House, 200 Euston Road, London NW1 2DB
American Branch: 32 East 57th Street, New York, N.Y. 10022

© Cambridge University Press 1974

Library of Congress Catalogue Card Number: 73–92788

ISBNs:

0 521 20441 0   hard covers
0 521 09853 X   paperback

First published 1974

Printed in Great Britain
at the University Printing House, Cambridge
(Brooke Crutchley, University Printer)

Contents

Acknowledgements

All the papers which appear in this book, with the exception of the first, were presented at a working conference held at King's College, Cambridge, in March 1973, and sponsored by the Nuffield Foundation. On their own behalf, and on behalf of the authors represented in the volume, the editors wish to thank Pat Thomas and David Yonge, of the Nuffield Foundation, for their help in staging the conference and their participation in it. Special thanks are also due to: those who acted as discussants, Jean Floud, John Goldthorpe, Theo Nichols, John Dunn, Harold Perkin, Michael Wolfson, David Lockwood, and Tom Bottomore; to Chris Otley for contributing a paper on 'The educational background of British Army Officers' which has since appeared in *Sociology*, Volume 7, No. 2, May 1973, but is not included in the present collection; to Bruce Headey who delivered a paper on cabinet ministers which is now part of his book, *The Job of Cabinet Minister* (Allen and Unwin, 1974); and to Ali Rattansi for managing to commit to paper the gist of discussions which were perhaps not always at the highest level of coherence. The article reprinted as the first chapter of the book, 'Elites in the British class structure', is included by way of providing a theoretical discussion of issues relevant to most of the papers delivered at the conference. Its author initially undertook to write a theoretical introduction to the present volume, but since it became clear that this would tend to retrace the exposition first set out in that article, it seemed both simpler and more effective to reproduce the original. Thanks are due to the editors of *The Sociological Review* for their permission to reprint; and to Professor W. B. Reddaway, editor of *The Economic Journal*, for allowing us to include the paper by C. D. Harbury and P. C. McMahon, which was published in Vol. 83, September 1973.

ANTHONY GIDDENS
PHILIP STANWORTH

[vii]

List of contributors

Anthony Giddens   *University of Cambridge*

W. L. Guttsman   *University of East Anglia*

C. D. Harbury   *City University*

Christopher J. Hewitt   *University of Maryland*

R. K. Kelsall   *University of Sheffield*

P. C. McMahon   *University of Birmingham*

Ray Pahl   *University of Kent*

John Rex   *University of Warwick*

W. D. Rubinstein   *Johns Hopkins University*

Philip Stanworth   *University of Cambridge*

Kenneth Thompson   *The Open University*

Frances Wakeford   *University of Lancaster*

John Wakeford   *University of Lancaster*

Richard Whitley   *Manchester School of Business Studies*

J. T. Winkler   *Imperial College, London*

Preface

This volume is devoted to an initial exploration of what, remarkably, is almost uncharted territory. While there have been a few studies of elite groups in British society, this part of the sociological landscape has mostly remained a desert visited only by a few itinerant travellers who have strayed, almost by chance it seems, from the well-trodden paths of British sociology.[1] In this very brief introductory conspectus, I shall not attempt to account for this situation, which I certainly believe is bound up with the specific development of British society itself, but shall rather attempt to suggest how we might begin to remedy it. The remedy involves, first and foremost, empirical research. But this, of course, implies the formulation of theory.

The theoretical literature dealing with elites and power, to alter the imagery employed above, wallows in a sea of ineffable confusion – a situation which results from variation in terminological convention, conceptual ambiguity, and profound divergencies in the theoretical stand-points of different authors. Most of these have their origins in the clash between 'elite theory', as first expressed in the writings of Pareto and Mosca, and 'class theory', particularly as formulated by Marxist writers. If Pareto, like Mosca, accepted aspects of Marx's analysis of the class struggle as, in the former's words, 'profoundly true', in adapting that notion to his own purposes he wrenched it out of the scheme of development in which Marx had placed it. Pareto looked to history in order to demonstrate that the mutability of events, the rise and decline of ruling groups, and even of overall civilisations, conceals the cyclical play of unchanging elements. In so doing, he tended to assimilate the terms 'elite' and '(ruling) class'; more significantly, the notion of 'governing class' – like that of 'political class' – substitutes what is essentially a political division, concerning those who rule and those who are ruled (the 'mass'), for the Marxian concept of class as founded in relationships of production. The confusion between the concepts of class and elite theory has since then been compounded by the introduction of such notions as 'power elite', 'ruling elite', etc., without clear indication of how they relate to the more traditionally established vocabulary of class.

The concept of class, in common with that of elite, has been endowed with a variety of shades of meaning. In its Marxian connotation, however,

[ix]

and in the writings of those influenced by Marx but not accepting his views in their entirety, class is necessarily a phenomenon expressing connection between the economic order and other institutions in society. In the Marxian scheme of things, the vital factor involved in these connections is private property, and most of those who have attempted to overhaul Marx's own ideas have not deviated very far from their emphasis, even if (like Max Weber) they have wished to allow room for market relationships that do not directly involve property ownership. From this standpoint, the advanced societies, in the West at least, constitute 'class societies': class differentiation is conceived to be a major, or the major, axis around which the society is ordered. While it is not at all true that the progenitors of elite theory neglected the significance of property in the modern order, it can quite readily be seen that, since its characteristic emphasis is political rather than economic, those who have made the notion of elite the centre-point of their works have tended to produce a distinctly different portrayal of contemporary society. The elite concept has in fact been used to support two (internally opposed) interpretations of the nature of the advanced societies. One is that favoured by the early elite theorists, involving a differentiation between a governing elite, who manipulate democratic ideals to support their dominant position, and the mass of the population who, any appearances to the contrary, do not participate in the processes whereby they are ruled. That such a conception of 'mass society' is not inevitably linked to any sort of conservative posture is indicated by its adoption by Mills to launch his acerbic examination of the American social and political system. But the concept of elite has been used by other authors to bolster precisely the sort of interpretation of modern society at which Mill's attack is aimed. According to this viewpoint, developed by Riesman, Dahl, Keller and many other recent American authors, the class society of nineteenth century capitalism has in the twentieth century become eroded by a series of social changes leading to an overall diversification of the social structure. At the higher levels of society, this has led to the replacement of the old ruling class by a plurality of elites. Such elites, it is held, have only limited spheres of influence, and the competition between them ensures that they do not come together to form a coherent class of 'power elite' set off from the rest of society.

It is clear that there are genuine, and very substantial, differences between these various views, but the terminological and conceptual ambiguities that have attended their discussion have made it difficult to drag these into the clear light of day. While it would be sophistry to pretend that the problems at issue here can be easily resolved, it is surely possible to set them out in terms which avoid the irregularities of much current usage. Thus Bottomore has written, contrasting the concepts of class and elite theory: 'While on one level they may be totally opposed, as elements in wide-ranging theories which interpret political life, and especially the future possibilities of political organisation, in very different way, on another level they may be seen as complementary concepts, which refer to different types of political system or to different aspects of the same political system. With their help we can attempt to distinguish between societies in which there is a ruling class, and at the same time elites which represent particular aspects of its interests; societies in which there is no ruling class, but a political elite which founds its power upon the control of the administration, or upon military force, rather than upon property ownership and inheritance; and societies in which there exists a multiplicity of elites among which no cohesive and enduring group of powerful individuals or families seems to be discoverable at all.'[2]

As described in 'Elites in the British class structure', I believe that it is possible to establish a series of conceptual distinctions that allow us to delineate some of the possibilities indicated in the foregoing passage. It seems fruitful to abandon the idea that use of the vocabulary of class theory is necessarily incompatible with that of elite theory; but this involves making a clear division between the two central notions, class and elite, and avoiding using such terms as 'ruling class' as (more or less) synonymous with 'power elite', 'ruling elite', etc. I have suggested elsewhere[3] that two main sets of problems confront class theory: those concerned with class *structuration* – that is to say, the identification of the factors that create definite types of social formation on the basis of differences in market relationships; and those relating to the *mediation* of economic and political power – that is to say, the identification of the modes in which possession of economic resources can be, and is, mobilised to pursue political ends, and vice versa. The notion of elite, appropriately defined (see below, p. 4) is important to both of these. Elites may be regarded as fundamental to the structuration of the upper class (in a class society); and what I refer to below as the 'hierarchy' of elite groups is one principal medium whereby the translation of economic into political power, or the reverse, is effected. Hence to discern, in any given society, the existence of an 'upper class' whose position is founded upon privileged access to private property, should be considered not as the conclusion but the starting point of analysis of the system of power that pertains in that society. In order to demonstrate how this class is a *ruling* class, it is necessary to specify the modes in which its economic hegemony is translated into political domination: which means examining, among other things, processes of recruitment to elite positions in the major institutional spheres, the relations between economic, political and other elites, and the use of effective power to further definite class interests.

The essays included in this book, of course, do not by any means all conform to the usages which I have suggested. The reader will find considerable variation among the authors represented here in the use of the term 'elite', as well as pronounced disagreements about how best to study elites and what the results of such study demonstrate about British society. But at least some such disagreements, I would argue, rest upon a false, or at least one-sided, perception of the problems under debate. I shall mention only two of these problems here. One is partly methodological in character; the other is more directly concerned with analysing the connections between elites, class and power. The methodological issue, which is of some relevance to virtually every paper in the book, turns upon the significance of studying processes of recruitment to elite positions. Many of the papers provide documentation, for example, of the extraordinary near-monopoly exerted by the public schools in general, the influence of the Clarendon schools in particular, and of Eton especially, over elite recruitment in this country. But so what? Inequality, entrenched privilege are certainly manifest in these statistics, but of what relevance are such findings to any sort of *system of power*? For as Kelsall, Pahl and Winkler and other contributors point out, we are surely not justified in making direct inferences from the social background, or even the educational experience, of elite groups to the ways in which they employ whatever power they possess once they attain positions of eminence. Because a man emanates from a specific type of class background, it does not inevitably follow that he will later adopt policies which are designed to promote class interests corresponding to that background. From this it seems to follow, as Pahl and Winkler in particular advocate, that elite studies must move away from concern with processes of mobility and recruitment, towards the direct study of the ethos and action of elite groups. I think this is right. But it is mistaken to suppose that there is some kind of opposition between these two types of approaches as, for example, the controversy between some American authors over so-called 'positional' versus 'decision-making' studies has tended to imply. This is a false antithesis. Studies of recruitment are important and necessary because, since they document the differential distribution of life-chances, they analyse a key link between elites and the class structure. This is a basic aspect of what, as Rex notes, I have called the 'institutional mediation of power': the form of state and economy whereby life-chances are *reproduced* (or modified) across the generations. Like him, I think it essential that the study of elites is not detached from the analysis of class structure. But, partly in order to accommodate the sort of problem that Pahl and Winkler point to, it is also important to recognise that such analysis must be complemented by examination of what I have labelled the 'mediation of control': that is to say, the actual use of power, and conflicts over power, among the members of elite groups. If the latter is treated in isolation, the result is a trivialisation of research, which becomes simply concerned with 'decision-making' – taking the social, economic and cultural structures within which decisions are framed for granted, and thus ignoring the 'hidden face of power'.[4]

But if the first of these is dealt with in isolation from the second, the tendency is to slip into the practice of making immediate, and illegitimate, inferences from position to action.

This leads me to the second of the issues which I wish to touch upon, concerning the hypothesis of the 'ruling elite', or what C. Wright Mills has called the 'power elite' – a matter which Hewitt takes up in some detail in his paper in this volume. I do not wish to suggest that Hewitt himself commits the errors I shall draw attention to; but certainly many other writers have done so in the past. One such error is an expression of the conceptual misunderstandings which have dogged class and elite theory: the identification of 'ruling elite' (meaning a cohesive, power-wielding group, which is consistently able to sway others to its opinions) with 'ruling class'. If we are able to discredit the existence of an elite distinguished by Meisel's three Cs – group consciousness, coherence, and conspiracy – then, so it appears, we have made a damaging hole not only in Mills' ideas, but also in more orthodox Marxian theory.[5] In fact, the Marxian notion depends upon both more and less than this: more, because it supposes a definite institutional mediation of power, i.e. a definite alignment of state and economy, involving the central role of private property; less, because it does not necessarily involve assuming the existence of an internally cohesive and all-powerful ruling elite. This latter idea I regard as a pernicious one, even if it can claim some reputable ancestry in the writings of both the classical elite theorists and of Mills. For the sort of unified, conspiratorial elite which Mills portrays, in spite of the qualifications he makes, has never existed, in American society or anywhere else. To suppose that this is a realistic model merely generates, and has generated, false problems and empty controversies. It certainly is desirable and necessary to attempt to examine the degree of cohesiveness of elite groups, in terms of their social and moral integration, but it is wholly misleading to measure these against the 'three Cs' model – or, at least, it should be recognised that this is no more than a pure type, a limiting case.

Any critic will readily discern that the contributions which appear below do not add up to anything like a comprehensive account of elites in British society. But they do, I believe, contain important guidelines for future research. In my opinion, it is essential that such research be interpreted against the backdrop of general problems of classes and the state; in this way it can help to further our understanding not only of the specific characteristics of the society in which we live, but will in addition serve to contribute to the continuing debate over the development and contemporary nature of the advanced societies as a whole.

ANTHONY GIDDENS

1   Elites in the British class structure

Over the past two decades, sociologists in this country have given a great deal of attention to studies of the manual working class, and to the 'new' middle class, but they have paid much less heed to the upper echelons of the class structure. The dearth is a striking one because there are various reasons why the upper sectors of the British class structure – and the changes which may have occurred, and be occurring there – are of particular interest in sociology. In the first place, on the general level, the study of social class has always been closely linked to the analysis of 'power' or 'domination'; and this is an area which can hardly be adequately understood if only one side of the coin is examined – the 'subordinate' classes. Secondly, and more specifically, the fate of the British 'ruling class' is of special significance historically and sociologically, since Britain was the 'cradle of the Industrial Revolution', and the first 'industrial society' the world has known. In spite of the lead which it assumed in this regard in the nineteenth century, Britain did not, of course, experience the forms of revolutionary outbreak against the existing order which were such an evident feature of the modern history of such nations as France and Germany. Consequently, if there is still today a distinguishable 'ruling class' in Britain, it has enjoyed a continuity and a record of successful accommodation to change which is unrivalled.

While these matters have been little studied by sociologists,[1] there is no shortage of apparently authoritative pronouncements about them. It seems to be widely accepted – except by Marxist authors – that there has actually been a decisive transformation in the upper levels of the British class structure in the course of the present century. This supposed transformation is usually portrayed as part of a generalised process of 'decomposition' of class relationships as they existed (or are thought to have existed) in nineteenth century capitalism. One pole of this argument concerns the lower levels of the class structure, whereby the 'traditional' working class is presumed to have become internally fragmented or diversified, and the boundaries separating it from the white collar 'middle class' blurred or dissolved altogether. In the shape of the thesis of 'embourgeoisement', this has recently been the subject of a well-known study, and no direct analysis of it is required here.[2] But the themes involved in the debate over embourgeoisement are closely echoed in assertions concerning the supposed

dissolution of class boundaries 'at the top'. In common with the embourgeoisement discussion, the issues involved here have their origin in
writings of a political character as well as in more academic sociological
works, and were evoked in relation to the electoral setbacks suffered by the
Labour Party in the 1950s. Thus Crosland and other Labour 'revisionists'
argued that the defeats of the Party could not be taken as mere transitory
losses, but were indicative of fundamental changes which have eroded the
traditional class structure – at all levels. As regards the upper echelons,
what has occurred is nothing less than the disappearance of the old 'class
enemy': the 'capitalist ruling class'. According to Crosland, it is 'rather
absurd to speak now of a capitalist ruling class'.[3]

In more general writings in academic sociology, of course, the decomposition thesis has been advanced as one major component of the critical
rejection of Marxism. All such critics are agreed that the evolution of
capitalism has not followed the route Marx anticipated, towards a
'simplified' class system, 'polarised' between capital and wage-labour.
Most hold, as Crosland argues, that the 'ruling class' which Marx
(correctly) identified in nineteenth-century capitalism, has today disappeared or become radically changed; and most are in accord that it is
the expansion of the joint-stock company, with its attendant progressive
separation of capital 'ownership' from managerial 'control', which is at
least one primary factor which has undercut the position of the old ruling
class. But from then on authors part company. Within the veritable welter
of theories which have been developed, however, two stand out. The first –
the decomposition thesis – holds the view that the ruling class has ceded
place to a more amorphous and differentiated set of 'leadership groups':
this is the sort of position taken by the many variants of the theory of
'pluralist democracy'. The other view, which, however, finds few adherents
today, asserts that, while the 'capitalist ruling class' has disappeared, its
place has been taken by a new form of 'ruling class' – such as Burnham's
'managerial class'. This is a theory of 'class succession' rather than
decomposition.

Discussion of these conflicting views, although plentiful, has been
severely hampered by conceptual confusions and ambiguities. No field of
sociology has been more subject to vagaries of usage and to nebulous and
shifting conceptualisations. Terms are legion: 'ruling class', 'upper class',
'governing class', 'political class', 'elite', 'power elite', and 'leadership
group' vie with each other for supremacy in the literature. Sometimes they
are applied as synonyms, sometimes they are deliberately opposed to one
another. In some cases terminological usage is merely careless; in other
instances terminological variations conceal ambiguities in conceptual
formulation. No-one, of course, can legislate upon the use of terminology,
and there will be no attempt to do so here. But is the principal objective of
this paper to examine and isolate some of the conceptual distinctions, as

well as the methodological issues, which have to be analysed if the decomposition, or class succession, theses are to be studied in a systematic
way. Attention will be concentrated here mainly upon the former rather
than the latter.

As used by Marx, the conception of the 'ruling class'[4] entails the dependence of political power upon economic control: the class which is
economically dominant also holds the reins of political power. This
theorem was questioned, of course, by most of the early 'elite theorists'
writing at about the turn of the century. For Pareto and Mosca the division
of society into 'elites' and 'non-elites' is most significant as a specifically
political differentiation;[5] hence their preference for concepts such as 'governing class' and 'political class'. This is one principal source of confusion
in the subsequent literature, which has drawn heavily upon both traditions,
because not only does this latter usage of the term 'class' imply a separation between the 'economic' and 'political' spheres, according primacy to
the latter – both of which emphases are missing in the Marxian conception – but it is not always clear, in the language of the elite theorists,
whether 'class' refers to a grouping from which those occupying 'elite'
positions are drawn or recruited, or only to those actually *in* those positions
at any one point of time.[6] In the writings of those who have advocated one
or another version of the decomposition thesis, related confusions and
difficulties appear.

   If these issues are to be clarified we must formulate a series of conceptual
distinctions which are either not adequately made, or which remain latent,
in the writings of Marx, the elite theorists, and later authors. I shall argue
that, although the precise names applied here are of very little consequence, it is useful to be able to distinguish *conceptually* between a
number of distinct structural possibilities involved in the discussion over
the decomposition thesis. Briefly, I shall suggest that we should be able to
recognise – given the distinctions discussed below – that there can exist a
'governing class' without it necessarily being a 'ruling class'; that there
can exist a 'power elite' without there necessarily being either a 'ruling'
or a 'governing class', that there can be a system of 'leadership groups'
which constitutes neither power 'elite', nor 'governing class' or 'ruling
class'; that all of these social formations are compatible with the existence
of an 'upper class'; and finally, that *none* of these categories prejudices the
question of the relative primacy of the 'political' and 'economic' spheres
within the class structure. Before moving on to the discussion of these
concepts, however, it is necessary to specify how the terms 'elite' and
'class' will be used in the subsequent analysis. Both terms, of course
have frequently been applied in the vague and variable fashion which is
apparently generic to the literature on social stratification.

   As often employed, the term 'elite' can apply to those who 'lead' in any social category of social activity: to actors and sportsmen as well as to political or economic leaders. There is, however, an obvious difference between, say, 'leading actors' and 'leading politicians', in that 'leading' in the first case refers to some sort of implicit scale of 'prestige', 'fame' or 'income', whereas the second (although the individuals concerned may be prestigious, famous, or rich, or all three) refers to persons who are at the head of a specifiable social organisation which has an internal authority structure. I propose to use the term 'elite group' here only in this latter sense, to designate those individuals who occupy formally defined positions of authority at the head of a social organisation or institution. The term 'elite' will be used very broadly, to designate either an elite group or a cluster of elite groups. It should be noted that this inclusive definition leaves two problems unsettled. One is where the division between 'elite' and 'non-elite' is to be drawn; because in spite of Dahrendorf's assertions to the contrary,[7] 'authority' normally implies a graded hierarchy of spheres of administrative autonomy – there is not always a clear-cut line between those 'at the top', and those who possess recognised authority but who are not in the 'elite'. The other is the question of the relationship between formally defined authority and 'effective' or 'real' power: the fact that an individual possesses certain formal trappings of authority does not, *ipso facto*, allow us to infer what effective power he wields. It is precisely one of the major objectives of the study of elites to examine the relationship between formal authority and effective power. Each of these questions is taken up further below. The problem of the concept of 'class' is, of course, intrinsically an even more complicated one. A full discussion of the issues raised here, however, would go well beyond the demands of this paper, and its purposes can be served without departing from conventional formulations. Hence the term 'class' is used here in Weber's sense of the term, to refer to an aggregate of individuals who share a common market situation.[8]

There are essentially three primary dimensions involved in the study of elites, as defined above: first, the factors entailed in *recruitment* to elite positions; secondly, the organisation or *structure* of elite groups; and thirdly, the distribution of ('effective') *power*, as exercised by those in elite positions. While these are no doubt elementary distinctions, they appear only rarely to have been clearly made in the existing theoretical literature.[9]

1. *Recruitment*. Recruitment to elite positions may vary in terms of how far it is relatively 'open' to those drawn from a diversity of socio-economic backgrounds, and how far it is 'closed' in favour of those drawn from a privileged class. However, it is not sufficient merely to distinguish the degree of 'openness' or 'closure' in recruitment; we must also study the *channels* whereby such recruitment takes place. Even where recruitment to elite positions is relatively 'closed', there must be certain typical 'avenues' of mobility from within the privileged class.

2. *Structure*. In analysing the structure of elite groups we have to be concerned with their level of both 'social' and 'moral' integration. 'Moral' integration refers to the degree to which those in elite positions share common ideas and a common moral ethos; and to how far they are conscious of an overall solidarity. 'Social' integration concerns the frequency and nature of the social contacts and relationships between elite groups. These may obviously take various forms, including the formation of marriage ties between families of those in elite positions, the existence of personal ties of acquaintance or friendship between those in different elite sectors, and the frequency of direct 'consultative' ties between them. We can normally expect social and moral integration to vary directly with each other, and hence can conflate them and speak of the degree of 'integration' of elite groups. But this is not inevitably the case: it is not impossible, for example, to envisage the existence of a morally homogeneous elite which is nevertheless not a highly integrated social unity. It should also be pointed out that the existence of a low level of social and moral integration between elite groups is not necessarily the same as a situation in which such groups are divided by conflict, since groups may be fragmented or separated from one another without necessarily entering into direct clashes. Normally, however, a low degree of integration between elite groups is likely to be associated with outbreaks of conflict. Here it is evidently important to distinguish between latent conflicts, i.e. conflicts of interest which are not acted upon by those involved; and manifest conflicts, where there is some kind of open struggle between elite groups.

3. *Power*. In dealing with the phenomenon of power, we must differentiate how far power – meaning, again, 'effective' power – is 'diffused' in society, and how far, alternatively, it is 'centralised' in the hands of elite groups; and also what might be called the 'issue-strength' of the power held by those in elite positions. While the former refers to limitations upon elite power deriving from constraints imposed from 'below', the latter concerns how far that power is limited because it can only be exercised in relation to a restricted range of issues. It is often held to be characteristic of modern societies that there are quite narrowly defined limitations upon the areas within which elite groups are able to exercise power (as in Keller's 'strategic elites').[10]

Combining certain of the distinctions indicated by the differentiation between the first two dimensions outlined above, we can first establish a typology of elite formations.

A 'uniform elite' is one which shares the attributes of having a restricted pattern of recruitment and forming a tightly-knit unity. It hardly needs emphasising that this is an abstract formulation, and that the classifications involved are never empirically of an all-or-nothing character. There has never been, even among traditional aristocracies, for example, a completely 'closed' pattern of recruitment; all elites open their ranks in some

FIGURE 1

Recruitment	Open	Closed
High integration	Solidary elite	Uniform elite
Low integration	Abstract elite	Established elite

FIGURE 2

Issue-strength	Broad	Restricted
Centralised power	'Autocratic'	'Oligarchic'
Diffused power	'Hegemonic'	'Democratic'

degree to individuals from the lower orders – and may, as has often been pointed out, enhance their stability thereby. A relatively closed system of recruitment, however, is likely to supply the sort of coherent socialisation process producing a high degree of integration between (and within) elite groups. But there are undoubtedly cases which approximate more closely to what I have called an 'established elite', where there is a relatively closed pattern of recruitment, but where there is only a low level of integration among elite groups. A 'solidary elite', as defined in the classification, might also appear to involve an unlikely combination of elements, since it might seem difficult to attain a high degree of integration among elite groups whose members are drawn from diverse backgrounds. In fact, at least some of the socialist countries seem to fit quite neatly into this category: the Communist Party is the main channel of recruitment into elite positions, and while it provides an avenue of mobility for individuals drawn in substantial proportions from quite lowly backgrounds, at the same time it ensures a high degree of both moral and social integration between elite groups. An 'abstract elite', involving both relatively open recruitment and a low level of integration of elite groups, approximates closely to the picture of some of the Western societies as portrayed in the writings of the 'pluralist' theorists.

Secondly, by combining the two aspects of the distribution of power as possessed by elite groups, we can set up a classification of forms of power-holding. Like the previous typology, this states an abstract combination of possibilities; it goes almost without saying that this is no more than an elementary categorisation of a very complex set of phenomena, and the labels applied here do not exhaust the variety of characteristics which are frequently subsumed under these terms – hence they are put between quotation marks.

The consolidation of power is greatest where it is not restricted to clearly defined limits in terms of its 'lateral' range (broad issue-strength) and where it is concentrated in the hands of the elite, or an elite group within the elite as a whole. Power-holding is 'oligarchic' rather than 'autocratic' where the degree of centralisation of power in the hands of elite groups is high, but where the issue-strength of that power is limited. In the case of 'hegemonic' rule, those in elite positions wield power which, while it is not clearly defined in scope and limited to a restricted range of issues, is shallow: i.e. subject to definite limits from 'below'. A 'democratic' order, in these terms, is one in which the power of elite groups is limited in both respects.

Finally, combining the classification already formulated, we can set out a typology of overall structural forms as follows:

FIGURE 3

	Elite formation	Power-structure
Ruling class	Uniform/Established elite	'Autocratic'/'Oligarchic'
Governing class	Uniform/Established elite	'Hegemonic'/'Democratic'
Power elite	Solidary elite	'Autocratic'/'Oligarchic'
Leadership groups	Abstract elite	'Hegemonic'/'Democratic'

While this allows us to clarify four of the terms previously mentioned – 'ruling class', 'governing class', 'power elite' and 'leadership groups' – it should be emphasised that these partially cross-cut some of the existing usages in the literature. Thus Pareto used the term 'governing class' as a replacement for the Marxian 'ruling class'; in this scheme a 'governing class' is 'one step down' both in terms of elite formation and power-holding, from a 'ruling class'. But while this cuts across some of the traditional conceptions in the field of elite theory, it nevertheless clarifies and explicates some of the relationships which have been obscured by the terminological confusions noted earlier.

In this classification, the 'strongest' case of a ruling class is where a uniform elite wields 'autocratic' power; the weakest is where an established elite holds 'oligarchic' power. Where a closed recruitment pattern is linked with the prevalence of defined restrictions upon the power of elite groups, a governing class exists, but not a ruling class: there is privileged access to elite positions, but the power of elite groups is limited. In this case, 'government' is largely the monopoly of those from a restricted class background; but those who 'govern' – i.e. are in positions of high authority – have quite severe limitations upon their power. It can be said that the existence of either a ruling or a governing class, in this sense, presupposes the existence of an upper class, but the reverse does not necessarily hold. The existence of an upper class depends upon the prevalance of market differentials – in particular, of course, those that derive from concentrated minority ownership of private property – which favour a privileged minority. In practice, in most cases, if there exists a distinguishable upper class in a society, it is clearly likely to supply most of the recruits to elite positions, and thus to form a ruling or governing class.

A governing class borders upon being a ruling class where a uniform elite possesses 'hegemonic' power; and comes closest to being a system of leadership groups where an established elite holds 'democratic' power. Where a governing class involves a combination of an established elite and 'hegemonic' power, it stands close to being a power elite. A power elite is distinguished from a ruling class in terms of pattern of recruitment, as is a governing class from a system of leadership groups. The latter exists where elite groups hold only limited power, and where in addition elite recruitment is relatively open in character.

There is one very important way in which the approach outlined here breaks with some of the traditionally established conceptions in the field. It leaves undefined the question of the relative primacy of the power of any one elite group over others. It has already been suggested previously that this is one of the main sources of confusion in the writings of those influenced by the Marxian concept of the 'ruling class': that it takes for granted the subservience of the 'political' to the 'economic', whereas the reverse is implied in 'classical' elite theory. The scheme offered here leaves these both as open possibilities which have to be examined in concrete research. Hence the term 'political class' is dropped, in favour of the terms 'political elite', 'economic elite', etc.; how far a given political or economic elite forms part of either a ruling or a governing class depends upon criteria established in the classifications outlined above. In determining the relative primacy of elite groups in terms of their possession of power, there are two main factors to be taken into consideration: I shall refer to these as the nature of the *hierarchy* which exists among elite groups, and the *institutional salience* of the forms of social organisation or institution which they head. The first relates closely to one aspect of power distinguished previously: the degree of 'issue-strength' of the power held by elite groups. A hierarchy exists among elite groups when one such group (e.g. the political elite) holds power of greater issue-strength than others, and is therefore able to exert a greater or lesser degree of control over them. 'Institutional salience' refers to the vertical dimension of power: it can be defined as residing in the degree to which a given institution affects the life-chances of the mass of those belonging to it.[11] Thus the institutional salience of the state, or of economic organisations, is very high, and these have rightly been given most prominence in studies of the distribution of power in modern societies. The institutional salience of the Church, on the other hand, has declined considerably in the modern world. The distinction between elite 'hierarchy' and 'institutional salience' is an important one, because it does not follow that those in authority in the most salient institutions are necessarily those who are dominant *within* the elite, or vice versa. Thus if C. Wright Mills is right in his analysis of the power of the military in the United States, this is less because of its institutional salience (which would, however, rise dramatically in time of war) than because of the strong influence which it is able to exert over the political and economic elites.

The classification of relationships outlined above is not a theory, but it provides a conceptual basis for recasting the theoretical suppositions which are involved in the decomposition thesis. Examination of writings on the significance of the separation of ownership and control for the decomposition of the ruling class characteristic of nineteenth-century capitalism, shows that the changes which are presumed to have occurred may be helpfully ranged upon the three basic dimensions outlined in the previous section: elite recruitment, structure and power. First, the emergence of managers as a segment of the economic elite has been held to be associated with changing rates and channels of social mobility. As Dahrendorf has written: '(For managers)...there are two typical patterns of recruitment, and both of them differ radically from those of capitalists and heirs. One of these patterns is the bureaucratic career...More recently, a different pattern has gained increasing importance. Today, a majority of management officials in industrial enterprises have acquired their positions on the strength of some specialised education, and of university degrees...There can be little doubt that both these patterns of recruitment – but in particular the latter – distinguish managerial groups significantly from those of old-style owner-managers as well as new-style mere owners.'[12] This tends to be associated, Dahrendorf asserts, with a tendency towards a more open system of inter-generational mobility: as education becomes more important as a channel of recruitment into managerial occupations, the chances of those from working- or middle-class backgrounds of moving into the economic elite improve.

Secondly, the emergence of the managerial sector is held to introduce an important source of disaggregation, and potentially of conflict, within the economic elite as a whole. The moral solidarity of the old property-owning elite becomes undermined: 'the crucial effect of the separation of ownership and control in industry (is)...that it produces two sets of roles the incumbents of which increasingly move apart in their outlook on and attitudes toward society in general and toward the enterprise in particular'.[13] Much has been made of the supposed implications of this process, particularly by American writers. The 'individualistic', profit-seeking entrepreneur is contrasted with the managerial executive, whose values stress efficiency and productivity rather than profit. Such a difference in ideals and values, it is held, tends to reinforce divergencies in styles of life and social contacts: the 'organisation man' is alien to the traditional entrepreneurial capitalist.[14] This in turn produces a certain conflict of interests, sometimes leading to open struggles, since the pursuit of maximum return upon capital is not always compatible with safeguarding the productivity and security of the corporation. While these arguments are commonplace, they appear to be based upon only a minimal foundation in empirical research – particularly in this country.[15]

Thirdly, of course, as the word 'control' indicates, the separation of ownership and control is held to introduce important shifts in the structure of economic power. Within the large joint-stock companies effective power increasingly devolves into the hands of the managers; the sanctions held by the 'owners' of the enterprise are merely nominal. This process is often considered to be associated, however, with an *increase* in the degree of centralisation of economic power: those who control the very largest companies (where the ratio of managerial dominance is held to be greatest) are thereby able to control, or at least significantly influence, broad areas of industry and the market. But, as has been mentioned previously, quite different conclusions have been drawn by different writers as regards the results of these developments for the 'issue-strength' of the power of the economic elite. The theory of the 'managerial revolution' entails the conclusion that political decisions are directly or indirectly controlled by the economic elite. But the opposite conclusion has also been drawn from the presumed rise of the managerial elite: that while this group may possess 'concentrated' power in the economic sphere itself, their capacity to influence the actions of political leaders has in fact become more limited, in part because the political elite now increasingly extends its control over economic affairs.[16]

The separation of ownership and control is not the only factor which is mentioned in discussions of the decomposition of the old ruling class. Other factors which are frequently invoked include: a general rise in rates of mobility, particularly intergenerational mobility, into elite positions in most institutional spheres; the occurrence of a general process of 'levelling' in pre-existing inequalities in the distribution of wealth and income; and the growth of 'citizenship rights' which have helped to redress the balance of power in favour of those in the lower social classes. Again it is worth pointing out that these refer to different dimensions (potentially) involved in the decomposition of the ruling class. The first, of course, affects the 'openness' of recruitment to elite positions; but it does not necessarily, as is often apparently assumed, have the result of directly producing a fragmentation of elite integration, a point which has been emphasised previously. Whether or not this occurs depends upon the available *avenues* of mobility. If a general process of economic 'levelling' has occurred (which is dubious),[17] this could have various implications, including the eradication of a distinctive 'upper class', and the reinforcement of the separation of ownership and control, if share-holding becomes more widely diffused. Among the various sorts of 'citizenship rights' that have been distinguished,[18] the most important in regard to the decomposition thesis are clearly those concerning rights of organisation in the industrial and political spheres for the mass of the population. The growth of the unions, the expansion in the range of political pressure groups, and the rise of the Labour Party, constitute both potential limitations upon the power of elite groups as well as perhaps actually changing the structure of those elite groups themselves.

All of the above sets of factors have to be examined if we are to consider, in a systematic fashion, the validity of the decomposition – or the class succession – thesis as applied to the social changes which have occurred in Britain since the turn of the century. No-one doubts, of course, that major changes have occurred; but the identification of just what transformations these may have produced in the ruling class demands detailed analysis. It is not the object of this paper to undertake such an analysis, but only to offer a framework within which this might be accomplished in the future. However, it is perhaps worth pointing out that the unitary 'capitalist ruling class' which is mentioned in numerous abstract discussions of the subject, certainly did not exist in nineteenth-century Britain. Through his detailed studies of British society, of course, Marx was well aware of the peculiar characteristics of the British ruling class at the mid-point of the nineteenth century. That class, he wrote, was an 'antiquated compromise', in which, while the aristocracy 'ruled officially', the bourgeoisie ruled 'over all the various spheres of civil society in reality'. The 'antiquated compromise', however, lasted considerably longer than Marx foresaw; the aristocracy, which Marx thought had 'signed its own death-warrant' in virtue of the adventures of the Crimean War, proved to be much more resilient than this in maintaining a strong foothold in the Cabinet, Parliament and Civil Service.[19] The proprietary fortunes and power of the large land-owners remained virtually intact until the end of the Victorian era; and the relatively amicable interpenetration of aristocratic land-owners and wealthy industrialists remains one of the striking facts of British history in the latter half of the nineteenth century.[20] This is important, because it means that the process of decomposition of this ruling class, from about the turn of the century onwards, insofar as it has occurred at all, has taken place as something of a *parallel* (and perhaps conjoined) process to the decline of the land-owning aristocracy and the transformation of the position of the industrialists through the rise of the managerial element, together with the other changes mentioned above.[21]

The analytic scheme developed in the previous section allows us to encompass this as well as other possibilities in evaluating the decomposition thesis. According to the scheme outlined previously, various potential lines of movement can be recognised. If whatever changes have occurred have primarily affected the structure of elite groups through modifying the power relationships in which they stand *vis-à-vis* the rest of the community, we may speak of the replacement of a ruling class by a

FIGURE 4

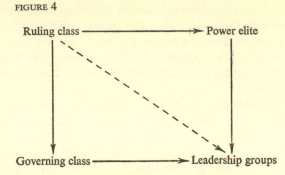

governing class. Where those changes which have come about have altered the structure of elite groups through transforming the patterns and avenues of recruitment to elite positions, the movement is in the direction of the supersession of the ruling class by a power elite. If the process of decomposition has proceeded further, we may conclude that a system of leadership groups has emerged out of a governing class or power elite. If, however, all the relevant sets of changes have occurred simultaneously, it is possible to conceive of an extended, but 'direct' process of movement involving the decomposition of the ruling class into a system of leadership groups (see Figure 4).

Methodological problems

In the first part of this paper I have indicated some principal conceptual distinctions which have to be made if the decomposition thesis is to be evaluated. The objective of this part of the paper is to discuss some of the methodological problems which are raised if research is to be undertaken to explore these dimensions in an empirical fashion in this country.

The initial problem is one which was mentioned above, but not resolved there: the problem of where to draw the 'boundary' defining the limits of elite positions. There are, in fact, two partially separable questions here: that of drawing the 'lateral' boundary separating those elites which are worth including in a systematic study of the decomposition thesis from those which are less significant; and that of specifying the 'horizontal' separation between those positions included as within, and those defined as lying below, the elite. It has to be emphasised that there is an arbitrary element in whatever lines are drawn with respect to each of these divisions. The first depends upon what I have previously referred to as 'institutional salience'. It is evident that, in this regard, the state and the economy are most important: the polity, civil service and judiciary on the one hand, and industrial organisations and trade unions on the other. But it seems advisable to spread the net as widely as possible, in order to include those institutions of declining salience (the Church, and – possibly – the armed forces, may be included in this category), and those of increasing salience (educational organisations and the mass media).

Various techniques have been proposed in previous writings on the subject for reaching an operational discrimination between elite and 'non-elite' positions – such as the so-called 'reputational method'.[22] The difficulty with such methods, at least as they have sometimes been used,[23] is that they tend to take for granted, or obscure, what is supposedly one of the main objects of investigation: the distribution of 'effective' power, as opposed to the 'formal' or apparent structure of authority. The simplest way out of the dilemmas to which this can give rise[24] seems to be to adopt a broad overall definition of 'elite' as referring to positions of higher authority, as has been done in this paper, and to recognise explicitly that it should be a principal endeavour of research to determine how far the distribution of effective power in fact diverges from this. It follows that, while the empirical choice of who is placed inside or outside the 'elite' in any given institution is something of an arbitrary matter, the research itself must examine how far this corresponds to a distinctive set of sociological 'realities' – by attempting to determine the inter-relationships between the three dimensions of recruitment, structure and power distinguished in the first part of the paper.

The scheme set out below provides a suggested portrayal of elite positions in Britain. Three sorts of structure are distinguished. Instead of employing a simple distinction between 'elite' and 'non-elite', a differentiation is made between 'elite', what could be termed a 'secondary structure', and the 'non-elite'. Two types of secondary structure can be distinguished, as shown below. A 'recruitment stratum' represents the 'pool' of individuals from whom those in elite positions are directly drawn. Thus judges are drawn from a 'pool' of barristers. The administrative apparatus of the judiciary – or what may be termed the 'administrative stratum' – is not the source of those who are recruited to the elite. In some cases, on the other hand, as in the army, the recruitment and administrative strata overlap completely. In other examples, such as in industry, the position is much more ambiguous; and it must be one of the objectives of research to determine in such instances the width of the doubly shaded area which appears in Figure 5.

It should also be noted that there may be similar 'overlap' *between* different institutions in terms of both recruitment and administrative strata. In the representation of elites which follows, there is one rather artificial example of this: the civil service occupies a dual place, since it is accorded independent significance in terms of an internal differentiation between 'elite' and 'secondary structure', but it also forms the principal administrative substratum of the political elite. A clearer case of overlap in administrative substrata, however, is to be found in those occupational positions linked both to the army and to a civil service.[25] An example of an

FIGURE 5

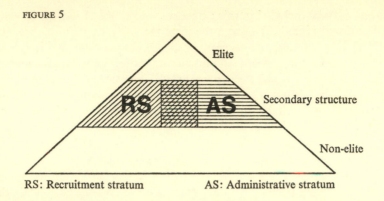

RS: Recruitment stratum   AS: Administrative stratum

important overlap in recruitment substrata is the recruitment of parliamentary candidates from trade union officials.

Problems of empirical analysis and measurement arise in relation to each of the three dimensions distinguished previously. The study of social mobility has been the subject of considerable discussion in the literature and there is no need to recapitulate the main themes of this here.[26] But it might be remarked that there seems to have been an excessive concern with the determination of 'rates' of mobility as compared with 'avenues' of mobility. The measurement of the 'circulation' of elites between the generations, which defines the degree of 'openness' or 'closure' of access to elite groups, is obviously of key importance; but if we do not know what are the channels through which this occurs, it is extremely difficult to interpret the significance of whatever mobility rates are found. There is a definite omission in much of the literature concerned with elite recruitment on this point. It is often assumed that, if it is demonstrated that recruitment to elite positions is becoming relatively 'open', it necessarily follows that this tends to lower the degree of social and moral integration of elite groups. But it may easily be mistaken to make such an inference from data on inter-generational mobility. To show, for example, that a given proportion of the political elite are from upper class backgrounds, or even attended public schools, does not *necessarily* entail that they either share a common moral ethos as elite members, or that they maintain close social contacts with one another. Apart from the fact that the inference that such individuals do manifest a common solidarity may be, technically, a case of the 'ecological fallacy',[27] it serves to direct attention away from the need for research which investigates both the typical stages in the career patterns of those who attain elite positions, as well as the processes of 'socialisation' involved. It may be that certain institutions function as a sort of 'switchboard' in the distribution of individuals to elite positions, and that the socialisation process which occurs there, or the social contacts

FIGURE 6. *Elite groups in Britain*[28]

Institutional category	Elite	Administrative stratum	Recruitment stratum
Polity			
Monarchy	Monarch	Royal household	Royal family
House of Commons	Members of Parliament	(Administrative class civil servants plus	Adopted candidates
House of Lords	'Active' Peers	senior diplomats)	'Passive' Peers
Economy			
One hundred largest industrial firms	Directors		
Large banks, insurance and finance houses	Large shareholders	Senior management	Senior management plus members of other elite groups
Nationalised industry	Board members		
Judiciary	Judges	Court officials	Barristers
Civil service			
Home	Under-Secretary and above	Administrative class civil servants	Administrative class and civil servants
Foreign	Officials, grades 1 and 2	Officials, grade 5 and above	Officials, grade 5 and above
Military	General Officers and equivalent ranks in other Forces	Colonels and above, and equivalent ranks plus senior civil servants	Colonels and above, and equivalent ranks
Trade unions	T.U.C. Council members	Senior union officials	T.U.C. delegates
Church of England	Archbishops and bishops	Assistant bishops, bishops suffragan and senior clerics	Assistant bishops and bishops suffragan
Mass media			
Newspapers, B.B.C. and I.B.A.	Directors and larger shareholders; board members	Editorial staff and senior management	Members of other elite groups
Universities and colleges	Vice-Chancellors; Masters of Oxbridge colleges, headmasters of Clarendon schools	Professors and heads of department	Professors and heads of department

which are formed there, are the crucial media which make access to those positions possible. Thus it may be the case, for example, that Oxford and Cambridge play the key role in influencing access to the higher civil service *regardless of prior class background or prior educational experience*. But the vital role of the two universities in this respect – supposing that this is actually true – is likely to be obscured by the fact that a high proportion of top civil servants can be shown to have attended public schools. The latter is obviously almost bound to be the case, given that a high proportion of Oxford and Cambridge students are drawn from public schools. But it may be that the public schools, as such, play only a minimal role in determining access to elite positions, as compared to the part played in this process by the universities.

A further factor which is possibly of considerable importance is that of 'occupational socialisation'. Research upon the connections between inter- and intra-generational mobility indicates that what is most significant in determining the career chances of an individual is the occupation he attains on his initial entry to the labour market.[29] Thus it may be that early career experience is the most important 'switchboard' controlling eventual entry into elite positions. The distinction between the two types of secondary structure is likely to be relevant here. Where the recruitment and administrative strata are the same, or overlap heavily, a process of bureaucratic selection is likely to determine recruitment to elite positions; advancement to the 'top' takes place within the organisation, and hence the manifest possession of technical skill and expertise will tend to be a primary criterion of mobility. Where, on the other hand, the recruitment and administrative strata are separate from one another, or only overlap marginally, the criteria used in the selection of elite members are likely to be (at least formally; not necessarily substantively) less clearly defined, and will tend to place emphasis upon generalised qualities of 'character', or possibly upon 'ascribed' rather than 'achieved' characteristics. Certainly there have been all too few studies of the role of occupational socialisation in influencing the process of elite recruitment and in consolidating – or fragmenting – elite solidarity.[30]

The 'circulation' of elites between the generations is only one sense in which the term 'elite circulation' has been employed in the literature; it has also been used to refer to the interchange or movement of individuals between elite positions themselves. To this can be linked the phenomenon of the multiple holding of elite positions (as in the 'interlocking' of directorships, or where political leaders hold business appointments). Now the investigation of these matters is undoubtedly important and instructive; but it is mistaken to assume that the existence of a high degree of interchange between, or interlocking of, elite positions is, *taken alone*, a sufficient index of the existence of a high degree of social or normative integration among elite groups. But it is just this assumption which has predominated in studies of the subject.[31] It is possible, however, that a marked amount of circulation between elite groups might signify the existence of *conflict* and dissensus rather than the reverse. One has only to consider illustrative cases to see that this may be so: a politician who is at loggerheads with others in his party in the Commons is 'booted upstairs' to the Lords, or is forced to abandon politics in favour of business; a director involved in a clash with shareholders, or with his fellow directors, in one firm, moves to take up a directorship elsewhere. It is, or should be, evident that the significance of observed *rates* of interchange between elite positions can only be properly determined if an attempt is made also to study the *nature* of that interchange. The same point applies to the analysis of the interlocking of elite positions. Much has been made of this also as an index of elite solidarity; but statistical details on the interlocking of positions are again of little value unless the nature of the connections are examined. This is particularly true as regards the operations of power. A man may hold several directorships, but may wield effective power in none of them.[32]

These considerations underline the importance of treating both the structure of elite groups, and the effective power which they wield, as phenomena which have to be investigated directly and in their own right. But the analysis of power relationships is a notoriously difficult matter and warrants some detailed consideration here. The difficulties are partly conceptual, but largely methodological. There have been many recent discussions of the concept of power;[33] but upon examination most of them turn out to be highly repetitive, and it is doubtful whether anyone has offered any brief definition of 'power' which is notably superior to that formulated by Max Weber: that power is 'the probability that one actor within a social relationship will be in a position to carry out his own will despite resistance...'.[34] It has sometimes been remarked that there is no agreement among sociologists as to the concept of power.[35] But this is surely exaggerated; Weber's formulation has actually acquired wide acceptance among secondary writers.

There are, however, several important points which have to be made clear if Weber's definition is to be employed here. The first concerns the problem of power as a 'capacity'. The term *Chancen*, which Weber employed very frequently in his writings,[36] here covers a certain ambiguity. 'Chance', in other words, can denote either 'empirical probability' or 'capacity'; the two are not the same, because the probability that an actor, who has the capacity to 'realise his will' if he wishes to, will in fact do so, may actually be low, since he may not choose to exercise that capacity. It seems important to recognise this possibility, even though it is a source of major difficulty on the methodological level; for it follows that there is no necessary connection between the possession and exercise of power. A second observation which should be made of Weber's definition concerns the connotation of the phrase 'even against the resistance of others'. It would be illegitimate to infer from this that power is only being used when resistance from others has to be overcome. But this assumption is very frequently made, especially where the use of power is presumed to be necessarily linked to the 'exploitation' of those over whom the power is wielded. Thirdly, although this does not figure in Weber's definition, we should recognise that power has both a 'distributive' and a 'collective' aspect. As Parsons has remarked in criticising what he calls the 'zero-sum' conception of power, the 'amount' of power within a social organisation or a society is not a fixed quantity.[37] Power can be 'created' by the formation of new institutional arrangements which deploy resources of men and materials in more effective ways than previously; recognition of this does *not* entail acceptance of Parsons' own definition of power, which treats power solely as a means to realise 'collective goals'.[38] The 'distributive' aspects of power – i.e. the fact that some possess 'more' and others 'less' – is clearly of vital significance in the study of elites.

These qualifications have to be borne in mind when approaching the methodological questions which confront any attempt to analyse power relationships empirically, although certain of them do not so much affect the attempt to 'measure' power as the interpretations which can be placed upon such 'measurement' once it has been undertaken. As has been emphasised throughout this paper, the analysis of power must be clearly distinguished from the possession and exercise of formal authority. Authority may be one 'base'[39] of power, but how far this is the case must be examined directly. Thus what has been called the 'institutional' approach to the study of elite formations,[40] if taken alone, is quite inadequate as a mode of documenting power relationships. Such an approach must be complemented, as Dahl has stressed,[41] by an investigation of the processes whereby policies are forged and 'significant' decisions are taken. But rather than ending, it is here that the difficulties begin. Lockwood has summarised these as follows:

> 'power must not only refer to the capacity to realise one's ends in a conflict situation against the will of others; it must also include the capacity to prevent opposition arising in the first place. We often hear that the study of power should concentrate on the making and taking of important decisions. But in one sense, power is most powerful if the actor can, by manipulation, prevent issues coming to the point of decision at all. Finally, of course, to determine the extent of power, we must know how significant its employment is; in other words, we must know what the goals and objectives of those who actually employ it are.'[42]

The comment is an interesting one, because while it neatly elucidates some of the dilemmas which face the analysis of power relationships, it is also misleading – for reasons which have been mentioned above. Namely: it assumes that the use of power necessarily implies 'opposition' and 'conflict', involving as it does a subtle misrendering of the Weberian definition in the opening sentence. While this is not the case, it is true that the only way in which we can study power as a *capacity*, through decision-taking, is when things in some sense 'go wrong' for the power-holders: the only *index* we have of the 'amount' of power held by the individual or agency in question is to be found in his ability to triumph over opposition.

I have earlier distinguished two aspects of power relationships which are relevant to the analysis of elite formations: the 'lateral' extension of the 'issue-strength', and the 'vertical' extension of the 'centralisation' of power in the hands of elite groups. The first depends upon the internal relationships between elite groups and certainly occupies a major place in the traditional debates in the study of elites. Here we are concerned with the connections which prevail between what Lockwood briefly refers to as the 'making' and the 'taking' of decisions. Decisions are 'taken' by those whose formal position authorises them to do so; but what is important is how far, and in what ways, these decisions are actually 'made' by others who themselves do not possess such authority. Several desiderata for the analysis of this process are given in Lockwood's observations. First, in choosing concrete issues to study it is not desirable merely to select those which eventuate in some clear-cut outcomes: if possible, some effort should be made to examine cases where a potential process of debate or bargaining between individuals or groups is 'blocked' at a relatively early stage. The limitations here are evident, but appear inescapable: the more effectively this is accomplished, the more likely it is that the whole episode will be concealed and thus go unrecorded. Secondly, in cases where issues are studied which eventuate in some definite 'decision', 'success' is not to be defined in terms only of the party which gains the outcome which it endeavours to achieve; in other words, a party may be 'powerful' even though it eventually 'loses'. Thirdly, since 'power' has been defined in terms of the realisation of the objectives of an individual or group, even where these are contested by others, we must obviously attempt to determine what these objectives are. It is only in these terms that it is possible to specify the respective 'interests' of competing parties. The point is a simple one, but it is often ignored in favour of an approach whereby 'interests' are inferred without evidence of the values and aims of the individuals or groups involved – as has conspicuously been the case in much of the literature concerned with the controversy over 'ownership and control'.

How far the materials are available which will allow us to examine concrete issues in a way which conforms to these requirements is, of course, a matter which can only be determined in actual research. It is clear, however, that such research must focus primarily upon the relationship between the political and economic elites, and should seek to isolate cases which relate to both 'directions' in the connection between the 'making' and 'taking' of decisions: where the 'taking' of the relevant decisions is vested in the political elite, but may be subject to influence by the economic elite; and, vice versa, where the authority to effect the policies or decisions in question rests in the hands of the economic elite but where these may be subject to influence from the political sphere.[43] It is important to emphasise, in this regard, that these interactions may centre upon a conflict over the extension or restriction of authority as such, as where the political agency seeks to acquire the legitimate right to intervene in industrial disputes between labour and management, or to operate a system of price controls.[44]

The relationship between the issue-strength and the degree of centralisation of the power of elite groups is one which has to be studied directly since, as has been argued previously, it does not follow automatically that these are correlated; those in the economic elite, for example, may wield a great deal of power both within industry and in other spheres, but still be largely subject to the control of political agencies within the elite as a whole. As in the case of the factor of issue-strength, the degree of centralisation of the power of elite groups can only be assessed through an examination of the mechanics of the processes whereby policies are shaped and decisions reached. One of the main objectives in this sphere, however, must be the assessment of power differentials *within* those groups which have been formally designated as 'elites'. Here again the point at issue concerns the nature of the relationship between the 'making' and the 'taking' of decisions: thus political programmes may have to be ratified by the authority of a parliamentary majority before becoming law, but it seems clear that effective power has increasingly devolved upon the Cabinet, or perhaps particular elements in the Cabinet, and upon certain spheres within the civil service.[45] The difficulties involved in systematic research upon these matters, of course, are among the most severe and intractable of any which have to be faced in the study of elite power. Concealment, subterfuge, but above all probably the ubiquity of informal and personalised relationships and procedures – something which, although no doubt common in the connections between elite groups, is likely to be much more prevalent inside them – create large blank spots which no form of sociological research is likely to penetrate satisfactorily.

As represented in the first part of this paper, the decomposition thesis embodies a statement of a set of changes which are presumed to have transformed the British class structure since the turn of the century. No such hypothesis – or, as I have tried to make clear in this paper, complicated series of hypotheses – can be adequately explored except by the gathering of trend data. In this respect, however, research which might be undertaken in this field shares a handicap which is generic to many other areas of sociological enquiry. A number of social changes are supposed to have taken place over a period of time, such that the present state of affairs is very different from that which existed previously. The difficulty is that not only do we need to undertake sociological research in order to attempt to show how far the present state of affairs is in fact the same as that which is hypothesised, but we cannot even be confident of how far the previous circumstances approximate to what is claimed to have been the case. This is apparent in many discussions of the separation of ownership and control: theories concerning the values, ambitions and attitudes of contemporary managerial executives (about whom rather little of a systematic character is known) are contrasted with those of traditional enterpreneurs (about whom even less is known) and who (therefore) tend to be portrayed in terms of traits borrowed from the 'economic man' of classical economics.[46]

W. L. GUTTSMAN

2 The British political elite and the class structure

In this paper, I shall attempt to present a brief social analysis of the personnel of the British government and of the 'ancient and honourable House of Commons', whose political role is performed not only in Parliament but also in the constituencies, where at least in the past the M.P.s had sunk deep roots and where they occupied positions of prestige and often of great power. The broad outline of such an analysis is today reasonably well known, and references to 'Tory grammar school boys', 'Labour intellectuals' or to 'public relations men' in Parliament belong with floating and disillusioned votes to the stock-in-trade of the political journalist.

A study of the British political elite in relation to the British class structure must also ideally seek to answer some wider questions. It should throw light on some general problems which have interested students of social stratification, notably the factors influencing the process of social mobility and the circulation of elite groups over time. It should help to assess the influence which social milieu, upbringing, education, occupational choice and the career pattern so largely determined by these, have on the political selection or aspirational process. And finally it should throw light on the social cohesion and political efficacy of decision-making groups and on the decision-making process itself.

R. H. Tawney must have thought primarily of the latter aspects when he pointed out that the House of Commons 'included diversity, not only of opinions, but of social status, occupational interest, education, age and political experience. A knowledge of these traits is not a key to unlock all doors but it facilitates a more realistic view of a famous institution...than is possible without it.'[1] And although he referred specifically to the seventeenth-century Parliament the general points of his statement refer to all ages.

At the same time a study of the British political elite, especially if it seeks to follow a historic approach, cannot avoid posing questions about the close connection between those who exercised formal political power, locally or nationally, and the upper strata of British society, the holders of hereditary titles and the members of landed families and all those closely allied to them, who have often been loosely described as *The Establishment* or the *English Ruling Class*.[2] The analysis presented here is inevitably based largely on data previously gathered and presented in published form and reference to the original interpretations is made where appropriate, but I hope that there is nevertheless some novelty in presentation and interpretation.

In taking the membership of the House of Commons and of the Cabinet as my frame of reference I am not suggesting that they, and only they, constitute the British political elite. Nor am I asserting that power in British society is, or was, exercised primarily, or in the last resort, by the holders of political office. To concentrate on the changing composition of Parliament and of the political Executive seems amply justified in heuristic terms. As political institutions they go back even longer than the period here surveyed. Their respective sizes have not changed much over this period.[3] The essential elements in the conduct of parliamentary business have not changed radically over a long period; the principal internal division between opposing parties has been with us for two centuries. The basic elements of the electoral system have also remained unaltered, viz. the constituency as the electoral unit and the principle of simple majorities with a single ballot, and the voting for individual candidates.

On the other hand, the locus of electoral choice has changed radically in sociological and territorial terms. And both have had deep effects on the social background of the elected.[4]

The extent to which we can equate the membership of Parliament with political power and its relationship with the upper class is also dependent on certain institutional and demographic factors. In terms of population, the eighteenth century House of Commons formed a comparatively large part of the total group of those who held positions of power and influence. Namier has estimated that in the middle of the eighteenth century *ca.* 70,000 men came of age annually. With an average number of 50 new entrants into Parliament every year and the restrictions, in terms of wealth, of those who could expect to get them elected, Namier concluded that 'not many men with an enduring will to get there failed to enter the House in which a miracle of seats seems to be performed for every generation'.[5]

Neither was there in the middle of the eighteenth century a strict separation between political office and what we would today term 'Senior Civil Service appointments' while those who occupied positions of command in the Army and the Navy frequently sat in Parliament. The Commander in Chief was expected to be in the House and the Duke of Argyll did not exaggerate when he claimed in 1741 that 'most of [the] flag-officers are in the House of Commons'.[6]

The close links between membership of Parliament and the higher echelons of the bureaucracy or the military establishment, whether contemporaneously or during the complete *cursus honorum* of individuals declined partly with the passing of certain disqualifying legislation in respect of the membership of the House of Commons, partly with the advent of a permanent career Civil Service whose members increasingly owed office to qualification rather than patronage. There remained, however, throughout the nineteenth century, close ties based on social background, upbringing and even kinship, between the members of the political elite formally speaking, and the holders of leading positions in the State, especially in the Armed Services, the Foreign Office and the pro-consular positions throughout the Empire.

Remnants of such ties between the parliamentary elite and those who hold principal public offices outside it still persist in the second half of the twentieth century. We can still observe a movement of men from positions of power outside politics into Parliament and also, though recently apparently on a declining scale, from the political centre to positions on the political periphery.[7] War and the immediate post-war period, saw the creation of new organs of central control which entailed a somewhat higher level of inter-elite movement, at least on a formal plane. In the 1960s this process seems to have slowed down and we have returned to a more normal pattern of recruitment into governmental office and relatively little movement from it into strategic positions outside parliamentary politics.[8]

The (formal) relationship between elite positions outside politics and the political (i.e. parliamentary) elite proper, already sketched out in broad terms, is, however, indicative primarily of the degree to which political status is linked to high social positions outside it. Membership of the House of Commons was and probably still is widely sought as an end in itself and for *affective* reasons – the conferment of prestige and the receipt of deference within the orbit of the local community or on a national level.

Over and above the relationship between Bagehot's 'deferent nation' and the prestige of the politician – whether antedating his accession to Parliament or consequential upon it – we must not overlook the economic significance of both the electoral process and the political parties.

In the eighteenth century and continuing into the second half of the nineteenth century, contests for a seat in the House of Commons, though comparatively rare, did imply expenditure of sizeable amounts of money with (temporary) effects on the electors and permanent ones on the elected. County elections in the eighteenth century might cost up to £30,000 – largely spent on the fetching and entertaining of voters. And even after 1868 expenditure incurred by candidates for their elections, etc., computed on an annual basis was upwards of £500 for boroughs and £1,100 for county constituencies. And subsidies to constituency organisations by sitting members or prospective candidates did not disappear in the Conservative party until after 1948.

A political career thus implied, until the advent of mass party organizations or pressure groups, e.g. trade unions, able to sponsor candidates, the possession of considerable wealth and the deference for it. 'The spirit of the present House of Commons is plutocratic, not aristocratic', Bagehot wrote in 1872. But this has unduly obscured the extent to which a political career conferred *tangible* social and economic benefits. In the eighteenth century and in many respects still for a century or more to come, the desire to enter Parliament was linked strongly to the desire to gain – or maintain – recognition within the social context of the neighbourhood and with society of one's *county*. It could strengthen existing territorial and family connections, produce voting blocs and pressure groups on ministers which could procure offices or titles. Membership of the House of Commons could provide government contracts for merchants, help enclosures for landowners, obtain colonelcies and governorships for officers. The 'unreformed' House of Commons was a vast cousinhood as well as a network based directly on patronage. Of the 166 English peers, 55 exercised patronage or virtual influence in respect of 111 parliamentary seats while a further 56 commoners determined or influenced the elections in another 99 seats.[9] Of the 5,034 M.P.s who sat between 1734 and 1832 3,045 belonged to 922 families and a mere 247 families could claim to have been represented by 1,527 members while 31 families counted on average 12 members apiece.[10]

Territorial connection was still very noticeable a century later and Namier's 'inevitable Parliament Men' were still with us. A comparison of Bateman's analysis of land ownership, carried out on the basis of the Parliamentary returns of 1873, with the membership of the post-1867 House of Commons, suggests that over *one ninth* of the families of squires and large landowners were still represented in the House of Commons, and of 111 landowners with more than 50,000 acres, 59 sat in the 1868 House of Commons.[11]

In the eighteenth as in the twentieth century M.P.s could also claim a lion's share in the award of honours. Of the former group a substantial proportion obtained social advancement while sitting in Parliament or after a parliamentary career and, one imagines, as the result of it except in the case of succession to a title. From his detailed, though formal, analysis of the eighteenth century House of Commons, Judd concluded that 'about *one third* of the representatives died as baronets or peers'.[12]

Between 1901 and 1957 M.P.s received 317 out of a total of 556 peerages awarded and 180 of those ennobled had not held government office. Allowing for those backbenchers who succeeded to a peerage and for those who died as incumbents of a seat it is likely that during this period one private member in five could reckon to receive a peerage at the end of his parliamentary career or occasionally as an inducement thereto.[13] It is unlikely that such an expectancy did not enter into the motivation of men seeking a seat.

The role of the political elite in the process of social mobility, touched on above, raises wider questions about the relationship between changes in class structure and changes in the social composition of Parliament. Attempting an answer, we are faced with the problem that the kind of empirical evidence which we would need for any quantitative assessment is difficult to come by. Numerical data about the size of specific socio-economic groups (e.g. landowners, entrepreneurs, professional men) in the population or about the distribution of wealth for different periods here under review do not really exist until the second half of the nineteenth century and even then the vagaries of enumeration make comparison over time difficult.[14] And before 1868 we are in practice concerned with changes in the composition of the upper classes only. More specifically, the entry of 'new men' into Parliament must be related to the rise of new strata, such as the new industrial entrepreneurs, or alternately, to the ease with which individuals of the 'nouveaux riche' type could expect to be absorbed into the upper class.

On the other side of the question, our knowledge of the personnel of Parliament is unfortunately only on rare occasions sufficiently detailed to enable us to be very precise about the class background of M.P.s or of groupings of them. The difficulty which we experience even with the available data is that they rarely give details of *family* background and that statistics about education and career are not correlated in respect of individuals. Some general hypotheses about the links between 'rising' classes or sections of them and parliamentary groupings exist and others will be attempted here, but the nature of the data is such as to prevent exact correlation. Thus the Marxist analysis of the 'English Revolution of 1640' has sought to go beyond the general propositions of an emerging bourgeoisie and put forward the concept of a 'new class of progressive landowners... thrusting its way forward unhampered by feudal survivals... in the revolution it took over the state...'[15] opposing a group of traditionalists still living – and administering their estates in a feudal manner. Yet the analysis of the Long Parliament found no significant difference in the background of Royalists and Parliamentarians, Royalist families were not more ancient, nor does a medieval background always indicate strong Royalist proclivities. 'The mass of the Royalists were blended from the same background as the rest of the "political nation".'[16]

On the other side of the equation we are faced with the difficulty of accurately measuring social change between Parliaments. In some measure this is due to the lack of sophistication in past attempts at analysis. The absence of sharp breaks in the development of the political system and the rarity of political crises was paralleled by a comparatively high degree of continuity in the tenure of seats and a slow change in the character of party representation. The ideal way of analysing the social composition of successive Parliaments would use the techniques of cohort analysis.[17]

Failing this we can only attempt comparisons over a long period allowing for the inevitable vagaries in the classification used.

Table 1 attempts such a longitudinal study of the House of Commons over two centuries using as a common denominator data about the social, educational and occupational background of M.P.s. Inevitably, comparisons cannot be carried too far, and different factors are salient at different times. In the eighteenth century, when private education of noblemen and of others was common and Public Schools few, the relevance of education at Eton or Westminster is less than 100 years later. An eighteenth-century lawyer is not readily equated with a twentieth-century solicitor and the number of peers' sons must be related to the size of the peerage as well as its social composition. Pitt's peerage creations did not ennoble the un-established, let alone men of no 'family'. At the beginning of this century a peerage was no longer related to the possession of funded and trans-missible wealth, let alone property in land.

Landownership forms obviously one end of the social spectrum of Parliament, and at one time its dominant hue. The M.P. of 'unknown' social origins and the parvenu or self-made man form the other. For the former a political career was 'ascribed', entry into the House of Commons was based on family precedent, territorial possessions including the right to nominate or the prestige in one's county.[18] For the latter it was 'achieved' and might be the outcome of venality, the possession of talent so great as to attract a patron or the sponsorship by party or pressure group.

Diagram A attempts to quantify on a time scale the membership of the House of Commons according to whether M.P.s belong to the traditional strata from which Parliament had previously been recruited or whether we are dealing with new men. The criteria selected vary from period to period and the results are 'indicative' rather than exact. And above all, no attempt has been made to look at the social character of parties in Parliament.

It has generally been held that following on the First Reform Act the entrepreneurial middle class sided more with the Liberals than with the Conservatives and that, conversely, the Tory Party continued to attract a large proportion of the landed gentry. It is unfortunate that the only chronological analysis of the nineteenth century House of Commons which we have – J. A. Thomas' painstaking recording of the economic interests represented by members of the two major parties is for that very reason deficient as a tool for social analysis.[19] We are today more keenly aware of the interrelationship between different forms of wealth and of the ties between landownership and entrepreneurship.[20] Yet the series of figures reproduced in Table 2 are not without significance. They show that commercial and industrial interests are originally much more important in the Liberal than in the Conservative Party, but they also show how the gap narrowed as the century advanced, until, in 1906, they virtually reach parity. Yet the figures also suggest that as late as 1868 landowners and

TABLE 1. *Social composition of the House of Commons, 1640–1970 (social, educational and occupational background of M.P.s) (percentages)*

	'Long' Parliament, 1640–1	1754–90	Pre-1832 (1734–1831)	1841–7	Con. M.P.s		Con. and Lib. 1906	Con. and Lab., average 1918–35	1951	1970
					1874	1885–1905				
Elementary school only	—	—	—	—	—	—	—	25	13	10
Eton (and Westminster)	—	[20]	26.4	—	—	—	13.8	19.6	12.9	10
All public schools	—	—	[34]	—	—	—	38.1	57.3	48.7	47.5
Oxbridge	—	—	—	—	—	—	35.8	15.1	36.2	38.9
All universities	50.7	[40]	19.7	37.9	—	—	—	40.3	51.9	58.8
Aristocrats	—	[20]	—	28.7	[32]	14	—	—	—	—
Gentry	—	—	—	—	[18]	25	21.9	—	5.5	4.0
Army (and Navy)	13.6	10.6	—	—	—	3.5	10.1	—	18.0	19.5
Lawyers	—	6.1	13.9	17.0	[24]	19	20.8	—	13.0	21.0
(Other) professions	—	—	—	—	[24]	31	9.3	43.4	22.0	22.5
Commerce and industry	—	—	—	—	—	—	39.4	—	21.0	13
Manual workers and clerks	—	—	—	—	—	—	1.4	24	—	—

DIAGRAM A. *'Traditional' and 'new' members in the House of Commons*

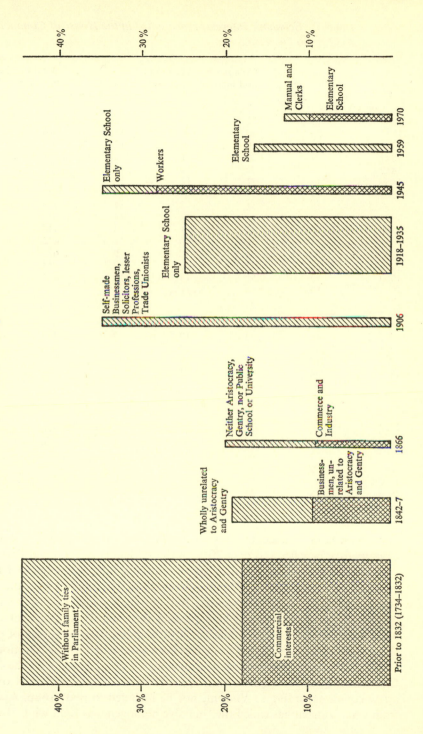

TABLE 2. *Economic interests represented in the House of Commons, 1832–1906 (percentages)*

	Land-owning	Commerce and industry	Legal and professional	Others	Total number of 'interests'
A. Conservatives					
1832	58	22	4	15	211
1837	58	20	10	12	446
1841	59	20	9	12	507
1847	53	23	11	12	481
1852	52	22	12	14	485
1859	50	21	12	17	382
1865	44	33	8	14	447
1868	46	31	9	14	477
1874	36	38	13	13	635
1880	35	42	11	12	446
1885	23	50	16	11	442
1892	24	49	18	9	679
1895	20	52	19	9	833
1900	20	52	18	10	832
1906	17	64	11	8	377
B. Liberals					
1832	50	29	11	9	672
1837	45	32	13	9	488
1841	42	33	13	11	403
1847	38	37	15	9	501
1852	34	39	21	6	505
1859	32	31	29	7	675
1865	28	51	14	7	704
1868	26	50	17	7	756
1874	21	55	19	5	614
1880	20	55	19	6	786
1885	15	57	23	5	640
1892	9	60	27	4	565
1895	9	58	29	4	371
1900	9	58	29	4	372
1906	8	65	23	4	766

those with some landed interest still accounted for about 80 % of the Conservative benches and over 20 % in the Parliamentary Liberal Party.

In the Liberal Party the number of business interests seem to have achieved parity with those of landed property by 1857 and to have drawn ahead rapidly from 1865 onwards. But although under Gladstone the leadership pursued policies which pleased the radicals the mass of the party's parliamentary representatives, not by any means members of old Whig families, did yet belong to or had been assimilated by the traditional strata who as such favoured the maintenance of the *status quo*. Of the 456 Liberals who sat for *English* constituencies between 1859 and 1874 only a few could, according to Vincent, not be included in that group. Apart from what Vincent has called the 'massive homogeneous right wing of the party', composed of landowners (198), officers in the armed forces (122) or relatives of peers (113) a great number of lawyers and business men in the parliamentary party can also, according to him, by upbringing, social ties and outlook be ranked with them. They are 'unmistakably established in Clubland'.[21]

Indeed, real change probably came only later with the rise of party organization at the *local* level and the further shift of electoral power to the working class through the enfranchisement of the householders in the counties and the redistribution from the agricultural to the industrial areas. The social background of the candidates at the General Election of 1910 tells a somewhat different story. Landowners and 'County Gentlemen' numbered only 100 (or 14 %) among the Unionist candidates and only 44 (sic) – or 7.5 % on the Liberal side. The proportion of professional men, on the other hand, was over one-third (35 %) among Conservative candidates and 43 % on the Liberal side. The majority of them were barristers but the lists also include the less prestigious occupations: solicitors (79), engineers (25), teachers (11).

The process of slow social dilution of the political elite emerges fairly clearly from figures about successive recruits to the ranks of the Conservative party in the House of Commons. Arranged in broad social/occupational groups this breakdown is given in Table 3 below.

TABLE 3. *Social structure of parliamentary cohorts: Conservative M.P.s, 1885–1900*[22]

	Percentage breakdown				
	Landed classes	Industry and commerce	Professional public service	Others	N
1885/6 Old	54.8	28.7	15.2	1.4	153
1885 New*	34.1	34.2	26.5	5.1	117
1886 New	36.7	27.5	29.2	6.7	120
1892 New	41.9	32.0	19.6	6.0	81
1895 New	36.0	28.0	24.9	10.9	136
1900 New	28.7	42.5	18.1	10.6	94
Totals	39.6	31.4	22.2	6.6	701

* New refers to M.P.s sitting for the first time.

The clearest instance of a substantial shift in the social background of a parliamentary party can be observed at the time of the General Election of 1918 when the ranks of the Conservative Party underwent a great sea-change. A comparison of the newly elected members with the group of pre-war M.P.s re-elected is given in Table 4 below. It shows the greatly increased share of businessmen and, to a lesser extent, of professional men, thus lending substance to Keynes' bitter jibe about the 'hard-faced men who had done well out of the war'.

TABLE 4. *Social structure of M.P.s elected (new) and re-elected (old) in 1918 General Election*[23]

	Old Nos.	New Nos.	Total Nos.	%
Landed interests	45	12	57	15
Services	34	24	58	15
Professions	67	51	118	31
Business	68	81	149	39
	214	168	382	100

TABLE 5. *The expansion of the electorate, party strength and working class representation in Parliament, 1868–1950*

	Electorate[a] ('000)	% of population[b] enfranchised	Party representation[c] (%) Con.	Lib.	Lab.	Working class (%)
1868–80	2,300	6.9	47	53	—	(—)
1885–1900	5,555	14.6	60	40	—	(1)
1906–10	7,487	16.6	40	53	7	7
1922–4	21,429	48.7	59	14.5	26.5	18.5
1929–50[d]	31,684	65.8	49	4	47	24.5

[a] Wherever possible the average of the electorates at the relevant elections has been taken.
[b] Population at nearest census dates, averaged where appropriate.
[c] Disregarding, if applicable, Irish Nationalists and minor parties, and percentage averaged on elections.
[d] Excluding 1931 because of confused state of parties.

The most significant change in the social character of the parliamentary elite, however, was the one that followed on the rise of class-based political pressure and especially the eventual organization of the working class vote in the Labour Party. This resulted from the extension of the franchise to the male householder which came in 1867 and 1884, but it followed with a considerable delay, especially if comparison is made with the speedier rise of the labour movement in Europe during the same period. It thus paralleled the developments which followed on the reform of 1832. The First Reform Act gave the vote to 'shopkeepers and tradesmen', but as the Whig proponents foresaw and contrary to what its opponents feared, this did not radically change the character of the House of Commons.

Table 5 seeks to relate the changing party composition of Parliament to the widening of the franchise, the rise of the Labour Party and the consequential growth of the proportion of M.P.s of working class origin. It shows in broad trends and global terms how the size of the Labour Party representation expanded in line with these trends. But it also shows how this development followed with a delay of more than a generation from the

TABLE 6. *Percentage of M.P.s with a working class background in the Parliamentary Labour Party*

	% of ex-working class M.P.s	Size of P.L.P.
1918	87	63
1922	71	142
1923	71	191
1924	72	151
1929	60	288
1931	77	52
1935	64	154
1945	43	393
1951	41	295
1955	37	278
1959	37	258
1964	36	317
1966	36	363
1970	27	287

date when the working class may be assumed to have formed the majority of the electorate.

Disraeli's 'leap in the dark' increased the electorate by nearly a million – or 88 % – and the majority of these were working men.[24] In the view of the future Marquis of Salisbury this was bound to turn politics into a 'question between class and class',[25] but this was not to be reflected in Parliament for more than a generation. This delay in the advent of a forceful working class party is as significant a factor in the relationship between class and political representation during the first half of the past century as the increasing correlation between class and party preference is for the period since World War I.[26]

The table also indicates the growing gap between the relative size of the Labour Party representation in Parliament and the percentage of M.P.s with a working class background, so that in a curious way the importance, relative, and lately absolute, of the working class in the political elite declined with the growth of the party claiming more than any other to represent it. For the Conservative Party, despite its 'national' appeal and considerable working-class following has in the past only sent a very small number of men with a working-class background into the House of Commons. Such figures as exist do not show in any one Parliament more than a handful of such M.P.s on the Conservative benches – over the last six elections Conservative M.P.s with a white collar or skilled worker background have numbered between 5 and 7.[27]

That the decline in the proportion of Labour M.P.s with a working class background should occur with the growth of the party's representation in Parliament may be explained in terms of an increase in the party's appeal

TABLE 7. *Occupational background of M.P.s, 1951–70: Conservative and Labour (percentage)*[a]

	1951		1955		1959		1964		1966		1970	
	Con.	Lab.	Con.	Lab.	Con.	Lab.	Con.	Lab.	Con.	Lab.	Con.	Lab.
Armed forces	10.0	0.7	13.7	1.0	9.9	1.2	9.2	0.6	7.5	0.8	7.2	—
Farmers	4.6	0.7	9.0	1.7	10.5	1.2	11.5	0.6	10.7	0.5	9.4	0.3
Professions	30.5	30.8	29.3	34.2	33.1	35.6	36.2	38.2	36.4	40.8	36.1	45.6
Commerce and industry	37.0	12.8	32.6	13.3	33.5	11.2	28.3	12.3	32.0	10.2	32.4	11.8
Politicians and journalists	7.8	13.2	10.5	12.2	10.2	12.4	10.2	10.7	7.5	10.5	12.1	13.2
Workers and white collars	1.5	40.6	1.4	36.7	1.4	37.2	2.3	36.0	3.6	36.1	0.9	27.5
'Private means'	8.4	—	3.2	—	1.1	—	1.3	—	2.0	—	—	—
Others	—	0.2	0.3	0.7	0.3	1.2	1.0	1.6	0.4	1.1	1.2	1.4
Total	321	295	344	278	365	258	304	317	253	363	330	287

[a] Based on statistics in respective Nuffield election surveys but occupations re-grouped to allow for separate enumeration of armed forces, farmers, politicians (political organisers) and *rentiers*.

in less solidly working class areas and the tendency for constituencies of this type to be contested more frequently by middle class candidates. But since 1950 Labour Party representation has fluctuated around a mean of 300 M.P.s, while, as Table 6 attempts to show, the percentage of M.P.s whose occupational background was skilled or semi-skilled manual work or white collar jobs has declined steadily.[28]

The decline of working class representation on the Labour benches has been accompanied by an increase in the professional element in the Parliamentary Party from 31 % in 1951 to 47 % in 1970. Today teachers, not miners, form the largest occupational group among Labour M.P.s.

This trend emerges clearly from the occupational breakdown of the Parliaments elected since 1951 based on the data available in the series of Nuffield election studies given in Table 7.

A summarized analysis only is given but some internal re-adjustment in the categories used there has been made. Thus 'member of the Armed Forces' and 'Chartered Accountants and Secretaries' have been extracted from the 'Professional' group and given separately or incorporated in 'Commerce and Industry'. Also by listing farmers, *rentiers* and politicians/journalists, some of whom, together with officers probably include, on the Conservative side, a fair sprinkling of the traditional strata from which the political

TABLE 8. *Educational background of average House of Commons, 1918–35 and 1951–70*[a]

Education	% 1918–35		% 1951–70	
	Con.	Lab.	Con.	Lab.
Elementary school only	2.5	75.5	1.2	28.3
Grammar school	19.0	15.5	23.2	52.1
Eton	27.5	1.5⎫	75.5	19.6
Other public schools	51.0	7.5⎭		
Oxford University	22.3	3.4	30.6	13.7
Cambridge University	17.0	4.3	22.0	6.4
Other	10.5	10.8	11.0	24.6
Total University educated	49.8	18.5	63.6	44.7

[a] 1918–35 figures derived from Ross, *op. cit.* and 1951–70 from the Nuffield surveys.

elite was recruited in the past, I have tried to create categories which may be a little more meaningful and which also allow for easier comparison between the parties.[29]

They show how the two parliamentary parties are becoming similar in respect of their social background and career pattern. And this emerges very forcefully if we compare the two party groups of M.P.s in respect of their school and university education during the inter-war period on the one hand and for the average House of Commons since 1951.

The similarity between the two 'party' sections of the political elite is even more obvious when we look at its apex, the Cabinet. At the end of its period of office Mr Wilson's Cabinet contained only three men of working-class origin; 80 % of its membership was middle class, a percentage almost identical with that which pertained in the Conservative Cabinet in 1964 except that for the working-class element we must substitute members of the aristocracy.

The development which led to this shift in the social composition of the Cabinet is illustrated in Table 9. It includes the total Cabinet personnel by party (including membership of the coalition governments of World Wars I and II). It shows how the increasing congruence of the two elites is the result of two converging trends: a steep reduction in the aristocratic sector of the Conservative leadership cadres and a more gradual decline in the proportion of working-class office holding in the Labour Party.

Entry into Cabinets has recently been achieved on average 14½ years after entry into the House of Commons,[30] and the Cabinet is bound to represent changes in the social character of the House of Commons, the body from which it is primarily recruited, with some delay. Yet the

TABLE 9. *Class structure of Cabinets according to party, 1916–70 (percentages)*[a]

	1916–35		1935–55		1955–70	
	Con.	Lab.	Con.	Lab.	Con.	Lab.
Aristocracy	35.8	8.8	32.3	2.9	21.0	3.0
Middle class	62.4	35.3	64.5	41.2	79.0	62.0
Working class	1.8	55.9	3.2	55.9	—	35.0
Total (numbers)	53	34	62	34	48	37

[a] For the period prior to 1955 class background has been based on father's occupation or in the case of the aristocracy on the possession of a hereditary title by at least one grandfather. For recent cabinet's 'aristocracy' is similarly defined but otherwise the first known occupation is counted.

DIAGRAM B. *Aristocracy and working class in Cabinets, 1830–1970*

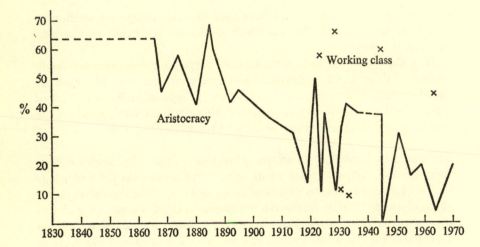

persistence of the aristocratic element, especially in the Conservative Party, is not fully accounted for by this. We are here concerned with a secular trend, illustrated in Diagram B where the number of aristocrats and of members of the working class in successive periods or Cabinets since 1801 is shown as a percentage of the total Cabinet membership. Read in conjunction with the data about the membership of Parliament given above, it is clear that a special selection mechanism is at work in their recruitment, a process which we must ascribe to the influence of social milieu, and the ties of kinship and friendship between members of the leading (and mostly landed) political families, and which at least during the nineteenth century seem to have produced a social inbreeding in political leadership cadres. The prejudices and predilections of Prime Ministers and of their political confidants are clearly at work here.[31]

However, it is difficult to speak in qualitative terms about the operation of social factors at this level over and beyond the figures already adduced: what we badly need is a kinship (and friendship) study of M.P.s and Ministers for the period 1832–1914. Occasionally we get glimpses of social tensions at the leadership level, such as that between J. E. Gorst, M.P. and Party Manager, and the Parliamentary leaders.[32] And it is clearly at the constituency and, eventually, at the grass-roots level that we must increasingly locate the political selection process. If we wish to go beyond those generalizations about the relationship between social class and political elite which are possible on this basis of broad trends over time we must look today as in the past at the politician in the setting of the (local) community and Party organization.

Within the context of this paper we can obviously not look at the evolution of more broadly based party organizations and the extent of party democracy in all its aspects. If, however, we can assume the existence of oligarchic tendencies in local political parties, we can then seek to relate candidate selection to the character of local party leadership. Direct personal influence began to disappear with the extension of the franchise.[33] In its place the constituencies were managed by a caucus the membership of which remained in the second half of the nineteenth century socially restricted even on the Liberal side. Local registration societies would use working men as instruments of propaganda and canvass but 'the vertebrate (sic!) remained a matter of families, firms and estates'.[34] The links between this group and the ward clubs or Liberal Working Mens' clubs was functional but tenuous. The 1860s and 1870s saw a broadening of the basis of organization without increasing the participation in decision-making. The local caucus remained a self-perpetuating oligarchy in social as well as political terms and 'rank within the party corresponded very closely to rank on the Exchange and in Society'.[35]

It is highly significant and relevant for the connection between political elite and class background that even in the more formal structure of party organization of the mid-twentieth century the higher echelons of local parties are markedly more strongly middle class in character than the parties at the grass-roots. Table 10 shows such a differentiation in the social background of two pairs of Conservative and Labour constituency parties in the 1950s analysed in respect of officers, members and supporters. The direct mechanism of candidate selection has so far defied analysis, but we can observe, at least in the Conservative Party, a close correlation between type of constituency and type of candidate. Candidates for safe Conservative constituencies tend to be to a greater extent men with a Public School background and a typical middle class occupational background

TABLE 10. *Social structure of constituency parties: Greenwich*[a] *and Glossop*[b] (*percentages*)

	Conservative						Labour					
	Greenwich			Glossop			Greenwich			Glossop		
	S	M	O	S	M	O	S	M	O	S	M	O
Middle class	6	35	36	27	47	77	1	2	11	5	7	34
White collar	34	32	54	22	14	15	7	9	45	18	17	33
Working class	60	33	9	50	39	8	92	89	44	77	76	3

S = Supporters.   M = Members.   O = Officers.

[a] According to M. Benney *et al.*: *How people vote*, 1956.
[b] According to A. H. Birch: *Small town politics*, 1959.

than those for impregnable seats where a candidature may be in the nature of a 'showing of the flag' and where competition for selection is weak or non-existent.[36]

If we take Public School education as a criterion of (upper) middle-classness we find the following gradations according to the type of constituency and, one would assume, social character of local party leadership.

TABLE 11. *Conservative parliamentary candidates, 1950–66, with Public School education, according to type of constituency (percentages)*[a]

Constituency	
Non-incumbent	
Impregnable	49.4
Marginal	63.1
Incumbent	
Marginal	62.9
Impregnable	80.5
Rural	84.4

[a] Based on Rush, *op. cit.*

This is not to suggest that class is the decisive influence in the selection: it is probable that in the final choice personality and experience and local connections are probably decisive. Rush suggests that social background is not discussed in the selection process but he does not doubt that working through a shared value system and a common frame of reference it constitutes an important influence.[37]

The absence of a reverse process in the selection of Labour Party candidates is equally significant. We saw already that the bourgeoisification of Labour's political elite in the post-1945 period was unrelated to the size of the party's parliamentary representation. An analysis of the selection process clarifies this development further.

TABLE 12.[a] *Labour candidates, 1950–66*

	% of candidates who were: Public School educated	Graduates	Workers
Incumbent C.L.Ps	37.5	68.2	5.7
Non-incumbent C.L.Ps			
Marginal	24.3	53.7	4.9
Impregnable	17.9	42.6	4.9
All	23.0	51.9	16.4

[a] Derived from Rush, *op. cit.* pp. 181, 206, 221.

In the competition for adoption by safe, non-trade union seats the more exclusive or more highly educated appear to have a better chance, and 'mere' workers a smaller opportunity to be selected by winnable constituencies.

And in the group of trade union-sponsored candidates, workers, although still in a majority (82 %) now receive competition from middle class candidates whose ties with the unions which sponsored them may be tenuous.[38]

We might then better understand the process by which an increasingly middle class elite is selected by local Labour Parties, whose membership is mostly predominantly working class, and which nearly everywhere includes a significant minority from affiliated trade unions, if we could relate it to the social character of the constituencies. There does not appear to be, however, a direct correlation here. The dispersal of the solidly working class city centre populations has produced a growing number of constituencies of a more mixed social character where a middle class candidate may attract votes. But as R. W. Johnson has shown, even solidly working class, e.g. mining constituencies, have experienced over the past 15 years a marked decrease in the representation by miners and other manual workers with a corresponding growth of university educated professionals.[39]

Unlike the situation in the Conservative party, where old-established avenues into politics have remained, we find in the Labour Party that the traditional career from a working class start, via office in union or party (often held in conjunction), has significantly declined, and also become further modified, both for sponsored candidates and for the few non-sponsored M.P.s with a skilled worker background. Increasingly, a second career of full-time trade union or party office or a white collar career is interposed between workbench and parliamentary benches.[40]

The concluding section of this paper must clearly seek to ask whether the data presented permit any generalization about the relationship between class and the recruitment to the political elite. It must seek to answer some of the questions posed in the introductory paragraphs about the significance of a political career in the process of individual social mobility, and of the interconnectedness between elevated rank in society and the prominence in politics which manifests itself in the membership of the House of Commons and other positions of political leadership. Finally, it must attempt to offer some explanation for the remarkable phenomenon which we have observed in our discussion of the development of the political elite in the period of a widening popular choice of representation: namely the late, limited, and eventually declining share of the working class element in the parliamentary representation.[41]

Nothing that we deduce from the recruitment pattern of the British political elite leads us to suggest that as an elite group it was in any way superior to other elite groups. The relationship was not hierarchical but, to follow Nadel, one of the extent of conformity and integration.[42] We saw that until fairly recently there was a considerable amount of interconnectedness between political office holding and the membership of landed families, but we must note in passing that a sizeable section of the families of the landed aristocracy never sought a political career either at a time or over the course of several generations.[43] And such present-day evidence as exists does not suggest that M.P.s are held in especially high regard either in terms of the ranking which is accorded to them in comparison with other occupations or in respect of the earnings thought to be appropriate for them.[44]

Entry into the 'Unreformed House of Commons' was on the one hand clearly linked to the *cash nexus* by which a fair number of borough seats might in the eighteenth century be sold like a commodity to the highest bidder (the legal qualification requiring of the prospective M.P. property in land to the tune of at least £600 p.a. was easily circumvented by fictitious transfers), but the number of those who thus bought prestige with the wealth acquired in their generation was small. Prior to 1868 the majority of politicians, actual or prospective, belonged if not to the gentry then at least to the 'pseudo gentry', a group of wealthy but not originally landed individuals, sometimes allied to landowners in commercial dealings and generally accorded social recognition by them.[45] Mercantile interests, such as those connected with the East India Company, were of course based on new sources of wealth but among its beneficiaries were many of established position. The late eighteenth century House of Commons knew a much larger number of men with East Indian interests than the two or three per cent. who could be described as 'nabobs', and who sought a seat in Parliament 'either as a symbol of newly acquired wealth or as safeguard against official enquiries into their conduct'.[46]

The eighteenth century political elite obviously expressed divers interests – of individual M.P.s, their patrons, the government (who may have bribed them) and even of the constituency (e.g. corporation boroughs seeking government favours) but none clashed with the basic interests of the landed and mercantile class who, in Namier's words, were 'primarily concerned with the nation's political business and therefore form[ed] the political nation'.[47]

Given the unrepresentative, proprietory nature of the eighteenth century political system this is not surprising. The reforms of 1832 were to extend further the bases of the interests represented in Parliament. Through the abolition of the rotten boroughs and the extension of the franchise they sought to reconcile the new and influential middle class interests to the constitution.[48] Why then did the social character of the political elite not reflect this? The answer would seem to lie in what recent students of the period have termed the 'deferential political community'.[49]

Admittedly, the 'deference community', composed of those who follow landowners and other local leaders, cannot be neatly divorced from the 'interest community'. Recognition of local leadership and of the protective activities on behalf of the local community undertaken by the local elite goes hand in hand with the representation of economic, social or religious interests.[50] What is remarkable and probably essential to explain the long continuation of political leadership by the landed classes and their appendages is that deference, once based more on the coercive powers of the local leaders, has in later times come to depend more upon voluntary community support. An investigation of the pollbooks for Rochdale showed that the social structure of the support for each party was broadly similar. 'By 1857 the Rochdale Tories included a large part of each class. Since their principle, however, was to ignore this remarkable fact and simply go on supporting the gentry, the Tory party remained in its explicit content and its final purpose, a re-enactment of the days when the local honorific hierarchies really had coercive power.'[51] A century later Birch suggests in his survey of Glossop that the attitude of the Conservative rank and file still displayed the attitude of deference which it had showed towards the more genuinely powerful local industrialists who had ruled the town a generation or two earlier, so that the new local leadership, composed of shopkeepers and small businessmen, still 'feel ill at ease in the company of professional men, retired army officers and country gentry who tend to dominate the party in the rest of the constituency'.[52]

One does not need to adopt Vincent's definition of the mid-nineteenth century classes in their political aspects as 'operational collectivities' (cutting across occupational hierarchies) and 'acting at national level to achieve or prevent general changes in the structure of the political order',[53] to account for the widespread existence of social deference on the political market place, the hustings and the committee room. Working class pressure, conceived in the solidaristic terms of economic groups, occurred primarily in the politics of 'out of doors' and much of its energies were directed at the trade union field. Parliamentary and party politics is not the whole of nineteenth century politics and the concentration on the formal political elite imposes artificial limitations just in this area and for that period. It was within the orbit of a truncated community dominated by a socially restricted caucus that the direction of local politics and the selection of candidates took place.

In the counties selection remained, in effect until after 1884, firmly in the hands of a committee of local landowners; it is the boroughs which present the test case for the operation of the system of influence and pressure at work on the electoral scene. Before the introduction of the ballot there was, of course, opportunity for sanction (as for bribery) but the canvass which elicited the support of artisans, shopkeepers and allied groups (the majority of the electorate in many boroughs) seems to have relied as much on personal influence as on economic and social interests. In the popular boroughs the social pyramid tended to be cut slant-wise with artisans and shopkeepers inclining toward the Liberals and the upper professional classes towards the Tories. But each party presented its own hierarchical structure and the existence of localized support for a particular candidate and the prevalence of splitting are further proof for the operation of personal standing on the electoral scene.[54] We noticed in the last quarter of the nineteenth century and in the first of the present one a considerable widening of the social dimensions of the meshes of the net that trawled candidates and M.P.s. But at the same time the 'social fish' which it caught had become more numerous. Thus the expansion should be linked to a widening of the occupations deferred to and to the entry of new occupational groups into the ranks of the local party leadership.

The system of political recognition as it operated at the end of the Victorian period responded eventually to the claims by local men of talent and enterprise but frequently of obscure social origin for social recognition. Politics thus served as a vehicle for the aspiring socially upwards-mobile members of the middle class, and political office as the accolade of its achievement. The process, like the one which widened the field of recruitment to the magistracy or led to the recognition of local government, or party, service by the award of honours, did not take place without difficulties of which the struggle between the traditional groups of the party leaderships at Westminster are examples, especially on the Conservative side. By 1885 the party which used to draw its strength primarily from the rural areas had become dependent on the urban borough voters, but the leaders cold-shouldered this new support, a neglect 'that reflected the social assumptions of a party of country gentlemen not in the least eager to welcome the support of outsiders...[or]...share the rewards of office with them'.[55] A generation later the coupon election of 1918 brought a majority of such men into Parliament under the leadership of one of its representatives.[56] Yet that election seems to represent the trough of the Conservative party's social decline. After the social upheaval of the

Second World War the group of newly elected Conservative M.P.s (1950) was again composed predominantly of men of the established, well-to-do (upper) middle class.[57]

The working class representation in politics had in its most salient aspects the character of class representation with a class appeal. And at least at one time, e.g. in the inter-war years, it came near to forming a counter-elite to the traditional Conservative ruling strata in a way which the middle class representation did not during the time of its political ascendancy. Yet during the 100 year period in which the working class has been a power in the electoral, and later in the parliamentary struggle, its relationship to the political elite has also had elements of the deference community, of the representation of interests, and of the upwards social mobility of its chosen representatives.

The leadership of the enfranchised working class, as manifested in the new model unions, subscribed in many ways to the middle class ideals of the period and sought remedial action within its economic and moral framework. In spite of the sporadic candidature of trade union leaders in the years after 1868, the movement held to the official tenets of Liberalism. The Labour Representation League in its short life in the 1874 contests felt bound to state that its opposition was primarily directed at Conservatives and that its leaders had 'ever sought to be allied to the great Liberal Party to which we by conviction belong'.[58] And a year later after the 1875 Act the Parliamentary Committee of the T.U.C. claimed that 'the work of emancipation is full and complete'.[59] During the following elections between 25 and 50 candidates appealed nevertheless to the working class electorate, mostly as trade union candidates and mostly unsuccessful (except for official Lib.–Lab. candidates) but the size of their poll does not suggest that the bulk of the working class voters were deserting the Liberal Party.[60] This element of interest representation which continued to characterise working class politics even after the foundation of a Labour Party – in itself until after the war essentially a pressure group on the Liberal Party in Parliament – meant that electors and candidates were men of the same background and experience who might well return to their old life if defeated. The working class character of Labour's political elite arose out of the institutional ties of the early movement with the trade union organizations, and the latter's support based on feelings of solidarity as well as on economic interest.

The social ties between supporters and elected might, of course, become weakened in the course of time by the inevitable removal of the M.P.s interest and life style from the working class community to the Metropolis and the middle class style of life at Westminster – and office may produce a further widening of the gulf. We must remember that politics provides a vehicle of upwards social mobility for the working class even more than for sections of the middle class. Indeed it was until comparatively recently one of the few channels of this kind, not only in prestige terms, but in purely economic ones. But we must not let the naive self-congratulatory notes about their achieved status, which grace the autobiographies of the early generation of Labour Party politicians (e.g. Clynes, Thomas, Hodge), make us overestimate the importance of *this* mode of 'embourgeoisement' of the Labour movement. The almost complete reversal in the social composition of Labour's political elite over a period of fifty years, which we observed, is an 'embourgeoisement' of much greater significance. It is, moreover, largely external to the working class. Although we lack important clues about the family background of (Labour) M.P.s there is little to suggest that we are concerned here largely with an embourgeoisement by the already embourgeoised, i.e. those who have experienced intra-generational mobility.[61] As we saw, this process is probably not primarily due to the changes in Labour's electoral support in objective class terms – the growth in the share of the vote which has come from white collar, professional and even sections of the business element – although this might well have led to the deliberate choice of middle class candidates in marginal constituencies.

We observed that in the local Labour parties the middle class element increases as we ascend from voters to supporters and office holders, but there is no evidence that the selection of parliamentary candidates is the result of this phenomenon. The failure by trade unions to retain or capture Labour seats seems the result of a decline in the number of constituencies where one union is pre-eminent or of a general decline in union pressure, not of middle class machinations. With the changed industrial pattern, the decline of predominantly one-industry communities and following on the dispersal of working class housing from the old city centres, the Labour Party is today less and less *the* community party. If we follow the 'affluent worker' thesis, the ties between the Labour Party and its supporters are today less solidaristic. This would suggest that the worker will feel less need to identify in respect of life style and experience with his political representative. At the same time a growing section of the industrial working class experience, as Goldthorpe and Lockwood suggest, affiliation with the middle class world of white collar labour, and this too must affect the attitude towards the middle class as such. And an 'instrumentalist' attitude to politics would reinforce such tendencies.[62]

The incongruence between the class background of the political elite and that of its supporters would thus seem to be due to power (cash and coercion), deference and, with regard to the working class, a more 'rational' attitude to politics.

CHRISTOPHER J. HEWITT

3 Elites and the distribution of power in British society

This paper is concerned in a general sense with elite relationships and the distribution of power in modern society. Its specific focus, however, is upon elites and their role in the national power structure of a single country during a particular historical period. It is offered as a case study of the distribution of political power in the United Kingdom during the 1944–64 period.

The term 'national power' structure is here understood as the pattern of relationships that exists between the State and various social groups.

> The power structure of modern societies is usually conceived as the interplay between the institutions of government and the multitude of politically active intermediary groups. It is often stressed that the role of intermediary groups determine the power structure even more than the formal governmental institutions.[1]

More precisely it consists of the relationships within and between three kinds of groups, political elites, social elites and non-elites. The term elite is used to describe those who occupy the leading positions in organizations or institutions. Political elites are those who occupy such positions in the State, that is the elected political representatives and the top civil servants. Social elites are those who control the non-political organizations that either embody sectional interests like 'business', 'labour', 'the professions' or represent attitudes and opinions. The non-elites are made up of subordinates and rank and file members in organizations as well as unorganized publics.

It should be stressed that the definition of the power structure that is being used here is restricted to a consideration of the distribution of power in the political system and hence to the influence which groups have over the activity of the State. The power relationships that groups have outside of this political sphere are not considered, so that such matters as the power of an elite over its organizational subordinates (of owners or managers over workers in a factory, for example) are outside the scope of the paper.[2] It is certainly true that the exercise of political power is affected by the exercise of non-political power and *vice versa*. Thus on the one hand the investment policies of private corporations must be taken into account by those responsible for Government regional policy-planning and such regional policies will on the other hand provide the context for corporate investment decisions. The term 'political power' will be used, however, only when it is exercised deliberately and directly to affect State action.

The Elitist–Pluralist Debate

There is a long-standing controversy as to the form that the national power structure takes in contemporary western industrial societies, that is societies characterized by the existence of political democracy, a high level of industrialization, and the predominance of 'capitalist' enterprise in the economic system.[3] Lenski introduces his discussion of national power in modern society by distinguishing two viewpoints.

> With the rise and spread of political democracy, students of power have become increasingly divided over the applicability of the concept of a governing or ruling class in industrial societies. Some claim to see no great change from the past, and write persuasively of the Power Elite and The Establishment; others deny their existence, and write no less persuasively of Political Pluralism, Countervailing Power and Strategic Elites.

The first of these theories will be labelled the 'elitist' view, since its proponents argue that a single group is dominant over other groups. The second theory will be referred to as the 'pluralist-democratic' view. Before giving my own formulation of the points at issue between the two theories, I shall quote the major elitist and pluralist writers summarizing their positions and those of their opponents.

According to Crockett,[4] the contemporary American New Left holds to

> ...the belief that a small omnipotent group consistently conspires to formulate national policy...the close co-operation between business and government in regulating the economy, appear to have heightened the influence of the corporate executive in politics. Perhaps most important, the inability or unwillingness of local, state, and federal governments to recognize and respond to major social problems, such as poverty, racial discrimination, and urban decay, and the ease with which powerful interest groups block legislation aimed at alleviating these ills, all lend credence to the charge that an 'Establishment' dictates policy for the rest of the nation...Many individuals experience difficulty in attempting to correlate democratic theory with everyday reality.

One of the first systematic studies of national power in America was by Hunter[5] who 'assumed that the most influential men in national policy-making would be found residing in the larger cities, manning the larger corporate enterprises, and using their influence to get the government to move according to their interests'. The second major American elitist writer was Mills[6] who saw the power of the elite as consisting of its ability to decide on the directions that American society would take. 'Insofar as national events are decided, the power elite are those who decide them.' He distinguished between those like himself 'who assume that there is an elite and that its power is great' and 'the opposite view of the elite as impotent...Far from being omnipotent the elites are thought to be so scattered as to lack any coherence as a historical force.' Mills saw three distinct though allied elites, the military and the owners and managers of the large corporations as constituting the power elite. The unity of the power elite is not due simply to the 'structural coincidences of commanding positions and interests' for at times 'it is the unity of a more explicit co-ordination'. The other important American elitist is Domhoff,[7] who considers the power elite as 'serving the interests of the social upper class. It is the operating arm of the upper class.' His summary view is that 'the members of the upper class...define most major policy issues, shape the policy proposals on issues raised outside their circles...members of the upper class have the predominant, all pervasive influence. In short they dominate it [the Government].' His work is an attempt to describe the 'specific mechanisms by which members of the upper class formulate and communicate political issues, reach a degree of consensus and act as a relatively cohesive force in the arena of policy formulation'. In doing this he accepts the pluralist argument that 'it is necessary to show that the hypothetical ruling group dominates a wide variety of issue-areas', and claims to be able to show that the 'power elite formulate and transfer their wishes into government policy' in matters of foreign affairs and social welfare legislation.

For Britain two post-war writers can be cited as examples of the elitist school. Aaronovitch[8] after describing their economic power goes on to ask whether 'the finance capitalists as an economic class rule politically?... Obviously the finance capitalists may truthfully be described as the ruling class if in fact the crucial political and economic decisions are taken by their representatives and in their interests.' His conclusion is that as a consequence of the control of the State by the finance capitalists 'decisions which affect the welfare and the very lives of millions of people are taken without public discussion or effective popular control'.

Miliband[9] attempts to remedy the deficiencies of the Marxist view of the State, but accepts its basic assumptions that it is 'but a committee for managing the common affairs of the whole bourgeoisie', and that contemporary Western democracies are regimes in which an 'economically dominant class rules through democratic institutions'. The question to which he addresses himself is whether 'the holders of state power are, for many reasons, the agents of private economic power – that those who wield that power are also, therefore, and without unduly stretching the meaning of words, an authentic ruling class'.

The elitist argument can be understood more clearly by considering the alternative theory, particularly since in defining their own position elitists use the 'pluralist-democratic' view as a negative reference point. Both Domhoff and Miliband explicitly see their works as providing a refutation of the pluralist theory of the State and in fact use the same quotation from Dahl as a summary of that theory.[10] Pluralists, says Dahl[11]

> ...suggest that there are a number of loci for arriving at political decisions; that business men, trade unions, politicians, consumers, farmers, voters and many other aggregates all have an impact on policy outcomes; that none of these aggregates is homogeneous for all purposes; that each of them is highly influential over some scopes but weak over many others.

Aaronovitch sees the alternative view to his own as one which believes that the State 'is independent of any particular interest but responds to the different lobbies according to the pressures exercised', and uses a quotation from Crosland to the effect that the State is now an 'independent, intermediate power' as the starting point for an attack on the position.[12] Both Crosland[13] and Strachey[14] do in fact argue that the State is not now an organ of the capitalist class (although they believe it was in the pre-war period), but is instead being used by the forces of democracy, that is by the ordinary people and the trades unions. Galbraith[15] makes a similar point for America and sees a change from the nineteenth century situation in which industrialists 'made ample use of the State as an instrument of their economic goals' to the contemporary period when 'workers, farmers and other groups have become politically conscious...[and] turned to the state'. Since the latter groups are 'great in numbers and hence in political power' they use the state to redress their economic grievances. Other pluralist writers have stressed not the existence of non-elite power, but the lack of cohesion of the elites themselves. Keller[16] argues that different elites have influence in different issue-areas, while other writers suggest an even more extreme pluralism in which elite influence and relationships are highly situational. Rose[17] puts forward the 'multi-influence hypothesis' and sees conflict as 'multi-lateral...with the sides changing at least partially from issue to issue'. Riesman[18] talks of power dispersed 'among many marginally competing pressure groups' with the politician playing the role of a 'new type lobbyist, who represents not one but scores of interests often competing ones, from truckers to chiropractors and who plays one veto group against others'.

Now although a detailed examination of the arguments of the theorists cited above suggests that some of the disagreement between them may be semantic in origin and although there are important differences within each school, there is manifestly a significant dispute between the two sets of writers. Furthermore the points of disagreement are quite specific, and appear to be recognized on both sides. Before discussing the kind of evidence that could be used in support or refutation of either view, it will be useful therefore to formulate the controversy somewhat more precisely.

1. All the writers agree at least implicitly that the controversy concerns the way that the state acts, that policy is made and decisions taken.[19]

2. Elitists consider that it is possible to identify a unified and cohesive 'ruling group'. This ruling group is sometimes seen as a social class (Domhoff) or as an economic class or interest (Aaronovitch, Miliband) or as an organizational elite (Hunter, Mills). Although there are certain disagreements between elitists concerning the correct conceptualization of the ruling group and its composition, in practice the different terms are used almost interchangeably.[20] In general the ruling group is considered to include the business elite plus other elites drawn from the same social class, and with common interests or values. Pluralists conceive of the elites as lacking in cohesion and frequently in conflict with one another (Dahl, Rose).

3. Elitists see the ruling group as active in more than one policy area (Domhoff). Pluralists consider elite involvement as specialized either in terms of issue-areas (Keller, Dahl) or even in terms of particular issues within a given policy area (Riesman).

4. Because of the opposition of other elites who are not part of the ruling group, or because of the activity of the public as a whole, pluralists would claim that the power of any particular elite to obtain what it wants from the political elites is greatly reduced. In contrast the elitists anticipate that public opinion will either be controllable by the ruling group, or that it and the demands of other elites will be ignored by the political elite who will function as the agent of the ruling group.

5. Both elitists and pluralists are making general statements about the power structure. The elitists do not see the ruling elite as totally cohesive, active in every policy issue, nor completely successful in getting their way, and the pluralists are not unaware of the existence of powerful interest groups. It seems, however, that the elitists are making the stronger statement if one accepts the way that Miliband formulates the matter 'The question is not whether this class has a *substantial* measure of political power and influence …The question is a different one altogether, namely whether this dominant class also exercises a much greater degree of power and influence than any other class; whether it exercises a *decisive* degree of political power.'[21]

Methodological issues in studying power structures

To determine which theory is the more accurate, that is what type of power structure exists either in a local community or the national society, three kinds of methods have been proposed, the 'reputational', the 'issue', and the 'positional' or 'sociology of leadership'.[22] The first method has been used frequently in studies of community power but only once to discover the national power structure.[23] The second method, which involves the analysis of a sample of policy issues, has been utilized occasionally for the study of community power but never for national power. The third method supplemented by various kinds of indirect evidence has been utilized by almost all the major studies of national power.

The absence of studies using the issue-method is somewhat surprising given that many if not most writers in the elitist-pluralist controversy have couched their hypotheses in terms of the ability of groups to influence the policy-making process.[24] The reasons why no studies of national power using this method have been made are due it seems to the practical problems involved. The more serious difficulties in its application involve the selection of a 'fair sample', gathering material on the policy issues, and the problem of how to analyse this material.[25]

Despite these methodological problems it is my contention that the study of national issues is in fact more practicable than critics have assumed. Furthermore there are grounds for considering that the results of the sociology of leadership method are capable of being misinterpreted, and that in fact most elitists have made some rather dubious assumptions about the significance of such data. Therefore the value of examining national power by an alternative and previously untried method seemed to justify studying national policy-making in a systematic fashion.

In order to select a sample of important national policy issues the following procedure was used. First, a list of policy issues was collected for the 1944–64 period from a survey of several history texts. Policy issues were considered to consist of (1) crises and the response to them, (2) authoritative decisions or actions taken by the political elites and the events leading up to them, or (3) controversies which were discussed by the political elites even if no decision was taken on the matter, that is if the *status quo* remained unchanged. The issues on the list were then divided in an *a priori* fashion into four different policy areas: foreign affairs and defence, economic affairs, welfare policy, and a residual 'social' policy area. A panel of five 'judges' then individually selected the ten 'most important' issues in each category. Finally, for each category, the three most frequently selected issues in the 1944–51 period and the three most frequently selected issues in the 1951–64 period were chosen for analysis. The twenty-four issues selected in this fashion were therefore drawn equally from two political regimes, Labour and Conservative, as well as being spread over four different policy-areas. Although there is an obviously subjective element in the selection process, this procedure does reduce the danger of the researcher deliberately selecting only those issues which validate a particular viewpoint and also selects out the less important issues. Published secondary sources were used as data and evidence was gathered for each issue on the following matters: the policy-preferences and activities of formal organizations, the state of public opinion, the attitudes of various political groups (Members of Parliament, party activists, civil servants) and the history and final 'outcome' of the issue.[26] The issues chosen were:

Foreign policy

1. Indian independence 1947.
2. The shift in Anglo-Russian relations from war-time coalition to the setting up of NATO and British re-armament.
3. The Abadan crisis of 1951 over the nationalization of the British oil industry in Persia.
4. The Suez crisis of 1956.
5. The attempt at creating an independent nuclear deterrent in the mid nineteen-fifties.
6. The creation of the Central African Federation.

Economic policy

1. The United States loan of 1946.
2. The nationalization of road haulage.
3. The nationalization of the steel industry by the 1945 Labour Government.
4. The abolition of resale price maintenance 1960–4.
5. Britain's bid to enter the Common Market under Macmillan up to the French veto in 1963.
6. The reorganization and 'rationalization' of British Railways under Dr Beeching.

Welfare policy

1. The Education Act of 1944 and its implementation.
2. The National Health Service Act of 1946.
3. The National Insurance Act of 1946.
4. The Rent Act of 1957.
5. The comprehensive schools issue throughout the nineteen-fifties and early nineteen-sixties.
6. The motorways issue throughout the nineteen-fifties and early nineteen-sixties.

Social policy

1. The Town and Country Planning Act of 1946.
2. The attempt to liberalize the divorce laws in the early nineteen-fifties.
3. The temporary abolition of capital punishment in 1957.
4. The introduction of commercial television in 1954.
5. The Commonwealth Immigration Act of 1962.
6. The Clean Air Act of 1956.

Organized groups

To a great extent the 'pluralism' of the power structure depends upon the unit of analysis that one chooses to adopt. Riesman's pluralist position, for example, is largely contingent upon his defining 'interests' in a microscopic fashion as specific organizations. If one follows such a strategy it is much more likely that one will discover that a particular interest is only involved in a very narrow range of issues than if one defines interests more broadly. The same point could be made in interpreting the results of the New Haven study in which Dahl found that very few individuals were involved in more than one issue area. Given that similar kinds of individuals with similar values were active in most issues the pattern would appear far less pluralist.

As a first stage in the analysis it is instructive to focus, however, upon individual organizations to see if they are involved in several issues or just in one. To answer this question every organization that was involved in each issue was noted even if the involvement comprised no more than the taking of a position. The lists of organizations were then compared to see how much continuity there was between issues. The results are presented in Table 1 below, the organizations being classified into seven types.

The classification of organizations is generally self-explanatory. The Business organizations (representing 'capitalist' ownership interests) include firms (such as Shell, ICI, etc.) and trade associations (e.g. the British Iron and Steel Federation). Two types of occupational associations were distinguished according to the class status of their members; the 'higher professions' (i.e. the self-employed, those in top administrative positions, and occupations requiring a university degree or its equivalent), and intermediate White collar occupations made up one category, while blue-collar unions formed the other. 'Promotional' groups were defined as organizations devoted to the advancement of a particular cause rather than to representing the sectional interests of their members. The category includes both permanent multi-purpose groups, such as the Fabian Society and *ad hoc* groups (created during the issue, or with very limited goals) such as the National Council for the Abolition of the Death Penalty, as well as some residual miscellaneous organizations.

TABLE 1. *Continuity of individual organizations between issues by type of organization*

Type of organization	Total no. of organizations	No. involved in only one issue	No. involved in two issues	No. involved in three issues	No. involved in four or more issues
Business organizations	173	145	16	6	6
White collar occupations	85	77	3	3	2
Blue collar unions	36	26	4	2	4
Religious organizations	11	4	1	1	5
Local government bodies	53	44	7	0	2
Research organizations	33	32	0	0	1
Promotional organizations	190	172	9	6	3
Total all organizations	581	500	40	18	23

The degree of continuity of individual organizations is clearly extremely low. Overall eighty-six per cent of the organizations were involved in only one issue and almost half of the overlapping organizations were involved in only two issues. Only twenty-three organizations (less than four per cent) were involved in four or more issues.[27]

Some caution must be exercised in the interpretation of these results. First it is clear that the activity of certain organizations may be ignored by the data sources used and furthermore that the sources are themselves of varying reliability. It seems probable, however, that it is the less important groups which will be most commonly ignored.

A second methodological problem lies in the fact that the sources sometimes make general references to the 'Building Trade', the 'Steel Companies', etc., or to individuals rather than to particular organizations. In such cases these were assumed, in the absence of any contradictory evidence, to be references to organizations and coded as such. Various objections could be raised to the conclusion that the low degree of continuity is significant. It might be argued that the most active organizations in any issue are more likely to be involved in several issues. Thus an analysis of the 'significantly involved' organizations alone would produce a different picture. To check this the continuity of such organizations was examined. Significant involvement by an organization was considered to include any of the following activities.

1. The initiation of some policy proposal that was accepted, or at least seriously considered in Parliament or by the Government.

2. Extensive lobbying of or consultation with ministers, civil servants, or some bloc of M.P.s.

3. Threatening some action against, or offering some inducement in support of a given policy, that was not obviously ignored by the politicians.

4. Propaganda activity aimed at changing or mobilizing public opinion.

5. Organizing concerted action by like-minded groups, providing support for active pressure groups (e.g. financial aid or other facilities) or serving as a 'transmission belt' for the opinions of important groups to reach the political decision-makers.

Very few organizations were involved 'significantly' in more than one issue, and the proportion of overlapping organizations was in fact slightly lower than for all the organizations.

The organizations that were involved in several issues could themselves be considered as the nucleus of a power elite. In fact, however, such organizations make up a rather disparate collection of interests, as well as including some organizations that were involved in only rather trivial ways. The organizations involved in four or more issues include the Federation of British Industries, National Union of Manufacturers, Associated British Chambers of Commerce, British Iron and Steel Federation, National Farmers Union, British Medical Association, National Union of Teachers, British Council of Churches, Catholic Church, Methodist Church, Church of Scotland, National Council of Women, Co-operative Movement, the London County Council, Association of Municipal Corporations, PEP and three of the six largest trade unions (TGWU, NUR, USDAW). The three most 'involved' organizations were the Fabian Society (11 issues), the Church of England (12 issues), and the TUC (17 issues).

Given that individual organizations are involved in a very limited range of issues the question then becomes whether or not organizations can be aggregated into larger groupings which do attempt to influence policy in all or most issues. Is it possible to consider the different business organizations, for example, as a cohesive entity? In measuring the cohesion of an interest bloc it seems reasonable to concentrate upon the *general* position of organizations since there are always likely to be minor differences over points of detail even within groups united by an overall consensus. The four main sectional interests, business, white collar occupations, unions, and religious groups were therefore examined to discover how cohesive they each were.

The cohesion of each category was measured in the following way. For every issue in which an interest group category was involved a judgement was made as to the position of the category *as a whole* (i.e. the position of most groups in that category). Then an aggregate measure for all the issues was calculated, and the degree of cohesion of a category expressed as the

TABLE 2. *Consistency of alignments within categories of organizations*

Type of organization	Total no. of organizational involvements	Total no. of organizational stands known	Total no. of consistent stands	Percentage of consistent stands to all known stands
Business organizations	225	172	160	93
White-collar occupations	100	54	42	78
Blue-collar unions	73	64	61	97
Religious organizations	41	39	36	92

percentage of times in which the organizations were aligned with the majority of the groups in that category.

In some issues the position of an organization changed over time. In these cases the organization was classified in terms of the position which it held for the longest period of time.

These results suggest that each of the interests is highly cohesive since even the most heterogeneous category, the white collar occupational group, is generally aligned as a bloc. The business group was seriously divided on only two issues and the unions on one. Although business interests provided substantial backing for the National Smoke Abatement Society, the Clean Air Act was opposed by the Cotton and Chemical industries and the Federation of British Industries wanted a much less stringent policy towards pollution. On the issue of Commercial Television, groups like the Newspaper Proprietors Association, and the Cinematograph Exhibitors Association were opposed to the introduction of Commercial Television, which was supported by advertising groups and the manufacturers and retailers of television equipment. Professional groups were split over the same issue, and also over Divorce Reform and Comprehensive Education. The Religious group was divided over one aspect of the Education Act, the role of the Church schools and state aid for them but united in support of the Act in general. Over the Nuclear Deterrent, individual Churches as well as the Religious bloc as a whole were divided. One category of organizations, the promotional type, is clearly heterogeneous and lacking in cohesion. This general category can be subdivided, however, into somewhat more homogenous blocs. The most numerous type of promotional organization includes those left-of-centre groups which advocate 'progressive' causes such as the Fabian Society and other offshoots of the Labour movement, Pacifist, anti-colonialist organizations etc. Even if one uses the term rather generously their right-wing counterparts are much less numerous (the Bow Group, various *petit-bourgeois* organizations such as the Middle-Class Alliance, People's League for the Defence of Freedom, anti-immigrant groups, military associations and the like). Various pro-business organizations such as Aims of Industry, or 'fronts' for business interests such as the Resale Price Maintenance Co-ordinating Committee, or the Popular Television Association constitute another small category of right-wing groups. The only other numerous types of promotional organization are charitable and welfare groups, tenants' and residential associations, women's organizations and groups which serve as fronts for several sectional interests. Overall the diversity of opinions embodied by promotional organizations and the large number of left-of-centre organizations appear to make the political process more rather than less pluralist.[28]

Given that the interest group categories are generally internally cohesive it seems legitimate to consider which of them are involved in each issue. Before doing this, however, it seems useful to examine the state of public opinion on each of the issues so that it can be compared to the positions of the various organized interests.

Public opinion

Some theorists have suggested that a precondition for democratic influence is the existence of competition between elite groups.[29] Other writers have seen the influence of mass public opinion as a limitation upon elite power. Given that the role of public opinion is a matter of concern to many writers, an attempt will be made here to characterize the state of public opinion on the different issues.

Both from the point of view of the politician in assessing what the public wants, and the observer who is trying to estimate the degree of democracy that the policy-making process reveals, public opinion situations can be classified into three categories.

> 1. Issues in which a clear majority of the public desires a given general outcome, such a majority being stable over time in aggregate terms.
> 2. Issues in which public opinion is fairly evenly divided and stable over time with no large net shifts.
> 3. Issues marked by an unstable and/or confused public opinion situation. These would be indicated by a high proportion of 'don't knows' in the polls, large net shifts in opinion or internally contradictory responses.

On certain issues it is possible to make a valid dichotomy of opinion; people can be distinguished into those who are 'for' or 'against' a given policy. Relevant opinion polling data exist for eleven such issues,[30] and are presented below in Table 3. When more than one poll exists, the average has been calculated.

On the basis of these statistics it is suggested that five issues (steel nationalization, resale price maintenance, National Health, capital punishment and immigration) fit into the first category. Based upon less direct evidence, six

TABLE 3. *Division of public opinion on selected issues*

Issue	No. of polls	Division of public opinion (%)	Don't know (%)	Majority opinion
Suez	6	44:40	16	Against intervention
Steel	2	52:26	22	Against nationalization
Railways	4	39:39	22	Beeching doing a good job
Resale price maintenance	4	52:28	20	For abolition of RPM
Common Market	8	43:29	28	For joining the Market
National Health	1	55:32	13	Approve NHS proposals
Rent Act	1	35:33	32	Against decontrol
Capital punishment	8	61:27	12	For retention of death penalty
Television	5	44:40	16	Against commercial TV
Divorce reform	1	43:31	23	Make divorce more difficult
Immigration	3	68:17	15	For restricting immigration

other issues are also included as cases in which a clear majority supported a given policy.

As regards the Education Act of 1944, the public appears to have been in support, and in fact to have been somewhat more 'radical' or advanced than the government, since forty-four per cent thought that the 'best' school leaving age was sixteen, while only twenty per cent favoured fifteen (the government proposal in the Act). Furthermore, as regards the other controversy of the Education Act, the role of the Church Schools, a large majority (61 per cent) thought that they should be taken over by the state.[31]

Over India there seems to have been little opposition to the principle of ultimate independence and the controversy revolved around the question of when self-government should be given. Twice during the war the public was asked whether India should be given self-government 'immediately, or after the war'. Fifty-one and forty-one per cent were in favour of granting independence after the war, although between the two polls the proportion of those favouring immediate independence increased from twenty-six to thirty-one per cent.[32]

On two other issues, National Insurance, and Town and Country Planning, there are no directly relevant poll results, but such evidence as we have suggests that the public supported the basic direction of policy and might even have favoured more radical change. A 1945 poll[33] found that over half would approve of the 'nationalization' of land with less than a third disapproving. We can therefore reasonably assume that the 1947 Act which merely controlled land use and profits was acceptable to the general public. Similarly with National Insurance, most contemporary commentators[34] assert that the Beveridge plan was hugely popular, and criticism seems to have focused on the government's slowness in implementing the plan or on restrictions in its scope.[35] After the 'Great Smog' of 1952, public feeling was strongly in favour of some anti-pollution law.[36] In the late nineteen-fifties poll data show that a large majority of the population favoured 'more and better designed roads' and supported increased expenditure on motorway construction.[37]

In three issues, as Table 3 above indicates, public opinion was evenly divided. These are the Suez, railway and commercial television issues. The other issues seem to be marked by a low level of public concern, or a high degree of instability and ambivalence.[38]

Group involvements, alignments and the policy outcome

In Table 4, the major involvements and positions of the main interest groups have been listed for all the issues as well as the positions of the general public. The table presents the data in a summary fashion and ignores minor involvements by certain organizations and slight differences between groups in their attitudes towards the issues. Setting out the data in this fashion allows one to make comparisons between groups regarding the number of issues in which they were involved, and also to see if any patterns of conflict or coalition are revealed between different groups.

The business group was involved in more issues than any other interest, but the union group was involved in almost as many. White collar occupations and the Churches were active in a substantial minority of the issues. In very few issues does one find that any particular group is the only one involved, and often several groups are concerned with an issue. Usually the business group and the unions are found on opposite sides if they are involved in the same issue, but apart from this the alignments between different groups do not appear to be very consistent. This seems to correspond generally to the hypothesis suggested by Rose of multi-lateral conflict in which the sides change from issue to issue.

The final question concerns the policy outcome, and leads to a consideration of which groups were favoured by government action. In some issues the overall policy pursued by the government or the final legislative outcome was clearly compatible with the preferences of certain interests and incompatible with those of other interests. The groups in favour of a 'hard line' policy on Russia, Indian independence, the National Health Service, National Insurance, the nationalization of road haulage, the control of Commonwealth immigration, the Central African Federation, the decontrol of rents, the abolition of resale price maintenance, the control of air pollution, Beeching's railway policy, a motorway construction programme, and no substantial change in the divorce laws were in this sense 'successful'.

In other issues, the final outcome generally favoured certain groups but substantial concessions were made to the opposing interests. Thus the Town and Country Planning Bill became law but considerable concessions

TABLE 4. *Alignments by interest on different issues*

Issue	Successful policy outcome	Business	White collar	Unions	Religious	Public opinion
India	Independence for India	—	—	—	—	Pro
Russia	Hard-line policy to Russia	—	—	Pro	—	—
Abadan	Sanctions against Iran	Pro	—	—	Anti	—
Suez	Military intervention	Anti	—	Anti	Anti	Divided
Nuclear deterrent	Independent deterrent policy	Anti	—	Divided	Divided	—
Central Africa	Federation	—	—	—	Anti	—
U.S. loan	Loan negotiated	—	—	—	—	—
Road haulage	Nationalization	Anti	—	Pro	—	—
Steel	No effective nationalization	Pro	—	Anti	—	Pro
Resale price maintenance	Abolition of RPM	Anti	—	—	—	Pro
Common market	No entry	Anti	—	Pro	—	—
Railways	Beeching's rationalization policy	Pro	—	Anti	—	Divided
Education Act	Education Act	Pro	Pro	Pro	Pro	Pro
National Health	National Health Service	—	Pro	—	Pro	Pro
National Insurance	National Insurance Act	Anti	—	Pro	Pro	Pro
Rent Act	Rent decontrol	Pro	Pro	Anti	—	—
Comprehensives	No support for comprehensives	—	Divided	—	—	—
Motorways	Motorway programme	Pro	Pro	Pro	—	Pro
Town and country	Town and Country Planning Act	Anti	Pro	Pro	—	Pro
Divorce	No change in divorce laws	—	Divided	—	Pro	—
Capital punishment	Abolition of capital punishment	—	Anti	—	Pro	Anti
Television	Commercial Television	Divided	Divided	Anti	Anti	Divided
Immigration	Immigration control	—	—	—	Anti	Pro
Clean air	Clean Air Act	Divided	Pro	—	—	Pro

were made as regards compensation prices. Over the capital punishment issue, the abolitionists got what they wanted but only for an experimental five year period. Similarly, substantial concessions were made to the opponents of commercial television as regards programming controls etc. The teachers' unions made considerable concessions to the Churches in the Education Act.

In other cases it is harder to define what the successful policy was because the government policy itself either appears ambiguous or changed over time. In some of these issues the uncertainty is increased by the fact that the ability of the government to achieve policy goals is limited by the activity of other national governments (as in foreign policy issues) or by the need to achieve co-operation from local government bodies (e.g. in the comprehensive schools issue).

The Steel Nationalization issue could be considered resolved finally in a way that was compatible with the wishes of the pro-nationalization groups, but the apparent unwillingness of the Labour government to act on the matter until just before the return of a Conservative government (which denationalized the industry) makes it more reasonable to consider the outcome of this issue as one which favoured the anti-nationalization groups. The Common Market issue can be seen as a victory for the 'marketeers' because negotiations were opened, or alternatively for the 'anti-marketeers' because the negotiations failed. It is assumed[39] that the negotiations failed because the anti-marketeers were able to impose such conditions on the concessions that the British negotiators could make, that a French veto was virtually inevitable. Over the Suez question one could argue that because the intervention failed, those opposed to the use of force were successful. On the other hand it is more plausible to argue that the intervention failed because of pressures from the United States, and to see the fact of intervention as a defeat for those opposed to the use of military force. The collapse of Sandys' independent deterrent policy was a result of the inherent impracticality of such a scheme for a Power with Britain's resources, although assisted to a degree by domestic criticism. Since the policy was maintained for so long, however, it is considered a defeat for those groups opposed to an independent British deterrent. The Government responded somewhat ambiguously to the nationalization of the British oil industry by Iran, since they resisted the call to use military force but instead tried to prevent the Persians from selling the oil. Although the resistance of many local education authorities was the primary factor, the lack of Government support also contributed to the slow development of the comprehensive schools system.

If these policy outcomes are compared to the preferences of the different groups it seems that no one group was generally successful in getting what it wanted. Neither the business group nor any other appears to be especially favoured by the government.

Discussion

From the evidence presented, it is clear that policy-making does not appear to be 'elitist' in the sense that any single elite or interest is dominant. Instead the picture of national power that is revealed suggests a 'pluralist' interpretation since a diversity of conflicting interests are involved in many issues, without any one interest being consistently successful in realizing its goals. Furthermore, each interest appears to be limited in the range of its involvement. These findings appear to be so divergent from the expectations of the elitist or ruling class theorists that some attention must be given to the question of why this difference exists, assuming that the picture of the policy-making process given in the previous section is generally correct.

First it could be argued that the ruling class or elitist theorists are not in fact concerned with the policy making influence of the business elite or the upper class, but with their general control over society. In other words their power over economic institutions may be sufficient for them to be referred to as a ruling class. However, as the quotations from the elitist writers cited in the first section of the paper reveal, most do in fact refer to the *political* influence and policy-making role of the ruling groups.

Another position which is increasingly popular is to conceive of policy influence in a negative fashion. This objection is more basic and argues that to interpret the results of decision-making studies as confirmation of the pluralist position is invalid since elite power may be exercised in restricting, through a variety of means, the issues that arise to those that do not threaten their position.[40] This 'non-decision making' aspect of power operating through the 'mobilization of bias' certainly does exist, but whether it is exercised as the elitists claim is highly problematical, and not much evidence has been offered to support their contention.[41] The fact that gross inequalities in the distribution of income and wealth exist and that no real attempt has been made to modify this situation does not in itself constitute evidence for non-decision making power.[42] An alternative and more likely explanation is that very few people know about or consider such inequality unjust or important.

Regardless of whether the political dominance of the socially advantaged groups in society is conceived of in a positive or a negative fashion it is still incumbent upon those who support such a view to explain why the political authorities should respond primarily to such groups. A variety of explanations can be found in the literature.

Many of the reasons given to explain why Government should be dominated by upper class or business interests represent, however, as Finer argues in his classic articles 'abstract possibilities...not effective capacity' and almost all the examples of such activities (e.g. the seduction of the police and armed forces, bribery, the maintenance of private armies, etc.) are drawn from non-British history.[43] Some plausible reasons remain; business as a source of party funds to the Conservative Party and the ability of business and certain professional groups to obstruct the government by not co-operating with its policies and 'refusing the Government the expert, scientific and technical advice on which it relies'. Both of these factors seem to be exaggerated. As Sampson[44] points out the disclosures forced by the 1967 Companies Act revealed that the majority of the largest 100 Companies did not give donations to the Conservative Party, and none of the fourteen largest did. Finer argues that Big Business even in the 1945–51 period did not deny the government its co-operation 'not only out of fear of reprisals, but from a strong sense of law-abidingness'.[45] The power of the business groups is also to a certain extent balanced by the 'countervailing power' of the unions with their powers of obstruction and non-co-operation, and political levy in favour of the Labour Party.

The evidence most commonly used in support of a ruling elite model is derived from the sociology of leadership method. This involves defining the key decision-making groups in the political process and then examining the socio-economic characteristics and career patterns of the individuals in such positions. An extensive literature exists on the background of M.P.s (and other political elites such as Administrative class civil servants, the Judiciary, members of Royal Commissions, etc.) and the results are fairly consistent. The political elites are 'firmly rooted in the general social elite' the higher socio-economic groups such as old Etonians, businessmen and professionals being over-represented and the working class drastically under-represented.[46] The problem then becomes one of deciding what can be concluded about the power-structure and the relationships between the political elite and other social groups from this evidence. Some analyses simply stop at this stage and *define* a governing or ruling class in terms of the social origin of the decision-makers.[47]

Frequently, however, the plausible assumption is made that such evidence can be used as an indicator of the attitudes and role of the political elite. The more sophisticated writers are careful to avoid any crude formulation of this argument, or are aware of the problems involved. Domhoff, for example, says that a 'drawback' of social background studies is that they 'do not demonstrate consequences from upper class control. Do upper class leaders have "special interests"?' Neither does social background analysis, he admits, answer the argument that 'real power' is in the masses. He is very evasive about this, and the related point, that the social background of the decision-makers may not affect significantly the outcome of the decisions.[48] However, this objection appears to be crucial, since if social background does *not* serve as a substantial predictor of the way that decision makers *act* then why study it – apart from the intrinsic interest of studying social mobility in any area?

There are many problems in assuming that the values and opinions of politicians can be inferred from their social class background, education and previous occupation. Even though there is a *general* relationship between social background and opinions in the population as a whole it may be a fallacy to make such an assumption about such a small, and highly self-selected group of men as M.P.s. Inferring from the general to the specific may be wildly inaccurate because of simple sampling error in predicting the opinions of prime ministers or Cabinet ministers from their origins. The 'unrepresentative' occupational histories of most M.P.s are shown by the very fact that they *left* their occupations to become M.P.s, and this self selection may indicate that their opinions are equally atypical.

Even if one provisionally accepts some connection between social background and attitudes the argument that Parliament is full of spokesmen for the socially privileged is exaggerated. This inference is often made by a semantic confusion of terms like 'non-manual' with 'middle class', 'upper-middle class' or 'bourgeois' in the Marxist sense. The true statement that the 'working class' (i.e. manual workers) are under-represented in Parliament is often used to infer that all the M.P.s of non-manual origins are upper class or upper-middle class individuals with a natural affinity for conservative *status quo* opinions.[49] One large non-working class group which is in fact generally 'radical' and 'anti-bourgeois' in its social and political ideology is suggested by Parkin. This group he locates in occupations 'in which there is a primary emphasis upon either the notion of service to the community, human betterment or welfare and the like or upon self-expression and creativity'. As a result of this work situation and ideological milieu, and the fact that their 'life chances rest primarily upon intellectual attainments and professional qualifications not upon ownership of property or inherited wealth' they have values and 'behavioural characteristics noticeably at variance with the overall middle class pattern'.[50]

If data on the formative occupations of M.P.s given in the Nuffield studies for the 1951, 1955 and 1959 Parliaments is re-analysed to distinguish *within* the non-manual category between the bourgeois and petit bourgeois, as well as between 'commercial' and 'welfare and service' professions[51] the composition of the House of Commons appears much less naturally conservative or solidly pro-capitalist than is often implied.

Comparable figures do not exist for the 1945 and 1950 Parliaments. Clearly they were much *less* bourgeois, as have been the subsequent parliaments since under a Labour regime the number of working class and 'welfare professional' M.P.s increases.

A final criticism of the sociology of leadership method, however, is that it often fails to predict the behaviour (i.e. the political stands and actions) of politicians even if it is accurate in inferring their personal preferences. If one considers the eleven issues for which there was a clear public

TABLE 5. *Social groupings represented in the House of Commons, 1951–9*

	1951		1955		1959		Average parliamentary composition 1951–9	
	Con.	Lab.	Con.	Lab.	Con.	Lab.	Number	%
Bourgeois	121	11	89	6	92	6	108	17
Petit bourgeois	23	17	23	29	25	20	46	7
Commercial professions	86	50	96	46	111	49	146	23
Welfare professions	31	96	39	83	49	77	125	20
Farmers	15	2	31	5	38	3	31	5
Armed services	32	2	47	3	37	3	41	7
Working class	1	108	1	97	1	90	99	16

opinion majority, in four either the M.P.s of both parties or the M.P.s of the majority party were in accord with the public opinion majority, and the outcome was compatible with this Parliamentary and Public consensus. These were the National Health, National Insurance, Education Act, and Town and Country Planning issues. On these issues the alleged unrepresentativeness of the politicians' opinions is not supported, but it is the remaining issues which are most interesting. For the sociology of leadership method to have utility, politicians' opinions must affect significantly what politicians *do* as well as what they would *like* to do. Yet the personal preference of most M.P.s of both parties against restricting immigration and in favour of divorce reform, and of M.P.s of the majority party in favour of Steel Nationalization, and retaining resale price maintenance were a poor guide to the eventual outcome of these issues, and the public opinion majority was in fact closer to the outcome. Only over the capital punishment issue did the effect of politicians personal sympathies lead to an 'undemocratic' outcome; that is one opposed to the wishes of the majority of the electorate.

While this general compatibility between public opinion and issue outcomes is not taken as validating any simplistic model of democracy it does seem to suggest that the policy process is not explicable in terms of the nature of the political elite. If as Bertrand Russell suggests 'Power is the production of intended effects' then we should look directly at how policy – the production of intended effects – is created through the interplay of public opinion, and organized pressure groups operating on the political system. The present essay is offered as a preliminary attempt to discover the power structure of Britain by using such a strategy.

4   The City and Industry: the directors of large companies, their characteristics and connections

Introduction

Group cohesion or solidarity is often regarded as an essential prerequisite of an elite[1] and backgrounds of, and connections between, elite members have been studied as constituting the preconditions of a high degree of cohesion.[2] To study changes in elites (defined here as sets of individuals in positions of authority over major social organizations sharing, to some minimum degree, common perceptions, beliefs and values, over time), however, and to relate these changes to the larger socio economic environment, some indication of the degree of integration of groups is required, preferably covering more than one dimension of connectedness. Lupton and Wilson[3] examined educational background, club membership and kinship links between 'top decision makers' and Brown,[4] among others, has discussed overlapping directorships, but connectedness between leading institutions has not been systematically analysed. A high degree of integration between leaders of major institutions has implications for their actions since it implies some common culture which mediates structural exigencies and creates the possibility of common, co-ordinated actions. Commonality of background and frequent opportunities for contact between leaders of similar institutions constitute favourable conditions for group solidarity, especially when combined with a considerable ownership of personal wealth. In understanding the nature of institutions, then, it is suggested that the degree of integration, and conditions favourable to it, are of importance since these lead to consideration of the group culture and rationality. Differing degrees of commonality and connectedness between leaders of institutions can be expected to lead to different responses to structural changes. Common educational backgrounds and life styles as evidenced, for example, through membership of exclusive clubs, constitute a basis for common definitions of socio-economic reality and associated actions. Similarly, structurally based connections between institutional leaders provide suitable conditions for developing and co-ordinating common definitions and actions. If leaders of similar social institutions are selectively recruited in terms of education, have access to prestigious social organizations and are related to the traditional aristocracy, as well as being connected through directorships, then it seems likely that they will share similar beliefs and values and so constitute an elite – although, of course, the existence of a common culture still requires direct investigation.

In an earlier paper[5] I outlined background commonalities and connections between directors of 27 large financial institutions, using published data, and suggested that the basis of a common culture existed. The assumption that directors are indeed powerful in such organizations was justified by reference to their active participation in mergers and acquisitions, investment and unit trust fund management, as revealed by the financial press. Although it is arguable that directors of very large industrial companies may not wield much power in terms of day to day administration,[6] the increasing sophistication of financial control techniques and importance of major financial decisions which traditionally are the preserve of the Board of Directors make it more, rather than less, likely that directors exercise substantial control. Here, then, I extend the earlier analysis to the connections between the 'City' and very large industrial companies, to see how similar are the networks connecting directors of financial institutions and those connecting directors of industrial companies, to examine how industrial firms are connected to financial organizations, and how similar in background are their directors. This seems a necessary prelude to both differentiating industrial companies with a view to relating different types of Boards of Directors to economic variables, and to charting relations between the 'City' and industrial companies over time in order to relate changes in these relations to changes in general financial policies. Brown[7] has suggested a threefold classification of the top 116 companies and has related this to some common economic variables. The basis for his allocation of firms to the categories is not entirely clear, however, and by directly examining directors of financial and industrial companies it is hoped to provide a systematic basis for future work.

Procedure

The financial firms covered in the present study include the big four clearing banks, merchant banks with authorized capital of over £5m., discount houses with authorized capital of over £3m., the Bank of England and the eight largest insurance companies drawn from the 1971 *Stock Exchange Year Book*. Although some changes have taken place in individual firms through mergers and acquisitions since then, it is unlikely that the general characteristics and connections of directors have altered to any great extent. The top 50 industrial companies were taken from the *Times 1,000* listing for 1970–1 and their directors similarly gathered from the *Stock Exchange Year Book*. This list is based on turnover, which is not always a reliable indicator of size since some service firms may have a large turnover in terms of paper transactions (e.g. commodity brokers) with a relatively small capital base. However, if capital employed is used as the indicator of size, only 13 companies were thereby found to be excluded from the top 50, and five of the 13 which were in the top 50 by capital employed shared directors with companies in the top 50 by turnover. Turnover, therefore, was retained as the criterion, but purely financial or brokerage firms were excluded on the grounds that they were really part of the 'City' and so more likely to be connected with leading financial institutions than non financial concerns. In examining Boards of Directors it is also relevant to note that subsidiaries of foreign companies may well operate in different ways from companies based in this country, so foreign owned subsidiaries were also excluded. It would, of course, be of interest to analyse these companies and their policies separately. These two sets of exclusions left 40 industrial companies, which are listed, together with their turnover, capital employed and number of directors in Table 1 with the financial firms.

Data about directors' background characteristics and connections were gathered from the usual published sources.[8] Unfortunately the proportion of directors of industrial companies for whom background data were available was not as high as for the directors of financial firms and educational and club details were located for just under a half (49 %) of the 'industrial' directors. Generally, information from published sources is biased towards the aristocracy and members of the traditional top status groups, but as far as can be inferred by comparing the various sources with each other, this bias is not large enough to indicate any substantial difference between the 50 % of directors for whom data are available and those from whom they are not. The measure of connectedness used here is based on Doreian's[9] integration score, normalised[10] to allow comparisons between groups of different sizes.[11]

Background characteristics

As remarked above, educational data were available for nearly half, 261, of the directors. These are given in Table 2, together with those for the 27 financial firms reproduced for comparison purposes. As can be seen, Eton and the major public schools figure much less prominently for directors of industrial companies than is the case for directors of financial institutions. However, Eton still educated 34 industrial directors and 66 % attended fee paying schools, still a substantial proportion, if not as high as the 80 % characteristic of directors of financial firms. This figure is, it should be noted, slightly less than the 71 % found by Heller[12] in his surveys of directors of the top 200 firms. The reduction in the proportion attending fee paying schools is, of course, largely due to the substantial number educated at grammar schools. This does not necessarily imply that all such schools were non fee-paying, simply that they were not 'independent'. Similar results occur when university education is considered. Two thirds of the industrial directors attending institutions of higher education went to either Oxford or Cambridge, compared with 87 % of the financial directors. However, the proportion going to university was about the same as that for directors of the insurance companies. Overall, these results

TABLE 1. *Financial and industrial companies included in the study*

Financial institutions		Industrial companies			
Name	No. of directors	Name	Turnover (£m)	Capital employed (Gross assets minus liabilities) (£m)	No. of directors
Bank of England	18	Shell Transport & Trading	2,352	1,909	10
Alexanders Discount	9	British Petroleum	2,242	1,769	15
Barclays	33	British American Tobacco	1,467	659	18
Cater, Ryder	9	I.C.I.	1,355	1,581	21
Clive Holdings	9	Unilever	1,144	548	23
Commercial Union Insurance	24	Imperial Tobacco	1,120	528	16
Eagle Star Insurance	24	Shell Mex & B.P.	1,028	344	16
Robert Fleming	20	B.L.M.C.	970	408	13
Gen. Accident Insurance	19	General Electric	898	606	15
Guardian R.E. Insurance	20	Courtaulds	626	510	15
Hambros	7	G.K.N.	511	320	16
Hill, Samuel	11	Dunlop	495	298	15
Kleinwort Benson	13	British Insulated Cal. Cables	404	211	19
Lloyds	33	Hawker Siddeley	402	234	12
Midland	22	Distillers	382	331	19
Minster Assets	10	Great Universal Stores	382	218	10
Montagu Trust	13	Marks & Spencer	360	169	11
National Westminster	27	Rank Hovis McDougall	359	158	11
Phoenix Assurance	18	Allied Breweries	345	318	16
Prudential	12	Rio Tinto Zinc	338	574	28
Rothschilds	19	Shipping Ind. Holdings	330	19	21

TABLE 1 (*cont.*)

Financial institutions

Name	No. of directors
Royal Insurance	19
Schroders	13
Slater Walker Securities	5
Sun Alliance Insurance	30
S.G. Warburg (Mercury Securities)	8

Industrial companies

Name	Turnover (£m)	Capital employed (Gross assets minus liabilities) (£m)	No. of directors
Bass Charrington	315	332	16
Reed International	314	258	10
Unigate	301	89	8
Rolls Royce	229	223	8
Tube Investments	294	246	17
C.T. Bowring	280	51	11
Sears Holdings	276	217	5
Coats Patons	268	207	8
Bowater	268	293	13
Thorn Electric	267	145	9
Cadbury Schweppes	262	188	18
Burmah Oil	253	764	15
J. Lucas	251	116	9
Allied Suppliers	250	60	10
Tesco	238	41	10
Rank Industries	237	179	17
Tate & Lyle	228	163	17
Boots Pure Drug	223	110	13
Union International	289	73	6

TABLE 2. *Educational background of directors*

School	Bank of England	Clearing banks	Merchant banks and discount houses	Insurance companies	Industrial firms
Eton	1	31	37	46	34
Harrow	0	3	7	9	5
Winchester	2	11	5	6	7
Rugby	3	5	6	4	6
Charterhouse	1	2	1	2	1
Marlborough	0	2	1	0	7
Other public	3	25	25	31	110
Private	0	0	2	1	3
Total fee-paying	10	79	84	99	173
Grammar	5	18	16	17	71
No secondary	1	0	1	0	0
Overseas	2	2	5	2	8
County Secondary	0	0	0	0	9
Total	18	99	106	118	261
No data:	0	16	50	48	269
Universities					
Oxford: Trinity	0	8	2	7	7
New	1	7	5	9	8
Magdalen	1	5	7	4	3
Other	2	11	20	11	35
Cambridge: Trinity	2	12	14	14	18
Magdalene	1	4	4	6	0
Other	4	13	13	13	34
Other U.K.	1	10	5	7	34
Military	0	2	0	3	2
Foreign	0	0	4	1	11
None	6	29	33	43	109
Total	18	101	107	118	261

indicate a fairly selective recruitment process but not so restricted as occurred in the 'City'.

Club membership was analysed using the same prestigious and aristocratically connected clubs as in the earlier study, selected from discussions in Graves,[13] Lejeune,[14] Matthews[15] and Sampson,[16] i.e. the Carlton, Boodle's, Brook's, Buck's, the Beefsteak, Pratt's, the Turf, St James and White's. 73 (28 %) of the 261 directors for whom data were available were members of at least one, and often more, of these clubs. Many more were, of course, members of other clubs such as the Athenaeum, Junior Carlton, Garrick, City of London etc. This proportion is considerably lower than the 46 % found for the directors of large financial institutions, which suggests that industrial company directors are less associated with the traditional social elite's life style than are the 'City' directors; whether this

TABLE 3. *Membership of nine prestigious clubs*

Club	Financial institutions	Industrial companies	
		No. of directors	Firms represented
The Carlton	25	18	G.E.C., R.T.Z., Cadbury Schweppes, Unigate, I.C.I., Tate & Lyle, Sears, Tube Investments, Rank, Hawker Siddeley, B.I.C.C., Boots, B.P., Union International, Dunlop
Boodle's	23	12	T.I., Cadbury Schweppes, Dunlop, Bass Charrington, Burmah Oil, Shipping Industrial Holdings, Bowater, B.P., Allied Breweries, Boots, Bowring
Brooks's	41	15	G.E.C., R.T.Z., Shell T. & T., Dunlop, Distillers, Rank, B.P., Burmah Oil, T.I., I.C.I., Rolls Royce, Unilever, Bass Charrington
Buck's	4	10	I.C.I., Tate & Lyle, B.P., Burmah Oil, G.E.C., Boots, B.I.C.C., Shell T. & T., Hawker Siddeley, Rank Hovis McDougall, Allied Breweries, Rolls Royce, Bass Charrington
The Beefsteak	6	3	Shell T. & T., Dunlop, Distillers, Lucas, Rolls Royce
Pratt's	20	7	I.C.I., Tate & Lyle, Shell T. & T., Dunlop, S.I.H., Rolls Royce, G.E.C., B.P.
The Turf	15	4	B.P., Burmah Oil, Marks & Spencer, Unilever, Bass Charrington
St James'	6	2	Rank, R.T.Z.
White's	32	16	B.P., B.L.M.C., S.I.H., Bowater, Tate & Lyle, Boots, Rank, B.I.C.C., Shell T. & T., Hawker Siddeley, R.H.M., R.T.Z., Rolls Royce, Union International

Proportion of firms in network = 29:40 = 73 %.
Integration score ($N = 29$) = 0.97.
Firms not in network: Shell Mex & B.P., Imperial Tobacco, Coats Patons, Tesco, Thorn Electric, G.K.N., Reed International, G.U.S., Courtaulds, Allied Suppliers.

implies a divergence in values and reality constructions remains to be explored. The firms represented by membership of the nine clubs are listed in Table 3, as is the integration score for the network which, although very high, only applies to 73 % of the firms under discussion. It should be noted here that this measure takes all entries in a matrix above 1 as 1 and so underestimates the actual number of connections between two firms. Unlike the 'City' firms, where the two 'newcomers' are not represented, there does not appear to be any single characteristic of the eleven excluded firms which would account for their lack of connection with these clubs. The background characteristics of the directors of industrial companies then, indicate a restricted social origin and, for a considerable minority, affiliation with prestigious social institutions.

Overlapping directorships

Direct connections between the 40 industrial companies by overlapping directorships only occur between 21 firms, and two of these, Distillers and Lucas, are not connected with the other 19. These connections are diagrammed in Figure 1 and it can be seen that this network is not highly integrated, having in fact an integration score of 0.52. Again, these figures are much lower than in the case of the 'City' firms, where 93 % were directly connected by overlapping directorships with an integration score of 0.82. This picture changes rather when connections with the 'City' are taken into account. The network becomes too complicated to present figuratively and is unfortunately too large to reproduce as a matrix. 56 of the 67 firms are now included in the network, 31 industrial companies and 25 'City' ones, which indicates that a further 10 industrial companies now appear because they are directly connected to large 'City' firms and therefore included in the network. The merchant bank with the largest number of connections to industrial companies is Hill, Samuel and the clearing bank most industrially connected is the Midland; their networks are shown in Figure 2. As can be seen I.C.I. is the most connected industrial company. As Speigelberg[17] points out, many of these connections are fairly recent and reflect a growth in influence on the part of the financial institutions. The firms which are not included are: Allied Suppliers, Coats Patons, Great Universal Stores, Marks and Spencer, Reed International, Tesco, Thorn, Unilever and Union International. Of these nine, six are dominated by a single man or family; only two of the other 31 appear to have this characteristic – Sears Holdings, which is included because Sir Charles Clore was on the Board of Hill, Samuel, and Tate and Lyle which shares a director, Lord Boyd, with I.C.I. The comparative isolation of the 'tycoon' and 'family' type company Board from the 'City', the traditional elite, and other firms is reflected in other ways. The integration score for this network of 56 firms is 0.92, which is high and, it should be noted, higher than that for the 'City' firms taken alone: thus indicating that the cohesion of this combined network is not solely due to the comparatively highly interconnected 'City'. Again it should be pointed out that very often more than one director is held in common between two firms, but the integration score does not take this into account.

If indirect connections between industrial companies through over-lapping directorships of other firms, obtained from the *Directory of Directors* (1971), are included, 36 of the 40 firms are connected by at least one director, showing an integration score of 0.93 as indicated in Figure 3. Here again, it is notable that three of the four companies not in the network, Allied Suppliers, Marks and Spencer, Tesco and Union International, are 'tycoon' or 'family' firms. Furthermore, Thorn Electric and Great Universal Stores each have only one indirect connection with other

FIGURE 1. Overlapping directorships, industrial companies

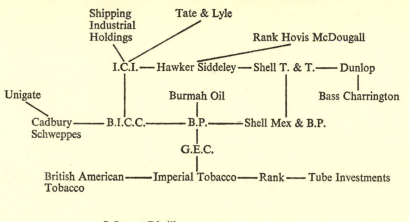

J. Lucas–Distillers

N = 19   Integration Score = 0.52

firms. Distillers and Unilever also have only one connection, with Lucas and B.A. Tobacco respectively, and Unigate and Tate and Lyle have two. When the financial institutions are included, 62 of the 67 are in the network, which has an integration score of 0.95. The omissions are: Allied Suppliers, Marks and Spencer, Tesco, Union International and Minster Assets. Firms only loosely connected (i.e. with only one or two overlaps) are Great Universal Stores, Tate and Lyle and Unilever. Thorn Electric has three connections. So again there seems to be a large, highly connected network of most major industrial and financial firms, with predominantly family or 'tycoon' controlled firms remaining largely isolated from this.

Kinship connections

This picture is substantially the same for kinship connections, except that for the industrial companies nuclear family connections are negligible. Using the same five criteria of kinship connection, based on common great grandparents, as in my earlier paper, fifteen of the 40 industrial companies are connected through directors mentioned in *Burke's Peerage* and *Burke's Landed Gentry*. Only seven of these, however, form a network greater than two, and as can be seen from Figure 4 this is only loosely integrated. These numbers are very low compared with those obtained for directors of the financial institutions, where it was found that 26 of the 27 firms were connected, with an integration score of 0.91. Obviously directors of very large industrial companies are much less associated with the aristocracy than are directors of large financial institutions. When the two sets of firms are combined, eighteen of the industrial firms are also included in the network to form one of 44 companies with an integration score of 0.94, which

FIGURE 2. Overlapping directorships: industrial connections of Hill, Samuel and the Midland Bank.[a]

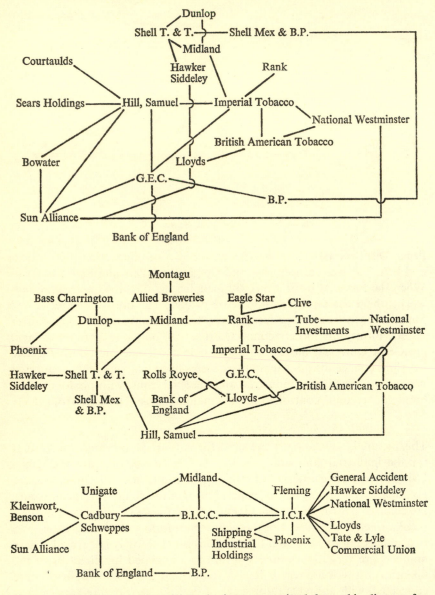

[a] Connections between Financial Institutions are omitted from this diagram for purposes of clarity.

is slightly higher than that for the 'City' firms alone. Hill, Samuel, Lloyds Bank and the Guardian Royal Exchange Insurance have the largest number of industrial kinship connections and R.T.Z. has the largest number of total kinship connections, as shown in Figure 5. With the exception of Tate and Lyle, none of the 'tycoon' and 'family' firms were in the network. These results show that although Boards of the very large industrial companies are not nearly so integrated with the traditional upper status group as are those of the large financial institutions, a considerable degree of connection between many large companies and financial firms does exist through the aristocracy. This may well have increased over the last 30 or so years as the management of large sums of money has become of increasing concern to the very large firm, and the need for sophisticated financial advice has correspondingly increased in conjunction with the growth of institutional investment.[18]

Conclusions

In comparing directors of 40 very large industrial companies with the directors of large financial institutions, both as distinct groups, and as one set, some fairly firm conclusions can be drawn. First, although the educational backgrounds of the industrial directors are not as restricted as that of the financial directors, they are still predominantly based on wealth, and a substantial number enjoy membership of an exclusive social institution, prestigious London clubs. Secondly, half of these firms share directors with at least one other in the set, although the network is not nearly so highly connected as the financial one. These connections are much increased when the 27 financial institutions are taken into account: only nine firms are not so connected. This suggests that the financial institutions play the central role in co-ordinating industrial companies' policies, and that seemingly disparate industries may be united through the financial elite. Obviously, however, the actual role of outside, financially expert directors remains to be determined, although according to data in Crawford[19] merchant banks often do put one of their directors on the Boards of client companies. Spiegelberg[20] also draws attention to the increasing influence of the merchant banks and institutions on large industrial companies. Furthermore, this network of directors from financial and industrial firms combined is highly structured. As would be expected, these figures are much increased when directorships of other firms are included, and again the 'City' and 'Industry' seem remarkably closely linked. Thirdly, while aristocratic kinship links do not appear to be particularly relevant for the industrial companies considered alone, they are important in connecting these companies to financial institutions and in producing a large, integrated network of the two groups combined. The directorship connections between industry and financial institutions, that is, are reinforced by, or alternatively can be seen as reflections of, kinship ties. The one group of

FIGURE 3. Indirect connections between 40 industrial companies by overlapping directorships. Integration score ($N = 36$) = 0.93. Firms not in network: Allied Suppliers, Marks & Spencer, Tesco, Union International.

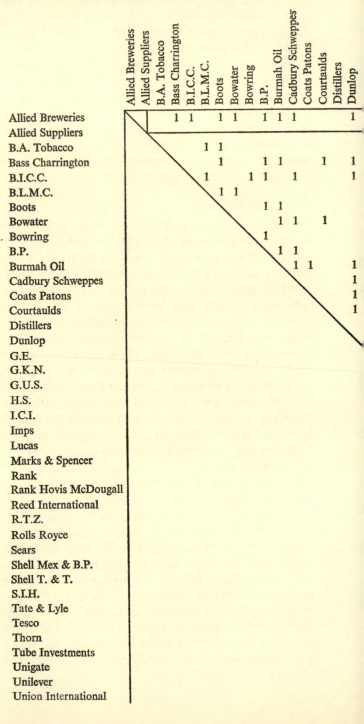

	Allied Breweries	Allied Suppliers	B.A. Tobacco	Bass Charrington	B.I.C.C.	B.L.M.C.	Boots	Bowater	Bowring	B.P.	Burmah Oil	Cadbury Schweppes	Coats Patons	Courtaulds	Distillers	Dunlop
Allied Breweries			1	1	1	1				1	1	1				1
Allied Suppliers																
B.A. Tobacco					1	1										
Bass Charrington					1					1	1			1		1
B.I.C.C.						1				1	1		1			1
B.L.M.C.					1	1										
Boots											1	1				
Bowater											1	1	1			
Bowring										1						
B.P.											1	1				
Burmah Oil												1	1			1
Cadbury Schweppes																1
Coats Patons																1
Courtaulds																1
Distillers																
Dunlop																
G.E.																
G.K.N.																
G.U.S.																
H.S.																
I.C.I.																
Imps																
Lucas																
Marks & Spencer																
Rank																
Rank Hovis McDougall																
Reed International																
R.T.Z.																
Rolls Royce																
Sears																
Shell Mex & B.P.																
Shell T. & T.																
S.I.H.																
Tate & Lyle																
Tesco																
Thorn																
Tube Investments																
Unigate																
Unilever																
Union International																

G.U.S.	H.S.	I.C.I.	Imps	Lucas	Marks & Spencer	Rank	Rank Hovis McDougall	Reed International	RTZ	Rolls Royce	Sears	Shell Mex & B.P.	Shell T. & T.	S.I.H.	Tate & Lyle	Tesco	Thorn	Tube Investments	Unigate	Unilever	Union International
		1	1	1	1				1				1								
	1	1	1						1									1	1		
	1	1			1								1	1							
		1	1	1	1	1	1	1	1				1								
		1	1					1										1			
		1	1		1				1				1					1	1		
			1		1					1		1	1								
			1		1				1					1							
					1	1	1	1	1		1										
	1				1		1						1								
	1	1	1		1				1	1			1					1			
													1	1							
1		1			1				1				1								
				1																	
	1	1			1	1	1						1	1							
	1	1	1		1	1	1	1	1				1		1			1			
1	1	1			1	1		1					1	1		1					
	1				1				1				1	1							
		1	1					1	1		1		1	1				1			
					1						1		1					1			
					1									1				1			
											1			1							
											1	1	1					1			
													1					1			
													1								
													1								

FIGURE 4. Industrial companies connected by kinship relations of directors

I.C.I. ————— Tate & Lyle
Boots Pure Drug ————— Hawker Siddeley
Imperial Tobacco ————— Shell T. & T.
Burmah Oil ————— Rolls Royce

Rank
|
Shipping Industrial Holdings
|
British Insulated————Rio Tinto Zinc————Tube Investments————Rank Hovis
Callender's Cables   McDougall
|
British Leyland
Motor Corporation

Integration Score (n = 7) = 0.23

The five criteria for determining whether a relationship existed between two directors were:

(*a*) a great grand parent in common,
(*b*) a great grand parent in common by marriage.
(*c*) a great grand parent in common by their siblings' marriage.
(*d*) a great grand parent in common by their children's marriage.
(*e*) a step great grand parent in common.

industrial companies which does not appear integrated into this combined elite is comprised of 'tycoon' or 'family' firms. It is also worth noting that 11 out of the 18 directors of Marks and Spencer, G.U.S., Thorn Electric, Sears and Tesco for whom educational data were available did not go to public school, a proportion much lower than that for directors of industrial companies as a whole. Not only, then, are these firms relatively unconnected through directorship, clubs or kinship to others and to the 'City', but recruitment to their Boards is not so narrowly limited as in the case of the others. Brown[21] has already pointed to some differences in growth and profits for 'tycoon' firms in the top 116,[22] an analysis which requires further extension. Brown also distinguishes between 'co-ordinator' and 'managerial' type boards, but on the basis of the evidence shown here there do not appear to be any purely 'managerial' companies in the top 40 except for Unilever and Allied Suppliers (in which, incidentally, Unilever has a substantial voting shareholding). Whether this is due to change in composition of the boards of large companies, or whether most 'managerial' boards are owned by overseas companies is not clear. A further point on these 'deviant' firms is that they are all fairly recent additions to the very large firm category. If the economists' ideas about the life cycle of the firm are applicable, then presumably these companies

FIGURE 5. Kinship relations of Hill, Samuel, Lloyds Bank, G.R.E., and R.T.Z. omitting connections between financial institutions.

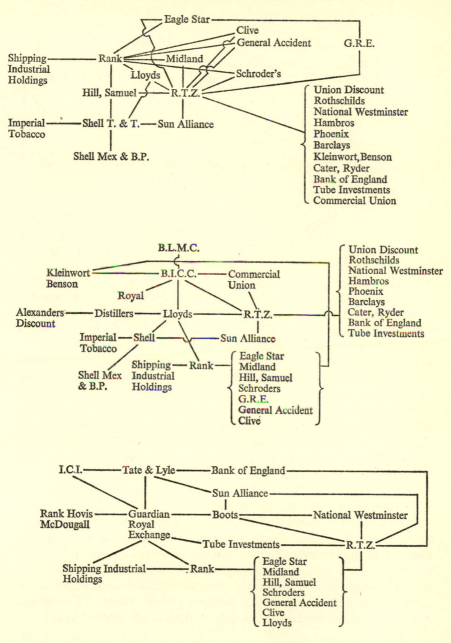

FIGURE 5 (*cont. overleaf*)

FIGURE 5 (*cont.*)

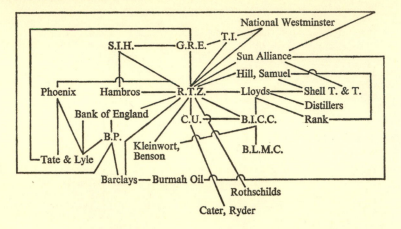

should eventually stabilise their growth rate and may well turn into connected companies with major institutional investors and merchant bankers on the Board.

In terms of seeing directors as an elite it appears that very large industrial and financial firms do recruit their Board members from a narrow segment in the population. These directors undergo a remarkably similar educational experience and, to some extent, have similar social circles as evidenced by club membership and kinship links. They tend, in other words, to be members of the same culture, or at any rate to have the background for sharing a common culture. The next step which needs to be taken is to ascertain to what extent these directors do, in fact, share a common view of social reality. Does, for example, the interconnectedness of financial and industrial Boards mean that the traditional opposition of the 'City' and 'Industry' has disappeared with the rise of giant companies, or do directors of merchant banks and of oil companies still see their basic interests diverging? Part of this question can be answered by finding out exactly how far the similarity of, and connections between, these directors have changed over the past 30 or 40 years. If they have indeed altered, then to what extent have these changes been associated with changes in financial and industrial strategy, and can we expect such changes to continue in the same direction? If we can ascertain the dimensions and dynamics of the culture of the financial–industrial elite, we may then proceed to suggest how this culture will mediate structural exigencies of developed capitalism, by constructing an overall theory of advanced capitalism which combines sociological and economic approaches.

5 An economic elite: a demographic profile of company chairmen*

Company chairmen are an elite within an elite. But, like the feudal monarchs with whom they are sometimes compared, their power and prestige varies widely. A small minority of chairmen, those whose rise to the top has been spectacular, or who have forsaken a total commitment to business activity in order to indulge a taste for public works, have become household names. The majority, sometimes partly by design, but most often because the manipulation of economic power is an affair shrouded with secrecy, keep well out of the public eye. Moreover, unlike the directors over whom they preside, they have never been the subject of systematic academic study.[1] We can readily distinguish, however, two principal factors, apart from the force of personality of the particular individual, which are likely to affect the position and power of the company chairman. One, of course, is the nature of the company he heads: the chairman who, for example, reaches this status as the end-result of a dynamic career within a rapidly expanding family firm will probably enjoy vastly greater powers than one who joins a firm which is already large and complex. A second, although not unrelated, factor is the definition of the chairman's role itself. Thus a chairmanship is not always a full-time job; a man may be chairman of a number of separate companies simultaneously, and may be little more than a figurehead in any of them.

Nature of the study

In this study (part of a broader study of business leaders) we set out to describe the social background and career structure of chairmen of large corporations and banks over a time period of some seventy years. A sample of firms was constructed initially by selecting the largest industrial companies, by asset size, at a number of different years – 1905, 1926, 1948, 1953, 1966 and 1971.[2] In order to facilitate comparisons between 'Industry' and 'The City', leading commercial and merchant banks were included, as were major railway companies prior to their nationalisation. In all, the sample included 199 industrial corporations and banks, distributed by sector as follows: 23 clearing banks; 26 merchant banks and finance houses; 82 firms engaged in 'miscellaneous manufacture'; 9 shipping companies; 5 oil companies; 21 brewery firms; 20 iron and steel corporations; and 13 railway companies.[3] Using the Stock Exchange Yearbook

TABLE 1

	No. of chairmen	No. included in study	No information (%)
Clearing banks	82	74	10
Merchant banks	45	38	16
Miscellaneous manufacture	202	161	21
Breweries	70	55	21
Iron and steel	56	41	25
Railways	37	37	0
Shipping	27	21	22
Oil	15	14	7
Retail	25	19	24
Total	559	460	18

names of company chairmen were identified from the turn of the century up to the present time. A range of sources was then combed in order to gather together as much biographical information upon these individuals as possible.[4] We were able to gain information upon three-quarters or more of the chairmen in each sector (Table 1).

In order to examine changes over the period 1900–72 we have grouped our chairmen into age cohorts. These findings are discussed later in the paper. In the first two sections, we analyse social background and career patterns in terms of an overall comparison of different economic sectors.

Social background and recruitment

It is commonly asserted that, while in other institutional settings, such as Parliament, the Civil Service, the Army and the Church, there has been a relatively 'closed' process of recruitment, in which social and material privilege has been perpetuated via the public schools and Oxford and Cambridge, the sphere of industry has been a haven of opportunity for the boy of lowly background intent on achieving high position. Certainly there is some evidence to indicate substantial rates of intergenerational mobility among industrial managers. Thus Clements' research, published in 1958, showed that some 30 % of managers in his sample were from manual backgrounds, and had indeed begun their careers on the shop-floor. He also showed, on the other hand, that there were definite limits upon the range of mobility which most of them experienced: no more than a handful of such men actually became directors.[5] If we examine directors themselves, the picture alters: only a tiny minority are from a working class background, and some two thirds have been educated at a public school; of those who are graduates, about the same proportion as this attended Oxford and Cambridge.[6] Moreover, there is a definite hierarchy according to size of firm: the larger the firm, normally the more marked the proportion of directors with public school and/or Oxbridge backgrounds.[7]

TABLE 2. *Social origins*

	Working class (%)	Middle class (%)	Upper class (%)	Unknown (%)	Total nos. of individuals
Clearing banks	—	3	74	23	74
Merchant banks	—	—	89	11	38
Miscellaneous manufacture	1	13	59	27	161
Breweries	2	11	75	12	55
Iron and steel	2	11	55	32	41
Railways	—	11	86	3	37
Shipping	—	10	67	23	21
Oil	—	13	47	40	14
Retail	—	32	21	47	19
Mean	1	10	66	23	460

We might expect to find this trend further accentuated for company chairmen, the elite within the economic elite, and our data indicates this to be the case. Of our total population (460 chairmanships), there are no more than five cases in which chairmen can be definitely identified as working class by social origin – although it seems probable that, given the nature of the sources from which we drew our material, which mainly depend upon whatever information a man chooses to provide about himself, the 'unknowns' may include a certain number of individuals from relatively humble backgrounds. Ten per cent of chairmen were of middle class origin, while 3 % were from a background of small business. But the vast majority, 66 % of the total, were upper class in origin, as we defined this latter term.[8]

Table 2 provides a more detailed breakdown of the social origins of our total sample. There are evident differences shown here between the banks and industrial companies – differences which express contrasts between 'the City' and 'Industry'. The chairmen of the banks are drawn overwhelmingly from the upper class (74 % of those on whom information was obtained) even if we assume that all the 'unknowns' (15 %) derive from the other classes, which is almost certainly not the case, the selective character of the recruitment process is very marked. There are also, however, clear differences between the two sets of financial institutions themselves: among the chairmen of the merchant banks, within which the hold of family interests is still very strong, we were unable to locate one case of an individual emanating from a background outside the upper class. The clearing banks do show a few such examples, with 2 % of chairmen being of middle class origin – although again there are none who have risen from a working class background. In the sphere of industry, on the other hand, these latter classes are somewhat more adequately represented, with 14.0 % of the total being recruited from them. But only a minute proportion have climbed to the pinnacle from a background of manual labour; most are of

TABLE 3. *Educational background*

	Public (%)	Other secondary[a] (%)	Private (%)	Unknown (%)	Total nos. of individuals
Clearing banks	86	8	1	5	74
Merchant banks	76	5	4	15	38
Miscellaneous manufacture	54	15	9	23	161
Breweries	76	7	5	12	55
Iron and steel	70	13	9	8	41
Railways	70	3	8	19	37
Shipping	62	5	—	33	21
Oil	57	36	—	7	14
Retail	21	5	21	53	19
Total	65	11	7	17	460

[a] This column includes a small number of persons who attended only elementary school.

white-collar origins. These differences between men in banking and industry are confirmed when we compare the proportions of chairmen in these two spheres whose forebears appear in *Burke's Peerage* or *Burke's Landed Gentry*. 24 % of those in banking as a whole have parents, and 23 % parents-in-law mentioned in the first, as compared to 17 % and 10 % respectively of those in industry (12 % and 9 % in manufacturing); for *Burke's Landed Gentry* the respective figures are 21 % and 15 %; 11 % and 9 %. Again, among the banking chairmen, the merchant bankers are clearly distinct, having a markedly higher proportion of parents or parents-in-law in both *Burke's Peerage* and in *Burke's Landed Gentry* as compared to the chairmen of clearing banks. The merchant bankers were the only group among our total sample of chairmen with a sizeable proportion of individuals (21 %) having parents or parents-in-law appearing in each of these chronicles of the British aristocracy.

In both banking and industry, the large majority of chairmen have been educated at public schools (see Table 3). Once more the preponderance of public school education is more marked among the bankers than those in industry as a whole; although in some sectors, notably brewing and railways, the prominence of those with a public school background rivals, or is equivalent, to that found in banking. It seems reasonable to assume that the 'unknowns' among chairmen in miscellaneous manufacturing include a considerable proportion of those who received a non-public school education; but even without such an assumption, this group emerges as the least privileged in terms of educational experience. This is further demonstrated if we examine the proportions of public schoolboys who attended one of the Clarendon Schools, and also if we look at the numbers who were educated at both public schools and Oxford and

TABLE 4. *Type of public school (not including those 'privately' educated)*

	Total individuals at public school	Eton (%)	Harrow (%)	Other Clarendon (%)	Total Clarendon as % of public school excluding 'private'	Total individuals at Clarendon schools
Clearing banks	64	34	11	22	67	43
Merchant banks	29	59	7	14	79	23
Miscellaneous manufacture	87	10	3	14	27	24
Breweries	42	43	14	10	67	28
Iron and steel	29	21	7	21	49	14
Railways	26	54	19	12	85	22
Shipping	13	23	7	46	76	10
Oil	8	25	—	25	50	4
Retail	4	—	—	—	—	—
Total	302	30	9	17	56	168

TABLE 5. *University education (total sample)*

	% known to have university education[a]	Public school and Oxbridge (%)	London/provincial university (%)
Clearing banks	58	53	5
Merchant banks	63	63	—
Miscellaneous manufacture	32	24	8
Breweries	47	44	4
Iron and steel	43	36	7
Railways	49	43	5
Shipping	43	38	5
Oil	36	36	—
Retail	11	5	5
Total	46	37	5

[a] These figures do not include a small number of persons educated at universities abroad.

Cambridge (Tables 4 and 5). Seventy per cent of banking chairmen who attended public schools were educated at a Clarendon school, and 55 % at either Eton or Harrow; only 27 % of manufacturing chairmen attended a Clarendon school. Breweries, railways and shipping again show the highest proportion of individuals having a Clarendon education within the general sphere of industry. A similar pattern emerges with university education. Only among bankers was there a majority who received university education of any sort. Of those who attended university, the vast majority went to Oxford or Cambridge, and virtually all of these had been at public schools.

Career patterns

Very few of our chairmen started their working careers in a manual job. Those who did so, as one would expect, were found in manufacturing industry and the retail trade, and 4 of these six cases began their careers in the nineteenth century, like the three who built up their own businesses from small concerns into massive empires. The poor boy who has succeeded in becoming the chairman of one of Britain's largest companies is rare indeed. Our data lend support to Blau and Duncan's thesis that first job is of vital importance in occupational mobility.[9] While a certain proportion (7 %) of chairmen started in routine white-collar employment, normally as clerical workers, by far the largest group began in higher administrative jobs. A smaller, though significant, number of chairmen started their careers in the professions, predominantly accountancy. This tendency strengthens as we approach present day chairmen. However, only in the case of the iron and steel industry, is a start in the professions more important than an early post in higher administration. In the retail trade the figures for higher administration and the professions are similar. In banking it is noticeable that the law is well represented among the professional element. The proportion of those beginning in professional occupations is lowest in manufacture; the vast majority of individuals here begin in managerial occupations, although not necessarily in the firm of which they eventually become chairmen, as will be indicated below. By no means all chairmen spend the whole of their career as businessmen. There is in the sample a sprinkling of individuals who have passed most of their lives in the civil service or in a military or political career, usually assuming a chairmanship only when that career is terminated, but such cases are relatively uncommon and becoming more so. In modern times the tendency has been for chairmen to be full-time professional businessmen. A recent survey, examining the two hundred largest corporations in Britain, found that the chairman also acted as managing director in over half of them.

Most individuals do not begin their careers within the organisation of which they become chairman; the majority of those who do are members of family firms. Within the clearing banks, 14 % of chairmen began inside the firm, 58 % outside;[10] for manufacture, the comparable figures are 38 % and 45 %; for the industrial sectors as a whole, the figures are 32 % and 44 %. Overall, the influence of family connections is pronounced: 23 % of bankers (47 % of merchant bankers) began their careers in firms which were either controlled by members of the same family, or in which they were strongly represented among the shareholders. 26 % of chairmen in industry did so. Moreover a certain number of individuals (13 % in banking, 4 % in industry) spent some time in other occupations before entering the family firm.

Chairmen are not a youthful group; most only reach their elevated position when they are far on into their working careers. Virtually all chairmen spend a long period as directors in the firm of which they eventually assume command; but only a small minority first become vice-chairmen. A handful of men, in family firms, become chairmen within a decade of beginning their business career (2 %); for most (60 %), the process takes at least thirty years. As a whole, those in sectors in which the influence of family firms is most pronounced succeed in reaching the chairmanship position at an earlier phase in their careers than those in areas where the representation of family figures is weaker – but this is not as clear a trend as one might anticipate.

A sizeable proportion of chairmen, including some of those who assume this position quite late on in their careers, have a very long tenure in the job; many continue long past a normal retiring age. A chairman may be brought into a company on a purely transitory basis – sometimes, for example, as a conciliator between two groups of directors whose conflicts may have stimulated the departure of the previous incumbent. But this is rare; out of our total sample, only 11 % of chairmen had a period of tenure of less than two years – although in the cases of the clearing banks and breweries this figure rises to 18 %. The average length of tenure of all chairmen was 10 years; an extended tenure was most common among those in breweries, iron and steel, and manufacturing, about 33 % of whom in each sector held their chairmanship for a period of fifteen years or more. There is a considerable amount of lateral movement in the upper reaches of finance and industry as indexed by the patterns of chairmen's careers. Many of the individuals covered in this study have been chairmen of several companies at different points in their career, and it happens fairly frequently that this process of lateral mobility is simultaneously one of upward movement between firms of ascending size and importance. It is much rarer, in fact, for a man to hold several chairmanships simultaneously, and in most cases where this does occur, the companies involved are subsidiaries of a parent firm of which the individual is chairman.

A certain proportion (17 %) of chairmen were involved in active political careers, both in national and local politics. Those who played a role in national politics normally did so in the early part of their careers, often while holding directorships in the companies of which they later became chairmen. Twenty-nine per cent of brewers and 41 % of railway chairmen were M.P.s at some point in their life history, and 19 % of those in the other spheres of industry. Nearly all were either Conservative or Liberal. The oil industry, a more recent arrival on the scene, of course, than the others, is the only one not to boast any M.P.s among the chairmen in our sample. Fewer chairmen engaged in local politics during the course of careers than participated on the national level, but many have maintained strong local connections – indicated, for example, by the fact that they have acted as J.P.s for their local judiciary. Chairmen present, in one particular sense, a distinguished profile. The great majority have received some form of honour, although not always ostensibly for their business activities. Of those without a hereditary title, 41 % received a knighthood and 37 % became baronets or barons. Those who did inherit a title are a sizeable group (10 %) and are especially well represented among those who became chairmen between the turn of the century and the First World War.[11] Disraeli's remark, that Britain is ruled, not by an aristocracy but by an 'aristocratic principle', 'an aristocracy which absorbs all aristocracies' is well exemplified here!

The chairman of a large industrial company or bank is, of course, normally in a highly advantageous market position, both from the point of view of protecting the interests of others, and of fostering his own interests. Consequently it is not surprising that many chairmen are at the centre of a radiating circle of business connections. On average, our chairmen held 10 directorships over the course of their careers.[12] Occasionally a man becomes a director of numerous firms before becoming chairman of one of them; far more common is for him to accumulate directorships during the time at which he is chairman of a major company. Such findings, however, have to be interpreted with caution. The individual who holds a large number of directorships does not, as is often assumed, wield more power or influence than a man whose business interests are more confined; on the contrary, the most influential men are often those whose formal connections with other economic enterprises are few. In fact, we may state as a principle that the demonstration of interconnections between directorships in itself gives us no indication of the actual structure of power which operates in economic life. Such interconnections, however, do give us a possible guide to the channels of information and established contacts which exist between different sectors of finance and industry.

The directorships held by chairmen during their tenure as chairmen were categorised into the sectors mentioned at the beginning of the article. Ignoring those concentrations of directorships within the sector within which the chairmanship is held, the importance of banking is particularly apparent. It is not so much that banking chairmen have many directorships in other areas, but that non-banking chairmen have directorships in banking (45 % or more of chairmen in spheres other than banking held banking directorships). Similarly it is noticeable that whereas the chairmen of one sector may have many directorships in another sector the chairmen of that sector may shun directorships in the latter sphere. Thus 55 % of iron and steel chairmen had directorships in the oil industry whereas only 6 % of the oil chairmen had directorships in iron and steel firms. The outstanding case of mutual attraction is that of the oil and shipping industries.

Changes over time

By grouping together all chairmen born within successive periods of
twenty years from 1820 to 1939, we established seven age-cohorts in terms
of which to examine changes in recruitment and career structure. Broadly
speaking, these document the increasing emergence of a centralised
economic elite, shedding some of the local attachments which are still
rather prominent in the early and middle part of the nineteenth century.
One index of this is the importance of local political careers (Table 6):
considerably larger proportions of chairmen were local councillors or
aldermen among the earlier than among the later generations. The proportions of those serving as J.P.s also declined, and the level of involvement in Parliament changed significantly.

Our data do not indicate that there has occurred a process of increasing
'openness' of recruitment to the chairs of the largest corporations but, if
anything, something the contrary of this. The numbers of chairmen
deriving from working-class backgrounds is negligible at all periods; but
the proportion from middle class origins seems to have declined slightly –
although the numbers involved are too small to make any precise judgements on this. Certainly in terms of educational background, upon which
the available information is more complete than upon father's occupation,
the public schools more than hold their own over the period, and the
Clarendon schools come to play an increasingly prominent role. It is also
evident that, towards the end of the nineteenth century, university education – virtually always at Oxford and Cambridge – assumes greater
importance (see Table 7).

But these phenomena vary to some degree according to the type of
economic sector in question. Banking is clearly shown to be the most
fixed and unchanging in terms of the class background and educational
experience of its chairmen. Among bankers born between 1840–59, 18 %
had parents and 23 % parents-in-law mentioned in *Burke's Peerage*, and
27 % and 32 % had such relatives who appeared in *Burke's Landed Gentry*;
among those born between 1900–19, the corresponding percentages are
30 % and 24 %; and 35 % and 12 %. Of chairmen in manufacturing born
in the 1840–59 period, 16 % had parents and 11 % parents-in-law appearing in the former source, and none at all in the latter; these percentages
compare with 7 % having parents and the same figure having parents-in-
law, in *Burke's Peerage*; and 10 % having parents, 2 % having parents-in-
law mentioned in *Burke's Landed Gentry* of those born between 1900–19.
Taking again the same two periods, 58 % of manufacturing chairmen
attended public schools in the earlier period, 53 % in the later one; of
these public schoolboys, 9 % of the 1840–59 generation, and 24 % of the
subsequent group, were at Clarendon schools.

Almost without exception, banking chairmen in the different generations,

TABLE 6. *Political and judicial posts*

Chairmen born between:	M.P. (%)	Local political (%)	J.P. (%)	Total of individuals
1820 and 1839	36	4	52	25
1840 and 1859	26	21	59	78
1860 and 1879	19	5	28	114
1880 and 1899	8	2	16	130
1900 and 1919	4	1	6	113[a]

[a] For the purpose of this table the very small number of individuals born before 1820 and after 1919 (3) contained in the sample have been included in the generation closest to their date of birth.

TABLE 7. *Education: public school and Oxbridge*

Chairmen born between:	% at Public school	Private school	% of public school-boys at Clarendon schools	% of public school-boys at Eton or Harrow	School unknown (%)	% attending public school and Oxford and Cambridge
1820 and 1839	75	8	33	22	25	28
1840 and 1859	58	13	66	51	21	32
1860 and 1879	59	10	61	43	19	34
1880 and 1899	70	3	51	34	11	39
1900 and 1919	74	1	48	31	12	42

in the clearing and merchant banks alike, begin their careers in professional or higher administrative occupations; the proportion of those beginning as professionals does, however, change, as we shall mention further below. In some of the other spheres of industry, the proportions of those who begin in professional occupations also varies over the generations. It seems clear that, in these spheres, whatever upward mobility is possible tends to be channelled through this route. A man from relatively lowly origins will, for example, enter chartered accountancy, become a partner in the business, and subsequently move over into the enterprise of which he finally becomes chairman. In both banking and industry, however, there is evidence of a general consolidation of career patterns. In the earlier years of the nineteenth century, it is not uncommon to find cases of individuals who spent large parts of their careers in commercial enterprises located in the Empire, especially India, returning eventually to Britain, there to assume the chairman's role. More generally, the type of career pattern whereby a man takes a job outside the family firm, then joins the latter firm ten or twenty years later, becomes less and less in evidence. On the

TABLE 8. *Locus of first job*

Chairmen born between:	Inside company of which chairman		Outside company of which chairman			
	Family (%)	Non-family (%)	Family[a] (%)	Non-family (%)	Unknown (%)	Total nos. of individuals
1820 and 1839	42	3	—	28	28	25
1840 and 1859	31	2	11	42	14	78
1860 and 1879	20	7	7	46	20	114
1880 and 1899	23	8	5	42	22	130
1900 and 1919	21	12	4	39	24	113

[a] This column refers to those persons whose first job was located outside the family firm of which they later became Chairman.

other hand, the persistence of a strong family influence into modern times is marked among chairmen both in banking and in industry. This is most prominent and direct, of course, among the merchant bankers, but is still notable in the other sectors, where unequivocal family control in terms of share ownership seems to have disappeared.

Table 8 classifies first job in relation to type of enterprise within which the individual began his career. The two left-hand vertical columns refer to those whose first job was in the company of which they later became chairmen; these are subdivided so as to distinguish individuals who began in a firm with which they had a definite family connection from those who appear to have had no such connection. The third and fourth vertical columns refer to those who started their careers outside the firm of which they later assumed the chairmanship. These individuals are sub-classified according to whether or not they subsequently became chairmen of firms with which they had a family connection.

A family connection refers not only to those companies in whose cases it has been established that the close relations (parents, grandparents, parents-in-law, uncles, brothers or cousins) of a chairman had a substantial ownership interest, but also to those companies of which the father of a chairman is known to have been a director. Although the decline in family influence is quite clear, it appears to have been an important element in the careers of many chairmen of recent times. Approximately one quarter of those who became chairmen of major industrial and financial corporations in Britain after the Second World War had a family link with the firm over which they presided. The outstanding examples of continuing family influence are those of the brewing and retail industries, and the merchant banks.

Over the generations, in spite of the fact that the proportion of those having a university education increases, implying that the men concerned enter work at a somewhat more advanced age than their earlier counterparts, the average length of time taken to reach the chairmanship position tends to decrease. Thus those born between 1840–59 become chairmen at an average stage of from forty to forty-nine years after the initial commencement of their business careers; those born between 1900–19 most often reached this position between thirty and thirty-nine years after they entered the labour market. Average length of tenure of chairmanships, by contrast, as one would expect, tends to increase.

These general points can be amplified by looking in more detail at differences between generations within specific sectors. Generations will be referred to as follows: generation I those born between 1800 and 1819; generation II those born between 1820 and 1839; generation III those born between 1840 and 1859; generation IV those born between 1860 and 1879; generation V those born between 1880 and 1899; generation VI those born between 1900 and 1919; generation VII those born between 1920 and 1939. The numbers of chairmen born in generations I, II and VII is so small that only rare reference will be made to them.

I. *Banking.* The exclusive nature of the social backgrounds of banking chairmen is partially evidenced by the character of their educational experience. Consistently 80 % of each generation of leading bankers have been educated at public schools, the share of the Clarendon schools increasing over time. In generation III 38 % of public school boys attended Clarendon schools; the figure for generation IV is 47 %, 70 % for generation V, and 71 % for generation VI. Eton has a particularly remarkable record. In generation III Harrow appears more strongly represented than Eton, but from then on its presence wanes while the Etonian element gains in importance. Accounting for only 6 % of generation III, the figure for Eton rises to 26 % in generation IV, 35 % in generation V and 47 % in generation VI.[13] In a similar fashion, graduates of Oxford and Cambridge are increasingly well represented. In generation III 44 % attended a public school and then Oxbridge; in generation VI this rises to 71 %.

Merchant bankers, as we have shown, appear to be more consistently upper class than clearing bankers in terms of social origins. However the evidence with regard to education suggests that merchant bankers reached a peak of exclusiveness in generations IV and V. The proportion of chairmen in this group who attended Clarendon schools rose from 50 % in generation II to 71 % in generation V, then declining to 53 % in generation VI. Similarly the Etonian element rises from 25 % of the sample in generation III to 66 % in generation IV, declining to 50 % and 41 % in generations V and VI. A further reflection of this is found in the figures for merchant bankers attending both public school and Oxford or Cambridge. In generation II 50 % are in this category; this rises to 71 % in generation V and then 'declines' to 59 %.

If attention is turned to data relating to first job it appears that while the proportion of those taking higher administrative posts and those entering the professions has remained fairly constant in the clearing banks, there is a notable increase in the professional element in generations V and VI. This may be another indication of the lingering effects of family control in merchant banks which has retarded the influence of the so-called 'managerial revolution.' In terms of the influence of family connections, only the well established brewing, and relatively 'new' retail, industries rival the merchant banks. Of generation III, 75 % of merchant banking chairmen assumed that position within family firms, and while this declines to 53 % in generation VI, it is still remarkably high. This is not the place to attempt to explain why the adoption of more 'modern' corporate forms, should be much more limited in some sectors of the economy than others but such an investigation would be a revealing study of the intermingling of the constraints of kinship and the exigencies of business life. Clearing banks evidence a much closer similarity to the general pattern of diminishing family influence (though perhaps this remains more significant than might have been expected), declining from 33 % in generation III to 12 % in generation VI.

In regard to direct political involvement the evidence on membership of the House of Commons confirms that the decline, mentioned previously in regard to combined totals, is borne out in the case of bankers.[14] Banking chairmen who were also M.P.s at some point in their careers are located primarily in generations III and IV. Similarly there is decline in local affiliations from generation III, when 56 % of chairmen were J.P.s, the same proportion being councillors or aldermen, to generation VI where the figures are 12 % and 0 % respectively.

II. *Brewing.* Brewing is an industry in which the leading companies have long family traditions, sometimes dating back to the early part of the nineteenth century.[15] It is not going too far to say that certain brewing companies have an almost unrivalled record of survival and growth, and must be among the 'oldest' capitalist organisations in existence. It is not, then, surprising, that throughout the twentieth century the chairmen of the major breweries have been consistently upper class in social background, although there is evidence of some middle class entry in generations III and IV, when approximately 6 % of the chairmen came from this group; 76 % of brewery chairmen attended public schools (80 % if those educated 'privately' are included) while 67 % of these public schoolboys attended Clarendon schools. Clarendon schools other than Eton are represented in generations II, III and IV, but it is noticeable that Etonians account for the total Clarendon representation in generations VI and VII. This no doubt partly reflects the family tradition of son following father and the success of a number of family firms with an Etonian tradition in surviving into the latter half of the twentieth century as top companies.[16]

There is also a clear tendency for a public school/Oxbridge education to become the predominant form of education. In generation III only 26% of future brewery chairmen attended both a public school and Oxbridge. By generation VI the figure was stabilising around 60%.

The brewing industry appears to have more formal ties, through the careers of brewing chairmen, with politics at the national level than any other sector of industry except that of the railways. Yet in the case of brewing these figures reflect the strong local affiliations of certain families which had established an almost proprietory right to certain constituencies in which their factories and homes were located. As we have observed elsewhere the peak appears among the earlier generations (II, III, IV). Similarly the proportion of chairmen who were also J.P.s is highest in generation II, when 50% of the future chairmen born in that generation served in such a capacity. The clear indication is that this kind of political activity on the local and national level by leading businessmen declined sharply after the First World War. As both politics and business became full time occupations at the highest levels so fewer chairmen found the time to become professional politicians. The introduction of salaries for M.P.s introduced a new competitive element into political activity, for hitherto only those with some form of private income could afford to be an M.P. Most of those brewing chairmen who served as M.P.s did so before the First World War, and only in very few cases do we find professional politicians moving into 'brewery chairs'.

The strong family influence in top positions in the leading brewing companies is evidenced by the fact that 64% of those chairmen had direct family links with the firm of which they became chairman. This proportion varies little over time.

III. *Iron and steel.* Analysis of the social origins of steel leaders by generations shows that, after a high and fairly consistent level of upper class representation the proportion of men with upper class backgrounds declines between generations IV and VI, from 67% to 44%.[17] In her classic work on the steel industry Erickson has shown that approximately 90% of steel leaders were from Social Class I backgrounds. The discrepancy between her figures and those quoted above reflects the more restricted sense in which the term 'upper class' is employed here rather than any real disagreement over the facts of the matter. The decline in upper class content probably reflects the 'voluntary abdication' of power to which Erickson refers when noting the waning of family influence which occurred in the 'thirties. At that time the industry suffered a period of serious economic decline which left many firms both technologically backward and increasingly questionable as a source of profit. The figures on first job reveal that the professional element was better represented than in other industries, and this is connected to the onset of this period of crisis. There are two distinct groups within the professional element in the industry which relate to two different sets of conditions. In the earlier generations the professionals were mainly the sons of steel leaders, who had entered law after going to a public school and possibly attending Oxford or Cambridge. Erickson argues that this can be interpreted as part of a search for social acceptance on the part of industrialists who in the long established tradition of new wealth were treading those paths which facilitated their entry, and especially their children's, into the ranks of established wealth. However, the character of this professional element changed in generations V and VI as the representation of barristers declined and that of actuaries and accountants rose. These latter were the men, often recruited from outside the industry, whose skills were necessary in order to attempt the rescue of foundering enterprises during the recurrent difficulties of the inter-war years.[18]

It is fair to conclude from an examination of the educational experience of the iron and steel chairmen that while this group was always characteristically privileged the quality of this selectivity changed over time. Public school representation reaches a peak in generation IV (92 %), expressing no doubt the success of the newly burgeoning schools in attracting the sons of established iron and steel leaders. However there appears to be evidence of a decline in public school representation in generations V and VI (although this is much less pronounced if we express the percentages as a proportion of those on whom we have information rather than percentages of the whole sample). Much more noticeable is the decline in the prominence of Clarendon schools among the public school element. The Clarendon representation is highest when public school representation is highest: in generation IV, when 73 % of the sample attending public schools went to Clarendon schools. Etonians are best represented at this time also; that is among the group who would have first attended public school between 1870 and 1889. However from then onwards the Clarendon group drops sharply to 17 % of public schoolboys in generation VI. If we assume that Clarendon schools are attended, in the main by representatives of the wealthiest and most prestigeful sections of the population, then the conclusion must be that as we move toward the present day then the leaders of the iron and steel industry, while being drawn from a fairly restricted section of society, became relatively speaking less 'select' than once was the case.

At the same time, however, the public school/Oxbridge 'channel' remains an important route of entry to the chairmanships of the companies in question. Twenty-five per cent of generation III chairmen travelled this course, while the comparable figures for generations IV, V, and VI are 25 %, 54 % and 44 %. The representation of other universities is in fact highest in generations III and IV.

Erickson has already charted the relative decline of the family firm in the steel industry in the latter quarter of the period 1860–1950. Our figures only apply to those who became chairmen of large iron and steel companies between 1900 and 1969. But they are in basic agreement with Erickson's much more detailed analysis. Between generations III, IV, and V the percentage of men having a family connection with the firm of which they eventually became chairmen declined from 62 % to 25 % to 8 %. This again reflects the introduction of the salaried administrator during a time of crisis. That these administrators were predominantly recruited from outside the industry itself is readily evident and confirms the observation that the industry was unable to provide the financial skills that were demanded during the Depression.

The pattern in respect to overt political involvements is the usual one. Those chairmen who were M.P.s belong predominantly to generations III and IV, and were in positions of business leadership either prior to the First World War, or during the period immediately after. Local affiliations, measured in terms of numbers of chairmen who were J.P.s or local councillors show a continual decline from generation III onwards.

IV. *Miscellaneous manufacture.* Miscellaneous manufacturing covers a whole range of industrial activities. This group contains the largest proportion of chairmen for whom we were unable to obtain information on their social origins (29 % of the total sample.) Confining ourselves to the sample on whom information was obtained (128) it is noticeable that there is a gradual increase in the proportion of middle class representation within each generation between generations II (17 %) and IV (24 %). The tendency is to drop to a lower level of middle class representation in the generations after that (V 8 %, VI 10 %), suggesting that a period of relative 'openness' had been followed by a 'closing off' of top positions as far as the major manufacturing companies are concerned. This occurred when social barriers against entry into elite positions by men of middle and working class origin were commonly assumed to be weakening. It should be noted that only one chairman of the companies in this category was born after 1919. Clearly it is going to be some years before the full impact of the 1944 Education Act and later educational changes of similar import can be assessed in terms of their effect on entry into elite positions both in industry and other sectors of society. However, the upper class content remained high throughout each generation, accounting for 75 % of all those for whom information was obtained.

The rather large number of 'unknowns' complicates the interpretation of the figures relating to the education of chairmen of manufacturing companies. The figures show a gradual decline, from 80 % to 58 % from generations II to IV in public school representation. After this, in generations V and VI, the public school representation moves up to 69 % and 66 % respectively. The decline in generation IV is partly due to the relatively large number who were educated 'privately' (17 %). It is also related to the penetration of middle class elements in this generation, and this is reflected in the fact that 25 % attended only elementary, local endowed or 'non-public' secondary schools.

The Clarendon schools are increasingly in evidence among the public school element up to generation V (39 %) and then decline in generation VI to 24 %. Thus the peak of Clarendon representation occurred at a time when non-public schools made a significant contribution to the sample. This may reflect the changing composition of the 'Top 50' over the past two decades. There appears to be a juxtaposition of at least two types of company: those large firms, long established as major concerns, with a characteristically upper class leadership; and those companies which have a recent history of rapid growth and whose chairmen are less consistently upper class.

As noted elsewhere, the public school/Oxbridge channel of entry has become established as a major characteristic of manufacturing chairmen. In generation III, 11 % of the total sample for that period attended public school and Oxford or Cambridge. The proportion then rises smoothly to 33 % in generation VI. Other universities are poorly represented, appearing only in the early and latest generations. One unambiguous trend is the decline in direct family connections. In generations II and III, approximately 70 % of chairmen had family connections with their firms; this declined to 27 % in generation IV, rose slightly in generation V, and then declined again subsequently to 18 %.

The gradual decline in the proportion of manufacturing chairmen who held a seat in the House of Commons mirrors what has been observed elsewhere. In generation II 33 % were M.P.s, while the figure for generation VI is 8 %. This pattern is matched in relation to the proportions who became J.P.s or local councillors. Sixty-six per cent of chairmen in generation II were J.P.s, 50 % in generation III, declining to 5 % in generation VI. This latter figure, of course, may rise slightly as these men complete their careers, but it is unlikely to change the general trend. Similarly council activity declines from 26 % in generation III to 5 % in generation V, and thereafter disappears. These figures are clearly an indication of the decline of 'local' affiliations on the part of top businessmen as their business becomes more national and international in its orientation.

V. *Railways*. Railway companies were, of course, among the earliest of the large industrial joint stock companies. In contrast to the merchant banks (and breweries) we look to them for examples of companies which even in the nineteenth century appear as predominantly 'public' companies. However what is noticeable about railway boards, and their chairmen in particular, is that they appear among the most selectively recruited in any sector of industry. More than in other industries, railway chairmen appear to have been recruited from outside the railway industry itself. Upper class representation in terms of social origins never drops below 78 % in any of the generations. The elite nature of railway chairmen is confirmed by the observation that 43 % had parents who appear in *Burke's Peerage*. However it is noticeable that the 'best connected' generations in this sense are II and III, when presumably the connection between the railways and landowners was still fairly strong.

The public school representation is extremely high throughout each generation of railway chairmen, and if we confine our attention to those chairmen on whom we have information, and include the 'privately educated' within the public school category, then 97 % of the railway chairmen received this form of education. Again Etonians are extremely well represented, comprising 38 % of the total, or 47 % of those on whom information in regard to education was obtained. Indeed 59 % of the whole sample attended Clarendon schools. As elsewhere, the public school and Oxbridge route is a well established factor in that 43 % of the total sample completed this type of education.

In contrast with other industries 86 % of railway chairmen started their careers outside the companies which they were later to lead. The proportion who were 'professional' railwaymen is minute. Thus the early start for railways as joint stock companies, the relatively low level of family control in the twentieth century, did not dramatically 'democratise' entry into the senior positions on the board.

The fact that railway chairmen were often recruited from other fields of endeavour is reflected in the relatively high level of political position-holding in comparison with other sectors. However, the decline in formal involvement in politics, on both the local and national levels, is in evidence here as elsewhere; the peak of this involvement is in generations II and III, and then drops away quite sharply.

VI. *Retail*. The retail sector stands out as that with the most plebian leadership. It is also characterised by a strong family element. Here we find examples of the shop assistant who worked his way to the top within the firm he first joined after school. The trend, however, is towards greater upper class homogeneity, for now the sons and grandsons of the founders of the great retail chains go to public school and Oxbridge, while their fathers and grandfathers learnt their trade in small businesses and served catering and retail apprenticeships. The numbers of retail chairmen in our sample, however, as with those in shipping and oil, are relatively small, and precise statistical analysis would not be particularly meaningful.

VII. *Shipping*. The most striking characteristic of the shipping industry over time is the tendency toward greater social and educational homogeneity, although the low numbers require caution in interpretation. The

Clarendon element as a percentage of the total sample shows a progressive increase, from 43 % for generation IV, rising to 100 % for generation V! The public school/Oxbridge combination characterises the educational backgrounds of 29 % of generation IV, but 80 % of generation VI.

VIII. *Oil.* The oil industry has, of course, come to prominence relatively recently in comparison with other industries. It is a 'new' industry, in which a small number of very large organisations have from early days dominated the British scene. The number of chairmen (15) is very small. It is, however, noticeable that there has been a tendency for the social origins of the chairmen to become more select as generations pass and the industry has grown in size and importance. Similarly, the proportion of oil chairmen who have received a public school education increases over time, as does the public school/Oxbridge pattern of education.

Family influence appears low, and since most companies were formed relatively late in the day, most chairmen started their career outside the companies of which they became chairmen. However, nearly all fulfilled long periods of overseas service once in the oil industry, and this is reflected in the almost complete absence of local political and judicial involvements.

Conclusion

The changes which we have analysed in the previous section should be interpreted against the broad backdrop of the development of industry over the past century.

Nineteenth century Britain was the first capitalist-industrial society, but it was not a society in which the entrepreneur or business leader was accorded a distinctive status *as such*. In this respect, the modern history of this country differs both from cases in which a distinctive 'business ethos' has been created, where business success is accorded an intrinsic prestige – as, most notably, in the United States – and those in which industrial leaders were scornfully held at arms length by traditionally established landowning groups. In Britain, during the course of the vast industrial expansion in the first few decades of the nineteenth century, a process of mutual accommodation between established and rising elites occurred which seems to have few direct parallels elsewhere. It was a process of accommodation handled in large part by the reorganised and mushrooming system of public schools, and, towards the end of the century in particular, by the powerful medium of socialisation provided by the conjunction of public school and Oxbridge education. The persistence of aristocratic titles, and their use as a mode of reward for business success, is symptomatic of far more than a continuation of the trappings and symbols of an old order into modern times. If the United States developed, in Baltzell's phrase, a 'business aristocracy', Britain made both gentlemen of businessmen (or, more appropriately, the sons of businessmen) and businessmen of gentlemen. Of course, it is true that major tensions and rivalries existed between these groups throughout the nineteenth century, and of course the processes of accommodation and assimilation were never anything like complete; but nonetheless we may correctly speak of the emergence, towards the turn of the century, of a consolidated and unitary 'upper class' in industrial Britain.

The period during which this came to fruition was the very time at which the lead in industrial prosperity that Britain had previously enjoyed was being rapidly cut back by other newly industrialised powers. This era of so-called 'entrepreneurial decline', which was really one of the successful penetration of industrialists into a re-formed upper class, has been linked by some economic historians to presumed failings in the economic leadership of this country in the late nineteenth and early twentieth centuries.[19] However this may be, the phenomenon of what Coleman has referred to as the 'Gentlemen and the Players' is scarcely debatable.[20] The social ascent made possible by the accumulation of business fortunes, as Coleman rightly stresses, was not in any way something confined to the industrial period – indeed it might be said that the history of the English aristocracy and gentry since the Wars of the Roses has been written in the ledgers of merchants and financiers. But the transformation of the society into an industrial and urban one might be thought to have posed a challenge to the continuity of established elite groups that could not possibly be adequately met. The ideal of the 'gentleman' became purged of most of its feudal residues in the nineteenth century, but in its newly refurbished form it provided the key element in the ethos which legitimated the partial fusion that was accomplished between rising and entrenched groups.

> As the industrial revolution went its successful way, so did the 'practical man' come into his own. Respect for practical achievement mounted; the acknowledged virtue of the 'practical man' grew greater. The leadership role exercised by the Gentlemen in the countryside was now assumed in industry by the Players. But it was also universally seen and acknowledged that the ultimate goal of the 'practical man', the Player, was still to cross the social divide and become a Gentleman. As industry consolidated its success and emerged as a recognised possible route to this ancient goal, so did further social developments follow. New occupational patterns were extruded: the industrial 'practical men' were to be found amongst, for example, the ranks of mill and factory managers; in general, amongst the layer which, in time, was to stretch downwards to top foremen but upwards to stop short of the board room. Partners and directors, if rich enough, could become Gentlemen; Gentlemen might decently become directors. The 'practical men' continued to look

after practical, technological matters; they continued to be seen as needing training but not education. They remained Players. Promotion from the ranks was always possible. So the layers of 'practical men' came to constitute a reservoir from which there might be drawn directors and thus, eventually, Gentlemen. The partnership, in English manufacturing business, of the 'educated amateur' and 'practical man' had been formed, in concept and deed.[21]

By the turn of the century, amongst the larger industrial organisations, we see the emergence of a national economic elite, whose background and educational experience does not differentiate them in any obvious way from that of those men in the dominant positions in the spheres of politics, the civil service and the Church. Certainly some economic sectors, particularly banking, remain ahead of most others in these terms; but this does not alter the general picture. There is a lengthy time-factor involved in these matters: the chairmen who preside over the British economy today for the most part received their education in school or university some thirty or forty years ago. In their own life-times, the structure of industry has itself changed very substantially – especially in respect of the accelerating centralisation of economic power. It is thus in a sense too early to offer a conclusive assessment of changes occurring over the past thirty or so years from the end of the Second World War, insofar as these bear upon elite formation and recruitment. The reform of the educational system after 1944, together with the increasing prominence of the very large corporation within the economic system, might be supposed to have created a situation in which a new breed of 'grammar school executives', moving up within the large scale enterprise, will assume positions of industrial leadership.[22] But the plausibility of such a transformation of the existing economic elite must at the very least be regarded with a certain scepticism; while this may take place at other levels of industrial management, it is likely to stop short, as in previous generations, at the doors of the board-room.

6 The economic elite: theory and practice

This chapter will attempt to draw the implications for macro-sociological theories of elites from information gathered in the course of a study on company directors. While the main aim of this research concerned how directors perceived and negotiated their role, the data is equally relevant to the study of elites and the study of power in society in general. We will proceed from our specific fieldwork to its wider implications by presenting our material in two sections:

I.   Empirical Analysis: Power and decision-making at board level.
II.   Conceptual redefinition:
         1. Allocative vs. operational control.
         2. Ownership, control and managerialism.
         3. Positional vs. action elites.

Introduction

The research has consisted of four main phases. The first involved extended, open interviews with individual directors. The second consisted of obtaining diaries from 71 directors covering all their activity for one week, both in and out of work. The third was a short series of discussion groups with selected directors around themes that emerged in the first two phases. The final and principal phase involved following each executive director of a company's board through one complete day of his working life in as unobtrusive and non-interventionist a manner as possible, observing and recording his activity and interaction.

Access to these companies was obtained through the sponsorship of the Institute of Directors, which funded the research, through direct approaches and personal referrals. We studied nineteen companies in this way, selected as a rough quota sample of British industry,[1] covering a range of size, location and nature of industry. The firms varied in turnover from £250,000 per year to one of the ten largest in the country. They were involved in the production of primary materials, producer goods and consumer goods, in construction, distribution, property development and the rendering of financial, information and intellectual services. Their market situations were complex, since most of the companies were active in multiple markets with different characteristics, but considering only their principal products/services there were two effective monopolies, two companies so specialised there was little real competition, several variations of oligopoly, one case each of an exclusive supplier and exclusive customer, and the remainder in open competition with numerous other firms. The manufacturing companies included unit, small batch, large batch, mass/ assembly line and process technologies, some with very simple and traditional operations, others highly scientific with large research and development expenditures. Twelve were public companies, seven private. While the firms had operations all over the United Kingdom and the world, our directors worked in Scotland, the Midlands, the West Country, the South-East, London and the City.[2]

Methods and assumptions in previous studies of elites

There have been four principal approaches or methods in the study of elites – the *institutional approach*, concerned with the leaders of important social institutions, the *recruitment approach*, concerned with the social background and characteristics of incumbents in elite positions, the *reputational approach*, a sociometric selection of influentials, and the *decision-making approach*, the reconstruction of those taking part in the resolution of a major issue.[3] The first two methods, favoured by sociologists, start from an assumption about who the elites are, based on previous information and theory. In the latter two approaches, used most commonly by political scientists, the purpose of the research is to determine who the elites are. Since the subjects of our research were leaders of business institutions, it might appear that our study was within the institutional tradition. However, we made no assumption that our men were members of an elite, viewing them simply as members of a certain social category, company directors, the given subjects of the research. Since we chose our method in order to study the processes of power among directors, we conceived it as a variant of the decision-making approach, its mirror image. Whereas the normal decision-making approach has started with a decision and sought the men involved in it, we began with a group of men and observed the decisions they were involved in making. The decision-making approach has been criticised for its tendency to over-emphasize the importance of those in formal positions of authority.[4] Inevitably most decision-making studies have been reconstructions of past decisions. We, however, studied decision-making in process and we confirm the argument of other critics of the decision-making approach on different grounds by suggesting that directors are not necessarily taking the decisions imputed to them.

Many sociologists concerned with the theory of elites have consistently been aware of the distinction between the structure of elite positions and the effective power which elites use to control the distribution of life chances in their favour. Nonetheless, because of the difficulties of observing elites in action, much of the literature is concerned more with the anatomy than the physiology of power. The *conception* of elites in most sociological writing has been *positional*, incumbency in positions at or near the top of important institutional hierarchies – economic, political, judicial, civil service, military, religious, educational, mass media, etc.[5] In the economic sphere, the most common *operational definition* of this conception has been a company directorship. In many discussions about economic elites' role in society, two crucial assumptions about the relationship between position and power are frequently made:

1. *That office is synonymous with control.* The question of elite power is translated into a question of access to elite positions.

2. *That social contact means substantial influence.* The question of an interconnected power elite is translated into a question of contacts between incumbents of elite positions.

Although sociologists have recognised the seriousness of the problem, they have not modified traditional approaches, and the consequent absence of a processual dimension in elite studies has attracted repeated criticism, from inside as well as outside the discipline. It is almost ten years, for example, since Worsley reminded us that 'what is crucially missing in most power-studies is any account of actual decision-making at the top (intrinsically difficult to obtain access to, of course except usually long after the event)'.[6] In default of detailed ethnography, sociologists have behaved *as if* they had this material and assumed, for want of any corrections, that those in elite roles had power by virtue of their office. This results in a very mechanistic description of power, as if organisations really worked the way they were drawn on the wall chart.[7]

If one does not have access, one can at least look at related situations where we do have evidence. Studies in industry and organisations from anthropological fieldwork,[8] from studies of local notables,[9] show that the power of office is always limited, hedged in by numerous constraints. While theoretical discussions of elites contain the appropriate qualifications, in empirical work sociologists have largely had little option but to set this recognition aside. Political scientists have in general been a good deal more sophisticated about this point and their empirical research is replete with distinctions between *de jure* authority and *de facto* power, between constitutional sovereignty and political strength, titular rulers and powers-behind-the-throne, front men and backroom boys, rubber stamps and pressure groups, office holders and influentials, strong leaders and weak ones, the politicians and the civil service, and in Bagehot's elegant phrase, between the dignified and the efficient. These distinctions do not, of course, apply only in the political realm, but in business organisations as well. Evidently the study of elites has to come to terms with the complexity of organisations.[10]

Thus, we shall begin this chapter with a description of power and decision-making as we observed it in our sample of conventionally-defined economic elites, company directors, with particular emphasis on the constraints, emasculations, and alternatives to directors' power. In this description, we shall bear in mind that power, particularly power in organisations, consists not simply in the ability to enforce one's will in the event of resistance, but in the ability to pre-empt issues from ever reaching the point of open contest.[11] As Hall notes in a different context 'the caucus is ubiquitous and continuously occurring at all levels of government and politics. It crosses partisan and organizational lines and can take place in every nook and cranny of life from the cloakroom, the office, the restaurant, the home and via the telephone. Even where conferences, meetings, and sessions have formal encounters where staged presentations are made, the work and agreements take place in the private and informal settings.'[12] We take it that in our context of economic life we are equally concerned to focus on 'the work and agreements'.

I. Empirical analysis: power and decision-making at board level

I. 1.   *Types of boards*

For the purposes of this discussion, boards of directors may be divided into two types, *pro forma* boards and functioning boards.

I. 1a.   *The pro forma board*

This type of board exists only to conform with the requirements of company law. It does not function in practice, either as a decision-making or consultative body. In some cases, it may not meet at all, and the board resolutions and minutes are genuine works of fiction. Boards become strictly *pro forma* either because they are superfluous or an encumbrance. A board becomes *superfluous* when a company is dominated by one man whose personal approval is required for every action of any significance, or when it is controlled by a small cabal. Such a cabal might, for example, in a family-owned company consisting of the kin who are in frequent social as well as business contact, or in a public company be formed by a small number of executives who work in close physical proximity and are thus, as one chairman expressed it, 'in continuous executive session'. The full-scale board meeting, if it takes place at all, merely ratifies decisions taken earlier by the autocrat or the oligarchs.

A board becomes an *encumbrance* when it is in part filled with men who are seen, by those in effective control of the company, as irrelevant to its functioning. There are many reasons why such irrelevant men occupy positions as directors. A once-effective director may have grown old or tired or ill; a long-serving manager may be rewarded with a seat on the board; a senior manager may be promoted to make room for younger men

in positions of real responsibility; the head of a company previously taken-
over may have demanded a seat on the main board as part of his selling
price; the heads of certain corporate functions, product groups or regions
may have 'traditionally' occupied a seat on the board, so all new incumbents do as well; a director may serve symbolic functions for a company
in its external relations; a man may be a director because he deals with
directors of other companies and a directorship is thought necessary to his
relationships with them; and other similar reasons. One particularly important type of director who *may* be irrelevant is the non-executive director.
Non-executive directors may also be appointed for reasons that have nothing
to do with the contribution they can make to the business – because they are
old friends of the chairman, because they are the company's solicitor or
accountant, because they are well-known and prestigious, because a
merchant banker thought an outside name would be useful at the time of
going public, etc.

At a point when the density of irrelevant directors crosses some nuisance
threshold, companies create a *circumvention device*, a group consisting
only of those who do count, where the consideration of substantial action
takes place. This group may be formal or informal. It may be an executive
committee of the board or a management committee, with regular
scheduled meetings, agendas, and minutes, or a coterie that usually eats
lunch together or meets for drinks in the leader's office after the normal
day is finished or occasionally comes in to the office on Saturday mornings.
These circumvention devices may include only directors or a substantial
number of senior managers without directoral status. Directors in such
companies would often have difficulty in remembering how frequently the
board met or how many directors there were, and would give grossly in-
consistent estimates when we asked them. They would make mistakes in
naming the directors, both including men whom we subsequently determined were not legally directors and leaving out some who were. In their
minds, meetings of the board became mixed up with meetings of the
circumvention device and directorship with membership in, or exclusion
from, the cabal. From spontaneous remarks in the normal course of
business interaction and from direct answers to questions from us, it was
clear that they, as well as we, perceived their boards as *pro forma*.

Our purpose in describing these types of *pro forma* Boards is not just to
demonstrate that some businessmen operate without using the traditional
instrument of corporate control.[13] More importantly, we want to draw
attention to the role of the *other* directors in such companies, the irrelevant
ones, the ones who are *not* in the cabal. Such directors do not take part in
any significant decision-making. They do not control their own life chances,
much less anyone else's. Yet they are by the conventional sociological
definition 'elites', that is they are incumbents in elite positions. But they
are not, we think, what those who write about power elites had in mind.

The definitional problem they present cannot be avoided by suggesting that such directors are few in number or exist only in unimportant backwaters of the economy. Many of the larger, more profitable, more expansionist, and more strategically important companies in Britain are vehicles for the aggressive, entrepreneurial spirit of one or a few dominant men. More pertinent methodologically, companies with *pro forma* boards are prominent in *The Times 1000*, which forms the sampling frame for most current studies on business elites.[14] Our research suggests that the boards of such companies all have what we will call 'non-elite directors', a contradiction in terms for most studies of economic or power elites.

I. 1b.   *The functioning board*

A more complex situation for clarifying the relationship between nominal authority and effective elite power is that presented by the functioning board. A *functioning board* is one that actually plays some role, however small, in the operation of a company. This role, at the minimum, consists in the power to veto some types of management proposals and may, of course, involve considerably more. It is possible to tell within minutes of entering a company whether it has a *pro forma* or a functioning board, simply because the regular meeting of a functioning board is the focus around which all other corporate and individual time scheduling is oriented.

Most importantly, companies with a functioning board have what is usually known as a *meeting structure*, a series of preparatory meetings in each function or product group or regional division, sometimes also liaison meetings between two or more of these sub-groups, and sometimes a meeting of all the executive directors shortly before the main board meeting. Secondly, such companies usually institutionalise *board papers*, documents discussing, explaining or apologising for performance since the previous board meeting, or proposing a course of action and/or requesting resources in an area which formally requires board approval. Time scheduling focussed on the board meeting affects not only those who will be attending the meeting, the directors themselves, but all levels of management, who must be ready themselves for the preparatory meetings and provide supporting evidence for superiors at their higher level meetings.

All the preparatory activity might seem to indicate that board meetings, the board itself, and its members, the directors, were singularly important, decisive for the conduct of the company. In fact, it indicates the reverse; the preparation is the basis of the board's weakness.

Any group which purports to be an instrument of decision-making in any institution, yet meets only once a month or less, as most boards do, is inevitably cast in the role of a gatekeeper, weighing proposals for future action, letting some go through, rejecting others. Unless it organises and exerts itself in a way we never observed, the initiative passes over to individuals or to a permanent secretariat/management. With initiative, expertise and control of information come opportunities for influence, guidance, manipulation and ultimately control. These we observed being taken in every company which purported to have a functioning board. All the advance activity is a preparation for manipulation.

Before relating the processes involved, a brief description of the three principal types of functioning boards will serve to clarify who is manipulating whom.

I. 1b (i).   *The non-executive board.* This is a board with a substantial percentage of non-executive directors – men not engaged in the company on a full-time basis. In such boards, it is the non-executive directors who are principally cast in the gatekeeper role, assessing proposals submitted by the executive directors and management of the firm. As mentioned earlier, in some boards non-executive directors may be irrelevant, chosen for reasons other than their business judgement. In other cases, non-executive directors do take a serious interest in the company's affairs and genuinely do try to perform their gatekeeper role. It is to this latter type to which we refer when we talk of a non-executive board. Among larger companies in the U.K. the average division between executive and non-executive directors is about two-thirds to one-third.

I. 1b (ii). *The subsidiary board.* This is the board of a subsidiary operating company in a group of companies. In such situations, one, two or more members of the main, parent or holding company board will sit in a non-executive capacity, with one usually holding the position of chairman. On such boards, it is the representatives of the principal company who perform the gatekeeper role vis-à-vis the subsidiary directors and management.

I. 1b (iii).   *The cabinet board.* This is one composed largely of the heads of the various functional divisions, product groups, or regional sections of the company. This is a board mainly of executive directors (e.g. the Production Director, the Food Products Director, the European Director). This is potentially a more complex situation because the executive directors must assess one another's proposals and there is not the clear division between outside gatekeepers and inside proposers.

I. 2.   *Manipulative strategies*

The consequence, in all companies we have encountered with functioning boards, is that the managements (including executive directors) have adopted a *manipulative strategy* vis-à-vis their boards. In the first two types of board, it is the non-executive directors and the main board visitors who are to be manipulated. In the cabinet board, it is the other executive directors, through the formation of coalitions and bartering. In all cases, the aim has been to get proposals through the board giving only a generalised estimate of the costs involved and a minimum promise of results expected. What they seek is generalised approval, a *carte blanche* to operate in a given field without constraints or performance targets. Successful manipulation in this way depends on the skilful structuring of the information which the board has available for assessing proposals. The power which the managers exercise over boards is power based on information control. Essential to such power is the sealing off of any sources of contradictory information. The result is conscious collusion among the management (or, in the case of a cabinet board, among sub-divisions of the management), to present a united front to the board.

We wish to make explicit early on that we are not here suggesting a covert form of managerialism in action. The collusion described above does *not* necessarily imply any diversion from the traditional capitalist corporate goals of profit, return on investment, asset growth, earnings per share, etc., nor the substitution of individual self-interest. The manipulation may be undertaken to improve long-term corporate performance against conventional business success indicators, when managers perceive the board as unduly fixated on short-term budgets and financial control. Our observations on this and other aspects of the ownership-control issue mentioned below have led us very definitely to reject the managerialist hypothesis. All these points will be brought together in a composite statement on managerialism towards the end of this chapter.

Viewed in this light, the pre-board meeting activity is not a period of intense preparation for a testing occasion, but a screening operation. It is a pure example of a pre-emptive mechanism, to which we referred above. It functions to select proposals to be put to the board, to eliminate discordant information, and to restructure the remaining information to make a coherent case for the actions that executives want approved. In some cases, this advance activity culminates with the chief executive (or, more subtly, his personal assistant) condensing and rewriting the board papers presented to him by individual subordinates into a summary statement for the board meeting, on the rationale that the full documents would be too much information for the non-executives and functional directors in other specialisms to absorb. Similar editing goes on at lower levels as well, of course, so the chief executive and individual directors themselves receive pre-screened information from their subordinates.

This situation is so commonplace that it has become the norm, the standard expectation of most of our directors (if not yet of management textbook writers and journalists) that the board collectively does not decide or even seriously discuss anything. The board meetings we attended were usually rather routine, without argument or substantial disagreement. When we asked our directors if board meetings were always so dull, the modal reply was that 95–99 % of items went through on the nod.[15] Moreover, it was repeatedly suggested to us that not only was this the way boards did behave, but the way they *should* behave. A director of our largest company said, 'If proposals get to the board that are really contentious, then management hasn't been doing its homework.' Pre-emption institutionalised. We regularly heard what might be called 'the chairman's proverb', 'If it comes to a vote in a board meeting, you've failed.'[16] In other words, pre-emption is the normal state of affairs.

It is important that this 'getting-it-through' spirit does not simply affect those who actually attend board meetings, but every level of management in the company. Every meeting in the meeting structure is a mini-board meeting for those involved. At every level, individual managers attempt to manipulate the meeting in advance, so that their particular projects are given a clear passage. The functional, product or regional divisions and sub-divisions, headed by senior managers and executive directors, also play collective strategies to manipulate meetings.

Nor are manipulative strategies employed only within companies; they may be used against the firm's providers of capital as well. In the course of the research we observed the preparation of a chairman's statement for an annual report, the composition of a prospectus for underwriters and investors for a £100-million loan, and a financial director organising the support of institutional investors to fend off a challenge from other shareholders. Again, the explicit principles of presentation were to give as few details as possible of what the company was intending to do and make the minimum promises of performance necessary to attract the required support/funds. Here it is holders of capital who were being manipulated, a point we shall return to shortly. (See below, p. 111.)

Once more, the purpose of this discussion on functioning boards has not been simply to describe corporate decision-making, but to provide evidence for the question of whether it is the formal authority holders, the directors, who actually make the decisions. To be sure, the final Yea or Nay, at a board meeting may be seen as the decision point, and may so appear in corporate histories (we witnessed the editing of one such book on a company's decision to leave its cartel). But the board actions we observed are better interpreted, we feel, merely as ratifications of decisions made earlier and elsewhere, sometimes by much more junior men, about which the board had no practical alternative. The distinction between 'making' and 'taking' decisions is relevant. Boards of directors are, we feel, best conceived as decision-taking institutions, that is, as legitimating institutions, rather than as decision-making ones.[17]

All that has been said here refers only to subordinates' ability to manipulate a decision in advance of its being formally 'taken'. There is also the ability, already well recognised in the literature, to alter a decision to suit their preferences during its implementation. They have two bites at the cherry.

The art of pre-emption is that the inevitability should never be obvious. The origin of a proposal that eventually receives board approval may be totally obscured in its successfully manipulated passage through several screening meetings and informal discussions. One of the current adages of good administration is that a superior should convince his subordinates that what he wants them to do was really their idea in the first place. Two can play that game. Skilful managers we observed regularly presented suggestions to their director as if they were really his idea, had been stimulated by an earlier remark of his, or at least were in accord with his known preferences. Indeed, such obfuscation is even more essential to the strategies of subordinates; if differences ever come into the open, they have the formal authority structure weighted against, not for them. The answers to the questions, 'Who initiated?', 'Who is ultimately responsible for a given decision?', 'Who has power?', 'Who controls?' will be buried by the normal practices of organisational politics.[18] We may catch them, if at all, only by observing decision-making in process. *Post facto* evidence will always be biased in favour of those in formal positions of authority. But once we recognise the processes of manipulation, screening and pre-emption, then any serious consideration of decision-making must allow that decisions may be thrust up from below.[19]

I. 3.   *Interlocking directors*

The implications of this analysis are serious for one mechanism of elite contact that figures prominently in many theories, *interlocking directorships*. Interlocking directors are, by definition, non-executive directors, and these are the easiest of all directors to manipulate, because they generally know less about the industries of the boards on which they sit. Ironically, the more boards on which an interlocking director sits, the more influential he is thought to be in many conventional studies of elites, yet the easier he is to manipulate because he has less time to devote to each. To be sure, the interlocking director who operates from some established position in the City of London may significantly influence the availability of capital for a company on whose board he sits. This might, on the face of it, seem sufficient to establish elite power. In fact, our research suggests that the non-executive, interlocking director may be *used* by company executives, and as much as he might wish to control the distribution of resources for his own ends, his class's ends, or elite ends in general, he is not necessarily able to convert the position into the effective power that would enable him to do so. He may be controlled, not controlling. Capital is not synonymous with control. Contact is not synonymous with influence. It is a well-articulated norm in the boardroom that non-executive directors should resign or withdraw from a situation of conflict and not stay to fight it out with executive directors.

I. 4.   *Delegated control*

The transfer of power down an authority structure need not only take place covertly. Some power is transferred openly; it is delegated. The management textbook view of delegation is that day-to-day, routine tasks are delegated, while the major, innovative ones that imply power are reserved at the top. We observed this, but we also observed the reverse. Particularly in the large companies, the directors we studied were frequently so engaged in co-ordinating sub-departments, dealing with immediate crises, assessing current budget and forecast figures and carrying out the ceremonial aspects of their role, that they confessed to having little time for 'original thinking'. Their solution was to delegate the consideration of major, future issues. The subordinate would prepare a proposal or alternative suggestions, on which the director would exert himself to varying degrees, from considerable discussion, revision, and even rejection to acceptance *in toto*. While an energetic director might keep control of such delegation, some openly acknowledged that in practice their role was simply to legitimate such subordinate-produced policies or to act as advocate for them in further discussions among the cabal/board.[20] At the minimum, initiative and opportunities for manipulation in line with his own preferences passed over to the subordinate. At the maximum, decision-making and power were directly transferred.[21]

In some cases, the delegation was directly down the authority hierarchy to a subordinate. In others, particularly from a chairman, the delegation was sidewards to a personal assistant. The chairman's personal assistant is one of the more common bases for non-directoral membership in a company's decision-making cabal. In larger companies and groups, this sidewards delegation is institutionalised in the form of staff advisors, either a planning department or headquarters elite staff.[22] On some major issues the sidewards delegation is outside the company altogether, to management consultants.[23] The significance of these various staff adjuncts varies from company to company, and their existence *per se* does not indicate any diminution in directoral power. But power may shift and at the minimum they provide institutionalised opportunities for manipulation and decision-making by non-directors.

I. 5.   *Information control*

The problematic nature of board and directoral power may be indicated in another way. There exists in the world of business an unarticulated, but well-understood and strongly enforced norm: a subordinate shall not surprise his superior with new information or new plans in public. To some extent, the board papers and other preparatory documents perform this warning function in a formal way. But much more important, when managers really want something, they approach their superior about it privately, they have 'a quiet word', they reach a decision in advance. The public meeting simply confirms that decision; which suggests why business-men always complain about committees. Viewed in terms of decision-making, they *are* a waste of time. The leaders know what the outcome will be in advance, and they have not yet been sensitised to the latent functions of ritual occasions. The norm of advance warning applies to every meeting, but naturally most strongly at board meetings. At this level there exists a rule of thumb equivalent to the barrister's injunction, 'Never ask a question in court to which you do not already know the answer.' It says, 'Do not put an item on the board agenda unless you have already reached a decision.'[24] When a director, or any superior, enjoys the confidence and support of his subordinates, this norm serves to ensure that he has all the information he needs to remain in control. From the subordinates' point of view, the norms provide an invitation to and opportunity for manipulation through information structuring.

Information control may also be exercised negatively. When a manager wants to sanction or attack his director, or a director his chairman, he may withhold information, give it to his superior's opponents, or spring it on him suddenly in public.[25] More generally, keeping his superiors in ignorance about the decisions that face him is one way for a subordinate to preserve discretion and hence power. Silence is a fundamental requital to authority. In Gouldner's terms, information control is one strategy employees may adopt to preserve their autonomy vis-à-vis their organisation and this applies as much to directors as others.[26] Accepting his point, which seems particularly reasonable in business organisations, that there will be a generalised tension over questions of autonomy and reciprocity between the institutionalised corporate control mechanism, the board, and individual employees, including directors, then we must expect it to be a normal state of affairs that employees play strategies which in part subvert the power of the board, and that individual directors are among the subversives. In the companies we studied, they had largely succeeded.

We wish to make absolutely clear the extent of what we are claiming. We are *not* saying that all directors are weak, that none are members of a business elite. Some of the men we observed were very powerful, members of elites by any definition of the term. What we have presented here is not a general description of power and decision-making at board level, but one which emphasises the limits, emasculations and alternatives to directors' power in order to illustrate the difficulties with the conventional conception which sees all directors as powerful and hence as economic elites. What we *are* saying is that sociologists can no longer go on treating the category 'company directors' as if it consisted only of economically powerful men, even in the largest companies. Many or most of those who are the sought-for economic elites may in fact carry the title 'director'. But all those who carry the title 'director' most certainly are not members of an elite. Office is not synonymous with control. Social contact need not necessarily imply influence.

II. Conceptual redefinitions: allocative vs. operational control positional vs. action elites

We will now use the description of the preceding section in an examination of some of the concepts sociologists use in the study of economic elites, those concerning the nature of the power which elites are thought to wield and the definition of the elites themselves.

II. 1.   *Allocative vs. operational control*

The essential element in the concept of an economic elite in capitalist society, following from the tradition of Marx and Weber, is market power. By market power is meant control over the *distribution* of economic resources, the power to employ resources or to withdraw them, in line with one's own interests and preferences. While labour power may also be used or withheld, the resource on which the sociological tradition has principally focussed is capital.[27] This control over the allocation process is analytically and also very often empirically distinct from control over the day-to-day use of resources already allocated. To be sure, the profitable use of capital generates new capital through the mechanism of retained earnings and this new capital in turn becomes the subject of an allocation process which may be controlled by people other than the initial distributors. There will be overlap between the two forms, in the sense that some individuals will have both. There will be a reciprocal relationship between them, in the sense that a man starting with one form may acquire the other. There will be gradations in both forms of control, in the sense that for any company or group they may be divided among several people who will have more or less control. Nonetheless, it is important to keep the two forms of control conceptually distinct. The difference between them becomes clear when the providers of capital choose to withdraw it, leaving the users in very changed circumstances, at the extreme with nothing to operate at all. This is most obvious when the providers of risk capital decide to pull out, but it is also shown in the course of a contested take-over bid, or when a holding company denies a capital allocation to an operating subsidiary. We will call these two concepts of economic power *allocative control* and *operational control*.[28]

The conventional examples of allocative controllers are the traditional financial institutions, clearing banks, issuing houses, discount houses, insurance companies, pension funds, and other institutional investors. But as the above remarks on the internal generation of corporate capital indicate, managers may have considerable allocative control themselves, and Britain has recently experienced the emergence or increased importance of new types of allocative controllers in both the financial and management worlds. Property developers, unit trusts and the new group of financial entrepreneurs, pejoratively known as asset strippers,[29] have exerted a marked influence on capital allocation recently. The flourishing of planning departments within companies[30] and of independent management and operations research consultancies have also provided new vehicles for allocative decision-making. In sum, the locus of control governing the allocation of capital for a given economic organisation may lie inside or outside the organisation or be shared between internal and external controllers. We make no assumptions about what positions these allocative controllers may occupy within their own organisations.

The institution of the unit trust illustrates an important point about the nature of allocative control most clearly. *Allocative control is not the same as, nor dependent upon, the ownership of capital.* Owners may control the allocation of their capital, but need not. In the unit trust relationship, they turn their capital over to others for allocation in the hope of higher returns. The same principle operates in a more complex way and less clearly in other institutions. In a capitalist society, effective economic power lies with those who have the ability to conceive and carry through schemes for the profitable allocation of capital. The unit trust legitimates the allocative role and, in theory at least, regulates the rewards of the allocative controllers. But the owners of capital also may be manipulated subtly, covertly, or illegally by those who propose schemes for its employment, just as our directors were sometimes manipulated by their subordinates.[31]

The purpose of distinguishing these two forms of control is to *suggest that we sociologists should henceforth limit our definition of economic elites to those exercising allocative control.* Those who exercise such control should be open to empirical investigation. Present conceptions of the economic elite include operational controllers as well as allocative controllers, together with many who exercise no control whatsoever. In making this proposal, we are *not* suggesting a new concept. We are advocating a return to the old Marxist and Weberian concept of economic elites as those in control of the distribution of resources, but attempting to define this more rigorously. The new terminology is necessary to adapt the idea to developments in the structure of capitalist economies that have occurred since they wrote, notably the separation of ownership and control. We are suggesting that sociologists have neglected to sharpen this old concept by not analysing this separation process rigorously enough and by adopting a crude positional definition of elites.

II. 2.   *New developments in the relation between ownership and control*

Recent analysis of the separation of ownership and control has suffered from a number of defects, the combined weakness of which has been demonstrated by recent developments in the British economy and else-where. The first was to lump all the rights of property together under the single heading 'control'. The classic sociological definition of property is the rights and obligations with respect to scarce and valuable goods.[32] The principal rights involved are those to use or direct the use of the good, to receive the rewards of its employment and to transfer the good to others. The crucial right that does *not* shift to management in the modern joint stock company is the right of transfer. While this is clearly recognised, the prevailing wisdom has been that since share ownership was relatively diffused and shareholders so unorganised, the right of transfer as a means of control over management, and hence power, became ineffective. Owners could sell their shares, but managers did not thereby suffer any interruption in their acquired rights. The right of transfer fell into a conceptual limbo and intellectual neglect. The joint stock company could be seen as the latest example of a tendency increasingly apparent at least since feudal times, for those who work with property to become its owners.[33] Share option schemes were simultaneously a vehicle and a sympton of the transition.

The second defect was to over-emphasise the importance of retained earnings, one of the foundation stones of theories of managerial capitalism. Retained earnings reduce managers' dependence on outside sources of capital (external allocative controllers), especially shareholders, since they do not have to issue new equities to raise funds. Approximately two-thirds of the total financial requirements of quoted British manufacturing companies are met through net profit after tax and depreciation.[34] We do not mean to suggest retained earnings are unimportant, but just to point out two qualifications. The issue is not simply that managers have access to their own sources of capital, but how effectively they use it. Do they perform well against those indicators of business success which principally determine the market price of shares, profitability, return on investment and asset growth? The conventional post-war interpretation, particularly in the 1960s, was that British management as a whole was not performing as well as managements in other parts of the world. Whether this inter-pretation is true or fair is not the point. It was perceived to be correct by businessmen, producing a sense of unfulfilled corporate potential and relatively low share prices. The second qualification is that to the extent a management does not capitalise its growth in the form of new shares, then the pool of owners to be captured by a potential take-over bidder is smaller.

The combined result of these first two mistakes was that sociologists continued, right into the1970s, to conceive of shareholders as weak relative to managers. Whatever the merits of this analysis in the past, it is no longer tenable today. The reason is simply that some capitalists adapted to the situation, particularly the builders of conglomerates and asset strippers. They recognised that shareholders were ill-organised and set about organising them – buying up scattered holdings and agglomerating them until they were able to force or 'agree' a take-over. The process is sometimes disguised by holding the shares in nominee companies until the time for acquisition is ripe. But when that time comes, what had once been a portfolio investment is suddenly converted into a subsidiary company and all the traditional rights of property dramatically revert to one owner – the right to direct the use of the property through a straightforward authority hierarchy and the right to receive rewards, not just meagre dividends, not even just total profits, but access to total cash flow. When nominee shareholdings provide inadequate cover for the plot, the enterprising market organiser arranges for independent friends to work with him, the concert party approach. The organiser need not want to take over the victim company himself. He may acquire a commanding holding in order to sell it to someone who actually wants to control and operate the company, the share warehousing approach. The premium he receives on the share price may be seen as an extravagant commission for a typical wholesaler's task, organising the unorganised.

The result was a gradual increase in total U.K. corporate acquisitions throughout the 1960s and a doubling of the rate beginning with 1967.[35] In the face of such developments, sociologists can no longer maintain an undifferentiated conception of passive, ineffectual shareholder-owners. *Some* shareholders are extremely aggressive and ultimately controlling owners. The significance for the study of elites is that they have capitalised, in both senses of the word, on the remaining unalienated right of owners, the right of transfer, which is to say the right to allocate or withdraw capital. By engineering a change in the structure of allocative control, they have drawn attention to a concept which has always been crucial but recently neglected by sociologists. Their aggression also appears to be affecting other allocative controllers. Even those most somnambulent of institutional investors, the pension funds, investment trusts and insurance companies have shown signs recently of stirring themselves to put more active pressure on managements. They have been encouraged in this by the Government and the Bank of England, which are inchoately articulating a theory of finance capitalism. Social scientists first developed the idea of the separation of ownership and control to cope with the changing practice of capitalism. We suggest that capitalism has evolved still further and our conception of the separation should be adapted accordingly.[36] Further, we feel that the implications of our research for the managerialist hypothesis should be clearly stated. Though there are several variants described by Nichols in *Ownership, Control and Ideology*, it broadly maintains that following the separation of ownership and control in the modern joint stock company, corporations controlled by salaried managers will be operated differently from those run by owners, possibly in a more socially responsible manner. Assessment of this hypothesis has been hampered by a paucity of direct evidence on the principal individuals concerned, executive directors in larger public companies.[37] However these formed a major part of our sample both in the observations phase and in interviews.

The principal rebuttal argument against the hypothesis has been that managers still operate in a capitalist market and hence must be just as oriented to the traditional capitalist goal, profit, as owners. This argument was completely confirmed by our observations. In our research we repeatedly encountered the concept of the 'professional manager' and directors who both embodied and articulated it. Their idea of professionalism is not that usually employed by sociologists, but more like that of actors, the ability to produce a competent performance in any circumstances, no matter how unpromising. The indicators of successful performance are profits, growth, and return on investment. The essence of the professional manager is his rigorous and exclusive dedication to financial values. He represents a return to the values of hard, unameliorated, unconstrained capitalism. We had in our sample several companies in various stages of a transition from family to professional management. The professionals' orientation to profit was not only explicitly recognised by the family owners and the new employed managers themselves, but both expected the managers to be *more* profit conscious. Indeed, the professional managers had been invited in purposely to improve company performance (and thereby increase return to family shareholders) above the level which the family owners could themselves produce. The professionals saw their purpose and their legitimation in improving profitability markedly compared with the last years of the family owners' management. In all cases we encountered, they were successful. Not only were they more oriented to profit, they were more capable of obtaining it.[38]

An argument, related to the managerialist hypothesis and often used in support of it, is that in technically complex modern industry decision-making has passed away from financially-oriented generalist managers to technical specialists. Our evidence suggests that not only are the financially-oriented still dominant, but if anything even more in the ascendancy under a new ethic of hard capitalism. The manipulative processes we described earlier implied no diversion from traditional financial goals. The technocracy argument is, we think, also untenable on a macro level in the face of the financially-stimulated escalation in corporate take-overs and acquisitions in Britain during the past decade. The argument may have been given unintended support by the positional definition commonly adopted for the economic elite, which lumped operational controllers, the potential technocrats, in with allocative controllers.

Evidence of a social responsibility ethic which we encountered was very limited and conventionally defined – a corporate philanthropy budget, conformity with government social legislation, and a grudging responsiveness to some of the more obvious social protest movements (e.g. pollution control and office development). There was no evidence of a shift toward a sense of responsibility for employees in general. Our directors, even the production and personnel directors, where the latter existed, had only the barest contact with workers, attended to them only at times of industrial action, resignation or retirement, and basically viewed them in the context of costs.

Two of the rebuttals to the managerialist hypothesis were not confirmed in our research. Interlocking directorships were not, in our experience, a significant instrument of shareholder-owner control; non-executive directors were easily manipulated. Nor did our salaried directors clearly share a sense of social unity with owners; a capitalist owning class was not their reference group. To be sure, most of our directors supported share option schemes and wanted a capital share in their businesses, but they supported all other forms of increased remuneration as well. The professional managers among our sample had a clearly articulated sense of a distinct social identity. Family owners were for them commonly objects of derision, mocked for their alleged leisurely indulgences. One of the more celebrated hard capitalists summarised the difference between the traditional owning class and the new professional managers as the difference between 'The Gentlemen' and 'The Players'.[39]

II. 3.   *Positional elites*

Empirically, we think our fieldwork demonstrated the inadequacies of positional definitions of elites. At the theoretical level, there are also problems.

First, positional definitions are liable to the problems of any categorisation of excluding those who should be in the category and of including those who should not. In terms of exclusions, we have already drawn attention to manipulative subordinates and advisors with staff status who do not occupy the appropriate positions. We have further indicated above the power of certain aggressive types of shareholders.[40] In terms of inclusions, a positional definition accords elite status to directors who are not within the decision-making cabals of their companies. It also selects an uncertain combination of allocative and operational controllers, but clearly one heavily weighted toward operational control. In sum, the positional definition errs on both sides at once, being simultaneously too inclusive and too exclusive. Secondly, suggesting that power is a matter of position encourages acceptance of an undifferentiated concept of power. We are suggesting that economic power at least must be disaggregated into allocative and operational control and that only one of these types defines economic elites. Thirdly, crude positional definitions based on whole levels in a hierarchy, inevitably set up a line drawing problem. However high in the pyramid the line is drawn[41] this does not get round the problem of weak men at the top.[42] Similarly, the notion of the 'real' elite behind the putative elite[43] simply underlines the point we are making about the

weakness of the formal positional approach. Further, attempts to acknowledge that those below the line do serve to constrain the actions of those
above it fail to face the reality of power from below as we have described it.
Giddens makes a useful contribution here by suggesting that we consider a
'secondary structure' between elites and non-elites from which the former
are recruited.[44] Such a notion helps in understanding the process of recruitment but does little to resolve the problems we encountered of non-cabal
directors above the line and manipulative subordinates below who control
those above it.

One could imagine a more sophisticated positional definition of elites
which tried to specify individual or functional positions rather than whole
levels (e.g. finance director or marketing director instead of just director).
This might be allied to theories, like Woodward's, that in different types of
companies different functions assume predominant importance.[45] In our
companies, however, membership in the cabal of controllers could not be
given any consistent definition in terms of position. While in two firms
there appeared to be a basis in specialist competence that might be translated into positional terms, inclusion in other cabals was founded on
varied characteristics that had nothing to do with position and cut across
levels – kinship, religion, membership in the founding group of the
company, social relationships outside work, a certain intellectualism, and
most significantly, the professional manager orientation described in
Section II. 2.[46] We do not believe the problems of positional definitions
in this area will be solved by tinkering with modifications. A different
type of definition is required.[47]

The fourth major problem is the relationship between formal authority
and effective power. In elite studies, this arises in three contexts: (i) in
determining who the elites are; (ii) in determining how they exercise their
power; and (iii) in choosing research methods.

On the question of delineating the elite, the problem is a construct of
positional definitions. The issue does not arise if one does not start with a
presumption that elites are office holders. Most elites may in fact hold some
office, but sociologists need not define them in terms of office. The alternative is to define them directly in terms of power.[48] This is what we are
suggesting here, that economic elites are those exercising allocative control.
The question of the relation between elite power and formal authority then
arises, where we feel it is a genuine issue, in the context of determining how
elite power is exercised, whether through formal office or otherwise.

Methodologically, many have seen positional definitions as a second best,
forced on sociologists by the difficulties of obtaining access to study the
powerful in action. Others have defended it as a useful starting point to be
followed by studies of how far effective power diverges from positional
authority.[49] While accepting that one must start with something, to begin
with positions and their incumbents is to risk building a conclusion into

one's methodology. Alternatives exist – to start with decisions or the places where they are made. We observed putative candidates for an economic elite without prejudging whether what they were doing was that which members of an economic elite are expected to do.

This is not just a methodological fine point. Positional definitions may have been substantively misleading in precisely that aspect of elites on which sociologists have done most of their empirical work, recruitment studies, examinations of the backgrounds and characteristics of incumbents in putative elite positions.[50] If positional definitions make errors of both inclusion and exclusion, if effective power diverges significantly from formal authority (and we suggest that in the economic realm as elsewhere this is the case), then the traits recorded in recruitment studies will differ from the traits of elites. We may obtain a distorted portrait.[51] At one extreme, Goldthorpe has suggested, what purports to be the sociology of elites may become just the sociology of occupations.[52]

The question is not the value of recruitment studies. We shall always be interested in how men become elites and their characteristics. The issue is recruitment to what? If we undertake recruitment studies into a set of positions before we are sure they are the significant positions, then we are operating back to front. The same point applies to processual studies. The traditional complaint about elite studies, noted at the beginning of this chapter, has been that it omits an investigation of the actual decision-making process. While we certainly agree, studying the application of power can also be substantively misleading if the group whose decision-making is being studied is not the elite one thought it was.

The immediate need in the sociology of elites, we feel, is to sharpen considerably our understanding of who the elites are. We have reached the limits of usefulness of positional definitions. The questionable relationship between formal authority and effective power raises theoretical doubts. Our own research has convinced us that these doubts are justified and serious and can no longer be ignored. Positional definitions distort organisational reality because organisations are more complex than authority hierarchies. Power is more than role structure. Men with power in organisations exist in various subdivisions, at various levels, and in staff positions outside the normal hierarchy.[53] We must expect to find elites scattered in the structure of our institutions. We have reached the limits of theoretical introspection and conceptual neologism. The need now is to get out into the field, observe the exercise of power and induce more appropriate definitions – to mate the sociology of elites with the sociology of organisations. We would like to locate our empirical work in this development. Our work with directors was *not* the study of elites applying their power pure and simple. We studied a variety of men, allocative controllers and operational controllers and some who controlled nothing of significance whatsoever, men who had effective power and others who had only the trappings of office. The result of this empirical work is a contribution to the redefinition of the concept of economic elites.

II. 4.   *Towards an Action Definition of Economic Elites*

At the *conceptual level*, we have already made clear our idea of the economic elite; they are those who control the allocation of capital. At the level of an *operational definition*, we are not yet ready to be so positive. Our research concerned directors, not allocative controllers *per se*. Our sample included a mixture of men, and the allocative controllers within it came from too limited a selection of the settings in which allocative control may be exercised for us to propose a firm definition. However, we think we can specify a few of the characteristics that such an operational definition must have.

First, *it will not be based simply on the possession of capital* by individuals or institutions, no matter how large the sum.

Second, *it will be a definition based on action*, control over the decision to whom and to what uses capital is allocated.

Third, *it will allow for power from below*, that allocative decisions may be made at levels other than the top of authority hierarchies. Some economic elites may be organisational subordinates.

Fourth, *it will probably include a minimum significance level*, some lower limit to the amount of capital being allocated which is of significance to the broader social structure.

Fifth, *it will probably include a notion of allocative feedback*, some distinction between the various uses to which capital may be put, having different consequences for the broader social structure and the generation of further capital.

To summarise then, we are making four points, that sociologists should: (1) recognise the inadequacy of 'Company Director' as a definition of the economic elite; (2) recognise the limitations of positional definitions in general; (3) clarify conceptually whom they mean by the elite (do they mean as we have suggested, just allocative controllers?); and (4) develop an operational definition precise enough to isolate this group.

Acknowledgements

This research was funded by a generous grant from the Institute of Directors. We especially acknowledge the help we have received from Dr Beric Wright of the Institute's Medical Centre. Early drafts of this paper were read to the Elites Conference at King's College, Cambridge, to the annual meeting of the British Sociological Association at the University of Surrey in 1973 and to seminars at the University of Kent at Canterbury. We have greatly benefited from these discussions. We are particularly grateful to Dr Derek Allcorn, Michael Gilbert and Richard Scase for their comments on an earlier draft. No one apart from ourselves is in any way responsible for what we have written and certainly not the Institute of Directors.

C. D. HARBURY AND P. C. MᶜMAHON

7 Intergenerational wealth transmission and the characteristics of top wealth leavers in Britain[1]

The role of inheritance in influencing the distribution of personal wealth in Britain in the 1950s was examined by one of the present authors in an earlier paper.[2] That study compared the pattern of inheritance in the 1950s with the one observed by Wedgwood during the 1920s and concluded that '...There was no very marked change in the relative importance of inheritance in the creation of the personal fortunes of the top wealth leavers of the mid-twenties and mid-fifties of this century'. The present paper extends Harbury's study to the 1960s to undertake the following tasks: (1) to investigate whether there is any significant difference in the importance of inheritance for the top wealth leavers of 1965 compared with those of a decade earlier; (2) to analyse attributes of the entire post-war data used for the study to discover which specific factors might be associated with the inheritance of substantial fortunes. The distribution of personal wealth in Britain is extremely unequal, much more so than that of income and that of wealth in other advanced countries. Studies based on the estate duty multiplier technique[3] have indicated a certain reduction in wealth concentration in this century. However, some observers contend that the decline in the share of the richest percentiles in the wealth distribution may be quite misleading, and reflect merely a rearrangement of wealth within families, rather than a redistribution of wealth from rich to poor families.[4]

The apparent failure of the high rates of estate duty introduced in the 1940s to bring about a significant reduction in wealth inequality, and the conclusion mentioned earlier that the importance of inheritance in the 1950s was substantially the same as that of the 1920s compels an examination of the possibility that changing rates of duty require a fairly long time to take effect. This question is considered in the first part of this paper by comparing the relative importance of inheritance for the top wealth leavers of 1965 with those of 1956–7. The second part of the paper is concerned with a cross-section analysis of certain characteristics of those both with and without inherited wealth.

The quantification of inheritance used here is approached through a comparison of fortunes left at death by two generations of the same family – mainly the estates of fathers and sons, but including also those of a number of other relatives. This involves severe limitations. An individual's inheritance cannot be measured solely by the financial benefits he receives.

Numerous advantages are also conferred by education, life styles, contacts and all that these imply and which are virtually unquantifiable. Furthermore, the value of a father's estate at death is only a very inadequate proxy for the financial benefits a son receives even from his father. The present study revealed cases of one-time wealthy fathers who died impecunious. Other cases highlighted the importance of gifts *inter vivos* rather than of legacies. Moreover, the size of a son's inheritance is not the same as the value of his father's estate at death but depends on the number of his brothers and sisters and other beneficiaries. Considerable effort was expended in attempting to obtain information on the size of individual legacies, but this proved impossible in practice, and the analysis here is based, therefore, on the estates left by two generations of the same family.

The method used to obtain the basic data was described in Harbury's earlier article.[5] A brief description is repeated here. Sample names of deceased males[6] who left estates worth £100,000 or more were drawn from the Register of wills probated or grants of administration made in 1956, 1957 and 1965. The 1956 and 1957 samples were complete; the 1965 sample included only males with surnames beginning with the letters A to M. The details are similar to those printed daily in *The Times* and other newspapers, though those are now known to cover only about 90 % of the total and are biased against the inclusion of 'self-made' men at the expense of those with inherited fortunes.[7]

The field work involved matching named top wealth leavers with the previous generation of their family – largely fathers, but extended in some cases to other relatives, especially fathers-in-law (see below pp. 000–00).

Tracing the values of a father's estate involved three essentially separate processes: (1) tracing the father's name, (2) tracing father's date of death and (3) tracing the probated value of father's estate at death. Methods of tracing involved the use of published directories, such as *Who's Who, Burke's Peerage*, etc.; searching in the General Registry of Births, Deaths and Marriages at Somerset House, the Probate Calenders of Wills and Letters of Administration in cases of intestacy, and divers other means.

The original combined samples for 1956–7 and 1965 produced 749 names, of which 58 were eliminated, mainly because the deaths had occurred abroad, or because the individuals were found to have predeceased their fathers.[8] Of the remaining 691 'rich sons', the values of their fathers' estates were subsequently traced (or estimated), with a high degree of confidence for 666 – a success rate of over 95 %.[9]

Fathers' names were easily traced in the standard directories for about a third of the total.[10] In about half of these cases, fathers' dates of death were also recorded, and led immediately to the discovery of the values of their estates in the appropriate volumes of the Probate Calendar. For about half of the remainder – some 250 persons – fathers' names were traced by the following procedure. (1) The entry in the Probate Calendar relating to the son, gives the date of death. (2) A search in the Register of Deaths yields a death certificate, which records reported age at death. (3) Finally, a search in the Register of Births around the appropriate year yields a birth certificate which records parents' names.[11] In the majority of cases this procedure yielded a single unambiguous birth entry and father's name.[12]

The next step was to search extensively through all Probate Calendars from the year preceding a son's birth to the present day for an entry recording the value of his father's estate. This procedure was, of course, necessary also for those whose fathers' names, but not their dates of death, had been found in one of the standard directories referred to earlier. The whole process was exceedingly lengthy, involving the reading of many wills in doubtful cases to match the correct father and son. Identification was also assisted by reference to occupations, addresses, relatives' names, obituary notices, company records, the Register of Marriages, etc.

The final method used in tracing fathers' estates involved correspondence with relatives, solicitors, executors and other persons associated with the families. Considerably more than 500 letters involving 281 cases where a father's estate had not been positively traced were despatched asking for help in tracing the predecessor's estate.[13] Replies were received to about three quarters of the letters sent and 233 fathers' estates were traced largely as a result. Barely 2 % of recipients expressed any degree of objection to the nature of the inquiry,[14] and a far higher proportion gratuitously supplied information about the creation of the son's fortune.

The final achievement – a success rate of about 95 % – indicates that the basis of the analysis is representative of British top wealth leavers in recent decades.[15] The lack of information from other sources of the quantitative aspects of inheritance made it imperative to achieve a very high success rate despite the exceedingly time-consuming task of tracing the fathers in the most difficult cases.

The discussion so far has been concerned with the representativeness of the sample data used in this study. It is also necessary to consider that wealth here is defined in terms of the gross value of estates as required by Probate (or Grants of Administration). These values suffer from certain deficiencies:

(i) It would have been preferable to use the net value of estates after the payment of debts and death duties. While such information is nowadays published, such was not the case before 1934. To ensure a consistent definition, gross values were used.

(ii) Probate valuations prior to 1894 excluded real estate. Hence the estimated wealth of landowners dying before this date would have been under-estimated. This affected some 10 % of the fathers in the sample. Fortunately, some correction for this deficiency could be made in most important cases by using information contained in the Return of Land-owners compiled by the Local Government Boards in the 1870s.[16]

(iii) Settled property is not adequately included in probate valuations. In the first place, although some settled property is included, that over which the deceased is not free to dispose is excluded, even though liable to duty.[17] Estimates made in the 1956–7 sample suggest that about 15 % of fathers had some such settled property which amounted to less than 8 % of probate valuations.[18] In the second place, and more important, probate valuations exclude non-dutiable settled property, especially if it is in discretionary trusts. This deficiency is quite intractable and in view of the prevalence of the various tax avoidance techniques[19] over the period, the data must unfortunately be treated with caution.

One final implication of the use of probate valuations is that account should be taken of changes in the value of money over the hundred-year period covered in this study. In the absence of an appropriate asset price index covering the entire period,[20] the price index of consumer goods and services was used as a deflator. Jeffreys' and Walters' Consumer Goods and Services Price Index[21] performed the function of inflating (and deflating) estate values. To minimise revaluation for the large numbers of sons drawn in the 1956–7 sample, the average of these two years was chosen as the base.

This section compares the distribution of fathers' estates for the top wealth leavers of 1956–7 with that of 1965 to see whether there is any evidence of a change in the relative importance of inheritance for the two years. The procedure is similar to that employed by Harbury in a comparison of the years 1924–6 and 1956–7.[22] Table I shows the cumulative percentage of sons having fathers who left estates of different size. Four classes of sons' estate, of £100,000 and over, are distinguished; additionally, the final row in the table telescopes them all into a single '£100,000 and over' category. This is to allow for an expected truncation in the upper echelons of the wealth distribution as evidenced by probate valuations. Tax avoidance among the very rich suggests that it is probably unrealistic to regard precise differences in amounts left by individuals with large estates as having any real significance. For example, if one man leaves £150,000 and another £300,000, this is as likely to reflect less effective tax avoidance in the former case as a difference in true wealth.[23]

Comparisons between the relative proportions of sons having rich fathers may therefore be made for the two sample years 1956–7 and 1965. To assist in the analysis we conducted a test for the significance of the difference between proportions. Denoting the population proportions for each period as π_1, π_2 respectively, we test for $H_0 : \pi_1 = \pi_2$ against the alternative $H_1 : \pi_1 \neq \pi_2$ using the t test. It must be stressed that this does not imply that we regard statistical significance as the sole criterion by which the existence of dependence should be judged, as will be seen from the following analysis.[24] However, where the differences between proportions for the two samples are statistically significant, the appropriate cells are marked with asterisks.

The first conclusion that might be inferred from Table I is that there was a tendency for sons dying in the mid-1960s to have a smaller proportion of wealthy fathers than those dying some ten years earlier. This is brought out particularly in the final row of the table, where the proportion of sons with fathers leaving all size estates over £1,000 is greater for 1956–7 than for 1965. However, the differences in proportions are statistically significant in only three out of the nine cells.

Table II presents cumulative percentages for all estates valued in terms of constant (1956–7 average) prices. The effect of this is to increase the value of most fathers' estates and to reduce the value of sons' estates in the 1965 sample.[25]

The evidence from Table II modifies the preliminary conclusion from Table I. In row five the two sets of cumulative percentages are much closer together. The proportions of 1965 sons with fathers in the highest wealth brackets are less than for sons dying in 1956–7, but this is reversed at the lower end of the scale. However, in none of the cells is the difference in proportions significant. There is a similar tendency to that noticed in Table I in the highest and lowest class of sons' estate for the 1956–7 sons to have had richer fathers. However in rows two and three the proportions of sons with fathers' estates between £1,000 and £500,000 are universally greater for 1965.[26] This table can hardly be said to lead to any conclusion other than that there was no very marked change in the relative importance of inheritance in the creation of large fortunes between the mid-fifties and the mid-sixties of the present century (see Fig. 1).

It is important to consider the extent to which this conclusion is affected by the increasing total numbers of persons leaving estates of different sizes as the nation's wealth has grown.[27] This influence may be tested in a similar way to that used to estimate its significance with regard to the importance of inheritance in 1956–7 compared to 1924–6.[28] The technique employed is to make use of the numbers of persons dying and leaving estates of various size as proportions of the total number of deaths in the median years of fathers' death for the two samples of sons. These may be interpreted as estimates of the probabilities, for any random hundred successors, of having a father leaving an estate of a given size.

The figures in Table III cannot be directly compared with those in Table II since the former relate to the whole population and the latter only to males.[29] They may, however, give a rough indication of the extent to which changes in the proportions of our samples of top wealth leavers having fathers leaving estates over £1,000 may be explained in terms of the increasing average wealth of the population. The table suggests that this explanation is likely to be of only minor importance for this study. Only

TABLE I. *Estates of fathers and sons 1956–7 and 1965 (valuations at current prices)*

Size of sons' estate	Year	Size of fathers' estate (cumulative percentages)										Sample size
		Over £1,000,000	Over £500,000	Over £250,000	Over £100,000	Over £50,000	Over £25,000	Over £10,000	Over £5,000	Over £1,000	All	
£500,000 and over	1956–7	12	23	31	42	54	69	77	77	81	100	26
	1965	0	11	33	33	56	67	67	67	67	100	9
£300,000 and under £500,000	1956–7	2	10	27	42	51	59	63	66	78	100	41
	1965	0	0	25	50	58	75	100	100	100	100	12
£200,000 and under £300,000	1956–7	1	4	15	29	47	63	69	71	83	100	72
	1965	0	6	6	24	47	65	65	71	94	100	17
£100,000 and under £200,000	1956–7	1	3	9	26	39	56*	66*	71	82	100	391
	1965	0	0	3	12	29	38*	50*	62	75	100	98
All sons £100,000 and over	1956–7	1	5	12	28*	42	57*	67*	71	82	100	530
	1965	0	2	7	18*	35	46*	57*	67	79	100	136

NOTE: An asterisk indicates that differences in proportions are statistically significant at the 5 % level of significance.

TABLE II. *Estates of fathers and sons 1956–7 and 1965 (valuations at constant prices (1956–7 average))*

Size of sons' estate	Year	Size of fathers' estate (cumulative percentages)										Sample size
		Over £1,000,000	Over £500,000	Over £250,000	Over £100,000	Over £50,000	Over £25,000	Over £10,000	Over £5,000	Over £1,000	All	
£500,000 and over	1956–7	35	42	46	62	77	77	81	81	85	100	26
	1965	17	17	50	50	50	50	50	50	67	100	6
£300,000 and under £500,000	1956–7	22	32	46	56	63	66	68	71	83	100	41
	1965	14	43	57	57	100	100	100	100	100	100	7
£200,000 and under £300,000	1956–7	13	24	36	56	67	69*	74	82	86	100	72
	1965	0	18	46	73	91	100*	100	100	100	100	11
£100,000 and under £200,000	1956–7	6	16	31*	50	61*	68	76	79	86	100	391
	1965	3	7	18*	38	49*	60	74	79	82	100	68
All sons £100,000 and over	1956–7	10	20	34	52	58	69	76	79	86	100	530
	1965	4	12	26	45	58	67	77	82	85	100	92

NOTE: See note on Table 1.

FIGURE 1

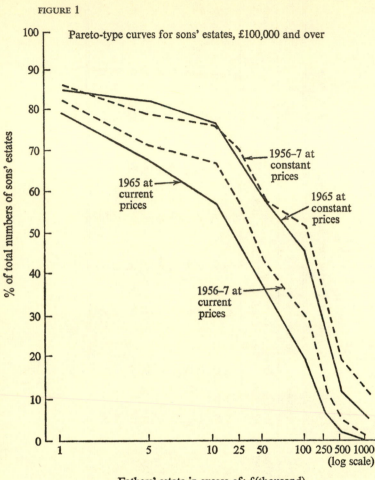

Fathers' estate in excess of: £(thousand)

TABLE III. *Numbers of estates as percentage of the population dying in 1915–16 and 1925–6 (Great Britain)*

Size of estate	1915–16	1925–7
Over £1,000,000	0.00	0.00
500,000	0.01	0.01
250,000	0.02	0.02
100,000	0.06	0.07
50,000	0.14	0.19
25,000	0.32	0.44
10,000	0.81	1.16
5,000	1.46	2.18
1,000	4.31	6.87

SOURCE: Reports of the Commissioners of Inland Revenue.

for estates of £1,000 to £4,999 could an increase of one or more percentage points in the proportions of sons having 'rich' fathers be explained by the rise in average wealth. For all the higher wealth categories, the difference in proportions is very much less than one percentage point.[30,31]

The results presented so far suggest that the 1956–7 and 1965 samples are drawn from a similar population. In this section both samples are amalgamated to undertake the analysis of further characteristics of this underlying population in order to identify those which appear to be particularly associated with inherited as distinct from self-made fortunes. Data were collected for each father and son on age at death, year of death, occupation, residence, number of company directorships held and whether a will was proved or the deceased died intestate. Tables are reproduced similar to Table II (at constant prices) for sub-groups in the sample. These are compared with the cumulative percentages obtained when both samples are amalgamated. Because the numbers in some of the cells would otherwise be small the single category of sons' estates of £100,000 and over was used for the analysis. It will be recalled that this procedure is in any event regarded as appropriate because of the expected upper truncations of sons' estates, previously mentioned. Thus, comparisons in the following tables are made between various sub-samples and the overall sample. The *t* statistic is again used to test statistically for differences between proportions of each of the sub-samples and the whole sample.[32]

(*a*) *V.I.P.s.* Our first set of comparisons relate to the approximate third of the sample where the predecessors of the later generations were most easily traceable – those who appeared in one or other of the standard directories, referred to now for convenience as V.I.P.s. No very surprising results appear from the first two rows of V.I.P.s in Table IV. As might be expected the importance of inheritance for Peers of the Realm, and persons cited in *Burke's Landed Gentry* (BLG) is markedly greater than that for our full sample of top wealth leavers, *e.g.*, approaching two thirds of these two groups had fathers who had left more than a quarter of a million pounds, roughly double that for the whole population in this study. All the *t* statistics are highly significant. The same is true for the much larger category of V.I.P.s in *Who's Who* (WW) or *Kelly's Handbook of the Titled, Landed and Official Classes* (K) which includes almost all of those in the previous two categories of V.I.P.s. For instance, half of these V.I.P. sons had fathers leaving more than £250,000, compared with only a third for all top wealth leavers. Again the *t* statistics are highly significant.

The only surprise in this section is the behaviour of Knights (Bachelor).[33] There is a remarkable similarity between the distribution of their fathers' estates and that of the whole sample. Thus, the recent generation of sons leaving £100,000 and over were not more likely to have had wealthy fathers simply because they had been knighted.[34]

TABLE IV. *V.I.P.s (valuations at constant prices)*

Sons' estate £100,000 and over	Size of fathers' estate (cumulative percentages)										
	Over £1,000,000	Over £500,000	Over £250,000	Over £100,000	Over £50,000	Over £25,000	Over £10,000	Over £5,000	Over £1,000	All	Sample size
All estates	9	19	33	51	62	69	76	79	85	100	622
BLG	21*	46*	60*	78*	86*	89*	93*	93*	95*	100	85
Peers	30*	44*	62*	84*	88*	90*	92*	92*	96*	100	50
Knights	12	15	35	53	62	71	74	77	85	100	34
WW/K	18*	35*	50*	69*	81*	87*	90*	91*	95*	100	202

(b) *Occupations.* The information relating to the occupations of sample members was gleaned from a variety of sources such as directories, death and marriage certificates, wills, entries in the Directories of Directors, etc. To minimise problems of demarcation between concepts of occupational and industrial groupings it was decided to use the Standard Industrial Classification as a basis for classification. Since the largest numbers of sons were in the 1956–7 sample, the 1958 version of the S.I.C. was used for coding purposes. Inevitably some of the allocatory decisions were rather arbitrary, but in the event it proved possible to classify about 90 % of the sample. An additional class (referred to as XXV) was constructed for those sons who had multiple directorships, but it may well be that several allocated to category XXV might better have been added to S.I.C. XXI (insurance, banking and finance).[35]

The aim in this section is to identify (1) individual S.I.C.s and (2) any combination of industry groups, where inheritance appears to have been relatively important. The results are presented first in Table V, which is confined to industry groups where the sample size exceeds 10. Analysis may proceed by comparing each row in the Table corresponding to the distribution of fathers' estates for a single S.I.C. with the overall average shown in row 1.

On the criterion of statistical significance the relative importance of inheritance among top wealth leavers appears greater in agriculture, forestry and fishing than in any other industrial group. This result could hardly be described as surprising. There are also, however, a number of other categories where inherited wealth appears to be relatively important, though this hypothesis is not supported by statistical significance for individual industry groups. These are in Public Administration, food, drink, and tobacco, distribution and the professions, and, more marginally, the textile industry.[36] It is also possible to discern industry groups where the self-made seemed to flourish. These are in metal goods n.e.s. (tools, cutlery, jewellery, etc.), construction, clothing, engineering and, more marginally, in chemicals, finance,[37] paper and printing, mining and transport. As stated previously, the differences in proportions between separate categories of inherited and self-made wealth and the total sample are not statistically significant. However, where the categories are amalgamated into two groups the differences are clearly significant. The results are presented in Table VI.

Caution is necessary for fear of deducing too much from the previous comments but it is interesting to note that the split favouring those with inheritance as against the self-made does not appear to coincide with a division between 'old' and 'new' industries.[38] The division is, perhaps, closer to one between industries containing a relatively large or small number of small firms. There are, of course, obvious exceptions to this. The only reasonable conclusion to be drawn is that the creation of sizeable fortunes by individuals in the industries mentioned in row 2 of Table VI

TABLE V. *Inheritance and occupations of sons (valuations at constant prices)*

| | Size of fathers' estate (cumulative percentages) | | | | | | | | | | |
	Over £1,000,000	Over £500,000	Over £250,000	Over £100,000	Over £50,000	Over £25,000	Over £10,000	Over £5,000	Over £1,000	All	Sample size
Sons' estate £100,000 and over											
All S.I.C.s ...	9	19	33	51	62	69	76	79	85	100	622
Sons' occupations S.I.C.											
I. Agriculture	16	31*	50*	67*	80*	86*	93*	96*	96*	100	70
II. Mining	9	9	18	46	46	64	64	64	73	100	11
III. Food	21	42*	46	71	75	79	83	83	92	100	24
IV. Chemicals	11	11	21	37	47	53	63	63	79	100	19
VI. Engineering	0	8	14*	33*	58	67	72	75	86	100	36
IX. Metal goods n.e.s.	0	0	0*	18*	36	36*	36*	55	64	100	11
X. Textiles	10	23	33	47	67	73	80	83	87	100	30
XII. Clothing	0	0	8	23	39	54	54	54*	85	100	13
XV. Paper, printing	7	7	43	43	50	57	57	57	57*	100	14
XVII. Construction	6	6	12	35	47	47	53*	59*	71	100	17
XIX. Transport	0	6	38	50	56	56	63	69	69	100	16
XX. Distribution	5	13	33	63*	70	76	85	85	88	100	86
XXI. Finance	11	19	25	38*	50*	56*	69	75	79	100	80
XXII. Professions	9	23	37	53	67	79	83	89	93	100	70
XXIII. Miscellaneous	0	7	14	29	36*	36*	57	57	71	100	14
XXIV. Public administration	18	41*	56*	88*	88*	88	94	94	100	100	17
XXV. Multiple interests	17	30	47	60	67	67	77	80	93	100	30
F/S same occupation	10	22	41*	63*	74*	82*	88*	90*	95*	100	282

TABLE VI. *Occupations of sons (valuations at constant prices)*

| | Size of fathers' estate (cumulative percentages) | | | | | | | | | | |
Sons' estate £100,000 and over	Over £1,000,000	Over £500,000	Over £250,000	Over £100,000	Over £50,000	Over £25,000	Over £10,000	Over £5,000	Over £1,000	All	Sample size
All S.I.C.s ...	9	19	33	51	62	69	76	79	85	100	622
Food, distribution, professions, public administration	9	22	38	62*	71*	78*	85*	87*	91*	100	197
Mining, chemicals, metal goods n.e.s., engineering, clothing, construction, transport, finance	7	11*	21*	36*	50*	56*	64*	68*	77*	100	217

appears to have been less hindered by the lack of inheritance than those in row 3. The former industries also allow scope for the entry of small firms with little initial capital. However, this aspect of the problem needs additional evidence and further analysis.

A similar analysis of the occupations of the fathers of the top wealth leavers of recent years was conducted and the extent to which the self-made and those with inherited wealth come from parents in different industrial groupings was examined. Fathers were allocated as far as possible to the same Standard Industrial Classification as used for the sons. Similar tabulations were performed and appear in Table VII. Exercising the usual caution we may, nevertheless, observe a remarkable similarity between the industry groupings favouring inherited and self-made wealth for both fathers and sons. We have therefore repeated the usual calculation for such cases – i.e., restricted to fathers and sons having the same occupation. The results are presented in the final row of Table V, which highlights the importance of inheritance in this situation. As might be expected the results are highly significant statistically. A distinction may be made between fathers and sons being in the same S.I.C. category and having the same occupation. The latter is, of course, stricter in view of the breadth of coverage of several minimum lists headings of the S.I.C. It was, therefore, used as the basis for classification in the final row of Table V.[39]

(c) *Age at death.* One other piece of information available about most sons and a very high proportion of fathers is their age at death. Table VIII provides this information in the usual way for eight age groups of each generation, chosen to maintain the numbers in the cells of the table. Separate analysis is necessary for fathers and sons.

(i) Sons' age at death. The distribution of ages at death in the case of sons could have a peculiar and highly significant implication for the study of inheritance. Atkinson has recently drawn attention to the inequality of wealth distribution by age groups.[40] Basing his conclusions on an analysis of the estate duty statistics published by the Commissioners for Inland Revenue he shows that there was no tendency among men in Britain in the period 1963–7 for the degree of inequality of wealth to decline with age. A possible explanation for the failure of such a decline to show itself is, according to Atkinson, a tendency for certain families to pass on their wealth well before death,[41] though he is unable to provide any substantiation of the hypothesis. Our data, however, are relevant to this question, and, indeed tend to support it, though without the firmness of statistical significance. For the most remarkable feature of the upper half of Table VIII is the fact that the first two rows show that the probability of having a father who had left a substantial estate was greater for those dying by the age of 60 than for the whole population of top wealth leavers. An assumption which would allow us to conclude that inheritance is relatively more important among those who die young is, of course, that they will not have

TABLE VII. *Inheritance and occupations of fathers (valuations at constant prices)*

| | Size of fathers' estate (cumulative percentages) | | | | | | | | | | |
Sons' estate £100,000 and over	Over £1,000,000	Over £500,000	Over £250,000	Over £100,000	Over £50,000	Over £25,000	Over £10,000	Over £5,000	Over £1,000	All	Sample size
All S.I.C.s ...	9	19	33	51	62	69	76	79	85	100	622
Father's S.I.C.											
I. Agriculture	9	26	38	57	67	74	85*	89	89	100	89
II. Mining	0	18	36	55	64	73	82	91	91	100	11
III. Food	29*	50*	54*	71	79	79	82	86	96	100	28
IV. Chemicals	13	13	27	60	73	80	80	87	93	100	15
V. Metal manufacture	0	9	64	73	82	82	82	82	82	100	11
VI. Engineering	0	8	15	35	58	62	73	73	92	100	26
IX. Metal goods n.e.s.	8	8	25	42	58	67	75	75	83	100	12
X. Textiles	16	26	42	51	77	84	90	90	94	100	31
XII. Clothing	0	9	18	45	64	73	73	73	82	100	11
XV. Paper, printing	7	7	29	50	63	71	71	71	79	100	14
XVII. Construction	0	0	10	29	38	48	52	57	71	100	21
XIX. Transport	8	13	38	50	63	63	71	71	71	100	24
XX. Distribution	4	15	31	54	62	69	76	78	84	100	124
XXI. Finance	21*	33	45	62	83*	88*	91*	95*	98*	100	42
XXII. Professions	7	10	19*	37*	52	58	73	77	86	100	62
XXIII. Miscellaneous	0	9	9	18*	18*	18*	27*	46*	64*	100	11
XXIV. Public administration	0	9	18	32	46	55	64	68	77	100	22
XXV. Multiple interests	30*	52*	70*	87*	87	87	87	91	96	100	23

TABLE VIII. Age at death and inheritance (valuations at constant prices)

Sons' estate £100,000 and over	Size of fathers' estate (cumulative percentages)										
	Over £1,000,000	Over £500,000	Over £250,000	Over £100,000	Over £50,000	Over £25,000	Over £10,000	Over £5,000	Over £1,000	All	Sample size
Age at death											
Son											
Under 56	11	19	38	54	73	84	87	89	95	100	37
56–60	10	19	36	55	74	74	81	81	90	100	31
61–64	3	11	33	50	58	78	83	86	92	100	36
65–69	12	22	33	51	63	67	73	75	78	100	67
70–72	8	22	36	50	64	68	76	76	84	100	50
73–75	12	19	37	49	60	65	75	79	83	100	57
76–80	9	21	31	48	57	63	70	73	80	100	127
81 and over	7	18	32	51	62	69	76	80	86	100	216
Father											
Under 56	6	10*	19*	33*	44*	50*	64*	66*	78*	100	90
56–60	0	13	28	53	75	84	88	94*	100*	100	32
61–64	12	21	26	42	56	65	70	77	88	100	43
65–69	12	28	40	55	61	70	79	85	91	100	67
70–72	8	15	25	51	68	72	81	85	89	100	53
73–75	9	16	33	56	67	71	78	80	87	100	45
76–80	12	23	48*	68*	72	81*	87*	88	92	100	75
81 and over	9	29*	43	59*	74*	80*	85*	90*	94*	100	96
All ages	9	19	33	51	62	69	76	79	85	100	622

had the time, or given sufficient thought, to passing on their own property to their heirs, and they are thereby 'caught' by the taxmen. Atkinson, incidentally, cites Wedgwood as arguing that inequality in the age group 55–64 might provide a reasonable guide to the degree of inequality of inherited wealth, on this account. Wedgwood, was, however, writing at a time when the catchment period for gifts *inter-vivos* was 3 years, whereas it had risen to 5 years by the time the population of sons in this sample had died. Moreover, the rates of death duty on large estates were then substantially lower and the 'punishment' inflicted on one's heirs by dying before distributing one's wealth was accordingly less. Hence, we might reasonably argue that the age group under 60 was the more relevant to present times. It is tempting to argue further, therefore, that the real significance of inheritance in present-day Britain is more nearly indicated by the figures in rows 1 and 2 of Table VIII than by the figures for the whole sample of top wealth leavers discussed at length in earlier sections of this paper. Such a conclusion can hardly be justified in the present state of knowledge, but it does seem fair to suggest that the overall figures underestimate the importance of inheritance in the creation of fortunes on this account.

(ii) Fathers' age at death. Inspection of the bottom half of Table VIII shows that the relative importance of inheritance tends to increase with age of father, being statistically significant at the two ends of the age distribution. This could perhaps be due to the fact that fathers' accumulate more wealth for sons to inherit the longer they live, but further work would be necessary to substantiate this proposition.

This section deals briefly with the evidence collected on the relationship between the estates of relatives other than fathers of our sample of top wealth leavers. It must, however, be emphasised that no systematic attempt was made to trace the estates of such relatives for all members of the sample population. The search for fathers-in-law was limited almost entirely to those cases where fathers' estates were small, in order to investigate the importance of wealth acquired through marriage.

Tracing a father-in-law's estate involves a considerable extra burden in the field work, as it is necessary to search additionally in each case in the Register of Marriages over spans of up to 30 years. This procedure entailed a lower success rate than that in the search for fathers' names, but it was possible to find the estates of nearly 50 fathers-in-law of sons in the sample. Row 1 of Table IX sets out the relationship between the wealth of such sons and that of the highest predecessors' estate, whether father or father-in-law. It may be compared with the second row in the table which shows the relationship between the same sons and their father alone.[42] The proportions of sons with rich predecessors naturally increase as a result of this operation. The numbers involved are not large, but include, for example, some six sons with relatively poor fathers, but whose fathers-in-law left more than £50,000. The highest predecessors' estates in these cases were then substituted for fathers' estates in the overall sample and the usual proportions calculated and shown in row 5 of the table. They may be compared with our standard bench mark for fathers only, shown in the final row of the table. The differences in proportions are not significant. This is, of course, mainly because only about 8 % of the sample was affected. It is also because the proportion of sons marrying into wealth that came to light was on the small side. Our impression is that this was not a very common explanation of the source of wealth of those who have so far been regarded as 'self-made'.

It must be stressed again that the search for fathers-in-law was mainly restricted to those of sons who appeared to have inherited little from their fathers. Were a study made of the wealth of the fathers-in-law of a more representative set of top wealth leavers, one would expect a higher frequency of rich sons having rich fathers-in-law to be discovered, due to the practice of intermarriage within one's social class.

A few cases were observed to support this view, where the small size of a father's estate led to a search for a father-in-law, but the father in question clearly belonged to the upper or middle classes despite his relative impecuniosity. For example, the wealthy (diplomat) son of an Oxford professor, who had left some £2,000, married the daughter of a wine shipper who had left nearly £200,000. Another son, a distiller, whose stockbroker father had left a mere £3,500, took as his (first) wife the daughter of a distiller, who had left over a quarter of a million pounds. A couple of other sons with 'respectable' but relatively poor fathers married into the Peerage.

Finally, it is worth reporting that in 35 additional cases the estates of predecessors other than fathers or fathers-in-law were traced, largely by chance during the search for fathers.[43] Rows 3, 4 and 6 of Table IX present the results of similar calculations used for rows 1, 2 and 5 with fathers-in-law, employing now the highest of any predecessor's estate found.[44] The results of this exercise naturally show again an increased importance of inheritance as here measured. Moreover, since no deliberate attempt was made to trace earlier generations for sons with wealthy fathers, and because trust property over which the deceased had no power of disposal is excluded from probate valuations, this probably means that the classes who tend to indulge in generation skipping as a tax avoidance device are under represented here.

This study is based upon an analysis of the fortunes left by the fathers of a sample of top wealth leavers in recent years, representing approximately 0.1 % of total adult deaths. The conclusions may be summarised as follows. No very marked change in the relative numbers of self-made men as distinct from those with inherited wealth occurred between the mid-fifties and mid-

TABLE IX. *Inheritances from fathers-in-law and other relatives (valuations at constant prices)*

Sons' estate £100,000 and over	Size of predecessors' estate (cumulative percentages)										Sample size
	Over £1,000,000	Over £500,000	Over £250,000	Over £100,000	Over £50,000	Over £25,000	Over £10,000	Over £5,000	Over £1,000	All	
Father/Father-in-law (*a*)	0	2	4	8	13	17	35	52	81	100	48
Father only	0	0	0	0	0	2	13	17	48	100	46
Highest predecessor (*b*)	11	18	27	36	43	54	64	74	88	100	83
Father only	4	4	6	12	12	14	28	32	54	100	80
All estates (*a*)	9	19	33	51	63	69	77	81	88	100	624
All estates (*b*)	10	21	35	54	66	73	80	84*	90*	100	625
Father only (*c*)	9	19	33	51	62	69	76	79	85	100	622

sixties of the present century. Moreover, in view of the results of previous studies by Wedgwood and Harbury, the role of inheritance in the creation of the personal fortunes of the top wealth leavers in the sense used here has not changed very much since the mid-twenties. Comparisons at current prices between the 1956–7 and 1965 samples indicate some statistical decline in the proportions of rich sons who had fathers in the highest wealth brackets. However, it has been argued that the size distribution of personal wealth derived from probate valuations is likely to be truncated as a result of tax avoidance practices. If attention is, therefore, directed at the experience of all top wealth leavers (£100,000 and over) and allowance is made for changes in the general price level, all statistically significant differences in proportions between the two samples disappear. Thus, for example, the proportion of sons leaving £100,000 and over and having fathers who had left more than £50,000 was 58 % both in 1956–7 and 1965. The fact that between a half and two-thirds of those who left £100,000 or more in the 1950s and 1960s were preceded by fathers leaving at least £25,000 illustrates the importance of having had a moderately wealthy father. If there were no connection between wealth of fathers and sons, one would expect less than 1 % of the population of sons to have had fathers with this size fortune. The apparent decline in the concentration of personal wealth using conventional estate duty multiplier techniques might be reinterpreted in the light of this observation. This has important policy implications for wealth taxation, in so far as it means that many wealth transfers have simply been of a kind which redistribute wealth between different generations of the same family.

The two samples for 1956–7 and 1965 were amalgamated to examine further characteristics of top wealth leavers. It was possible to identify a number of industry groups where inheritance appeared to be a more or a less important factor in wealth creation. In particular, it was found that rich sons in agriculture, public administration, food, drink and tobacco, distribution and marginally in textiles, were more likely to have had rich fathers than those in metal goods, construction, clothing and engineering and more marginally in chemicals, finance, paper and printing and mining. Analysis of the occupational groupings of fathers suggested a fairly close correspondence with that of sons. It is tentatively suggested that the split between the two categories of industry – those favouring inheritance or the self-made – is perhaps more likely to be based on a distinction related to the size distribution of firms by industry, than between 'new' and 'old' industries, with groups offering relatively more scope for the small man favouring the self made.

Analysis by age at death of son showed that those top wealth leavers dying relatively young were the most likely to have had rich fathers. This result may be regarded as some statistical evidence on the importance of gifts *inter vivos* among the wealthy. Furthermore, sons whose fathers' age at death was high were more likely to have inherited substantial wealth than those whose fathers died young. Analysis of Peers, landed gentry, Knights and those listed in *Who's Who* and similar directories confirmed an expectation that all such groups had a notably higher proportion of rich fathers than the sample as a whole, with the solitary exception of Knights Bachelor. Finally, about one in eight top wealth leavers with relatively poor fathers were discovered to have married into wealth, and there is evidence to suggest that wealth concentration within families is of considerable importance.

W. D. RUBINSTEIN

8 Men of property: some aspects of occupation, inheritance and power among top British wealthholders

After some forty years of neglect, the question of the wealthy in British society has again become the subject of a good deal of scholarly interest.[1] Many of the data about the wealth distribution of contemporary Britain are derived from the records of the Estate Duty Office, which are published annually in the Reports of the Inland Revenue. This series has the advantage for scholars of unbroken existence for many years – since 1894 – and is readily available in a useful form. However, it has the disadvantage of absolute anonymity: research on individual items in the Inland Revenue is forbidden for the extraordinary period of 150 years. Corresponding to the Inland Revenue series, however, is another which, although somewhat less comprehensive, contains the names of all individuals to leave property in Britain, and indicates the gross fortune left by each. This is comprised of the probate calendars at Somerset House, in Scotland and Northern Ireland, and, for the period between 1809, when this data begins in a usable form, and 1858, when the Somerset House calendars begin, the records of the various ecclesiastical courts, chiefly the Prerogative Courts of Canterbury and York. (Henceforth these records will be referred to as the 'Somerset House' series, unless otherwise noted.) Within their limitations, this series provides nothing less than a portrait of wealth in Britain since the Industrial Revolution, and it is astonishing that it has been so seldom used by researchers.[2] Aside from permitting us to establish the limits of individual wealthholding in a *Guinness Book of Records* sense, the Somerset House data provide, first, an entirely objective way of measuring what is frequently a matter of reticence and legend; they allow comparisons among members of different occupational and elite groups: was a wealthy banker richer than a wealthy cotton manufacturer? How much more wealthy was either than a wealthy barrister? How much richer were they than their employees? They allow us to identify individuals of great economic importance who have previously gone unnoticed, and whose invisibility cannot fail to distort the common impression of British economic, and, indeed, social and political history. They provide an excellent opportunity for measuring a specific type of intergenerational social mobility. They provide an excellent way of determining certain differences within elite groups. Finally, and most importantly, they provide a comprehensive measure of the outputs of the social system. Clearly sheer wealth is not the only output of British society: personal honours, professional and peer group esteem, and power-wielding at least complement economic rewards, but wealth remains, I would think, the common denominator of the system, and at the very least any long-term changes in the wealth of particular groups must surely be of considerable importance.

My own research has consisted in abstracting from Somerset House the names of all persons leaving £500,000 or more, and, for the nineteenth century, £100,000 or more. In this paper I shall try to accomplish two tasks: first to spell out what these sources reveal about some key aspects of Britain's wealth elite during the past century and a half, and secondly to demonstrate that there has been considerably more fluidity and mobility in Britain's wealth elite than is often supposed, such that the extent of social mobility into this elite compares not unfavourably with America, and is increasing; and to demonstrate that wealth and political power are becoming increasingly dissassociated. Comparing two sets of statistics about the amount of wealth held by, e.g., the top one per cent at different periods, as is often done, may well conceal a good deal of fluidity within that top one per cent.

It should be noted at once that the Somerset House series is less inclusive than the Inland Revenue data in several important respects. Before 1898, all real property (except freeholds) was excluded from valuation, and between 1898 and 1926, all settled realty. At all times, all settled personalty that did not cease being in settlement at the death of the testator, and, hence, over which he had no absolute disposition has been excluded from valuation. Also excluded is immobile personalty situated abroad, though not foreign shares traded in Britain. Furthermore, the Somerset House valuations are for the gross, and not the net value.[3] Finally, there is the separate issue, particularly in the most recent period, of estate duty avoidance.[4] This formidable-looking list of *caveats* is not, however, as prepossessing as it might appear. The wealth of top landowners in the latter part of the nineteenth century is, of course, known from the *Return of Owners of Land* of 1871–4; much 'foreign' property is included with the domestic total; and estate duty avoidance did not reach anything like its present level until after the Second World War. Probably the most important omission is that of settled personalty.[5]

The actual abstraction of the names of the top wealthholders from these sources was not quite as herculean a task as it might appear. Since 1901, complete lists have been published for almost all years in the *Daily Mail Yearbook*. The annual list is generally of fortunes over £500,000, though sometimes includes fortunes over £100,000. Similar lists are also published in a number of newspapers. These secondary sources do not include estates subsequently resworn at a different value, and therefore all estates over £300,000 have been checked against the original calendars. For the period 1809–99, however, it proved necessary to go through each of the calendars by hand.[6] The result is a catalogue of all persons leaving £500,000 of more – the monied elite of Britain.

Two very general points should, I think, be noted about British wealth-holders as a group. First, occupation percentages among the wealthy need bear little resemblance to either the income or occupational factors of the national product. This is perfectly clear, since bankers are apt to represent a very substantial portion of the wealthy, while banking as such is a minor element of the national product. To this extent, it might be noted, macroeconomic history distorts the actual wealth picture. Secondly, there are wealthy businessmen, and then there are famous ones, and the two groups are not identical. No Wedgwood, Marshall, or Rathbone ever left £500,000, or any sum close to this, although there have been many shipowners, flax-spinners, and several pottery manufacturers among the very wealthy. On the other hand, there are the inevitable unknowns. A single example will illustrate this. Few historians of the nineteenth century appear to be familiar with James Morrison (1789–1857), the son of an innkeeper in Hampshire, who arrived without means in London, worked in a drapery warehouse and married the boss's daughter, became a merchant banker, served as an M.P., and died leaving between 3 and 4 million pounds – probably the largest personal fortune ever seen in Britain up to that date – in addition to 106,000 acres yielding £53,000 *per annum*.[7] Nor did his fortune die with him – *vide* the following tree of his male descendants:

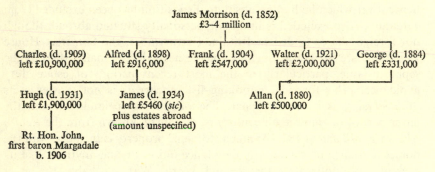

Of course, it is hardly the case that most of the wealthy are unknown: one of the two wealthiest families over the past century and a half, in terms of individuals leaving £500,000 or more, was that of the Rothschilds, twenty-one of whom have left fortunes in this class since 1836. The other wealthiest family, also with twenty-one members leaving £500,000, is the Wills tobacco family. Just below these is the Coats family, the Paisley sewing thread manufacturers, with sixteen, and the Colman and Palmers families with ten each. The Morrison family, with its female wealthholders, included nine top fortunes, as do the Rallis, the Greek family of merchants. The Goslings, an old banking family, produced seven such wealthholders, and the following families produced six each: Baird (iron), Courtauld, Garton (brewery sugar), Guinness, Joicey, Pilkington, Ratcliff (brewing), Reckitt (starch), Tate, Watney, Wilson (shipping), Sebag-Montefiore, and the dukes of Northumberland and their near relatives. Twenty-one families produced five members with fortunes in excess of £500,000, including the Crawshays, Fieldens, Frys, Goldsmids, Lyles, and Peckovers, while twenty-five families included three wealth-holders. As far as individuals are concerned, only fourteen fortunes of £7,000,000 or more have been recorded at Somerset House. Two of these belonged to foreigners: to the South African gold and diamond magnates Alfred Beit (1853–1906), who left £8,049,000, and Sir Julius Werhner (1850–1912), who left £10,044,000. By far the largest individual fortune belonged to Sir John Ellerman (1862–1933), the shipowner and property magnate, who left the incredible sum of £36,685,000 at the bottom of the Depression. Ellerman was a self-made man. His father, a corn factor in Hull, died when his son was nine, leaving under £600. Nine million pounds of Ellerman's fortune was in cash in the bank: it would be interesting to learn his rate of return on the rest, or what the value of his estate would have been had he died in 1928. He certainly deserves a biography. His only son, probably the richest man in Britain until his recent death, is reputed to be worth £150 million. Far down in second place is Edward Guinness, first earl of Iveagh (1847–1927), who left £13,486,000. Seven other fortunes of £10 million or more have been recorded: those left by Charles Morrison, James's eldest son; Sir George A. Wills (1854–1928) of the tobacco family; James Williamson, first baron Ashton (1842–1930), the 'linoleum king'; the second duke of Westminster (1879–1953); James A. E. de Rothschild (1878–1957); Guy A. Vandervell (1898–1967), an engine-bearing manufacturer; and Felix Fenston (d. 1971), a post-war property developer. In the 7–10 million pound range were the fortunes of Sir Ernest Cassel (1854–1921) the financier; James Buchanan, first baron Woolavington (1849–1935), a distiller; and Sir Alfred C. Beatty (1875–1968), the developer of Rhodesia's copper mines.[8]

Most in Britain's wealth elite could not, of course, approach this level of wealth: there are differences among the wealthy no less than among the poor. Even the largest of British fortunes, for example, can hardly compare in size with the top fortunes in America: Ford and Rockefeller, reputed to each be worth £200 million, were fifty times wealthier than any British non-landed wealthholder of the nineteenth century. In all, about 675 persons have left millionaire estates in Britain since 1809, of whom about fifty were women and twenty-five foreigners, who are excluded from the data below.[9] Below the millionaire class are the perhaps 1550 half-million-aires, and below them, the 30,000-odd who left between £100,000 and £500,000. Clearly no researcher can ever hope to master the careers of all of these men. In this portion of the paper, I will deal with the occupations of the millionaires, and with three groups of half-millionaires, those deceased 1858–99, 1925–9, and 1964–8. I am currently at work on the interstices of the half-millionaire group, and may in the future extend my research downward to a degree. But research on the very sizeable class below this can probably only be accomplished in representative annual segments, and it is here that the valuable research of Professor Harbury and Dr McMahon is particularly impressive and necessary. In particular it is to be hoped that the lower wealthholders of the nineteenth century may eventually be tackled.

Tables I and II are arranged according to what I have elsewhere termed the 'Old' trades, those very roughly that became profitable before or during the Industrial Revolution; the 'Intermediate', those that have been profitable throughout; and the 'New', those that have become profitable only during the past century. Roughly, too, these divisions correspond to the staple industries of the nineteenth century, plus land and finance, in the 'Old' category, and to what may be termed the consumer-oriented trades, including retailing, among the 'New'. A glance will show that the British wealth structure has shifted strikingly from the 'Old' to the 'New' trades,[10] to retailing, and to the production of consumer and consumer-related goods. For example, those classified among the 'New' trades accounted for about 13 per cent of all millionaire deaths among those deceased in 1900–9, but for about sixty per cent of those deceased in 1960–9. Among half-millionaires the story is much the same. In this sea of change, there has been only one relative constant: the wealth of landowners. (In these tables, the 'B' for 'Bateman' landowners are those whose real property, worth over the minimum figure for inclusion in that table, is not included in the valuation at Somerset House. I have taken a gross annual rental of £60,000 or more *per annum* as the minimum level for millionaires, and £40,000 or more *per annum* for half-millionaires. This is to assume that the value of land was equivalent to about 18 years' purchase in the case of millionaires, as it probably was after 1879. For the previous period, it is common to use the figure of 33 years' purchase. In any case, the place of landowning in the nineteenth century wealth picture was most substantial: it is likely that until about 1890, more than half of all really wealthy men in Britain were landowners.) It may appear surprising that the bankers, stockbrokers, foreign merchants, and insurance dealers have declined to such an extent: but certainly the old private or family banker, such as Barclay, Gurney, and Hoare has been superseded by banking corporations whose shares are widely owned, and whose managers are not themselves very wealthy. Even in the world of merchant banking, it would seem as if, e.g., the great Jewish financiers of the type of Lords Swaythling and Wandsworth, and, indeed, the Rothschilds, are no longer as rich as they were before 1914, as the cosmopolitanism of the pre-1914 period has disappeared.[11] A similar change is also evident in the occupational patterns among the half-millionaires in Table II.

TABLE I. *Occupations among millionaires*

	1809–58	1858–69	1870–9	1880–9	1890–9	1900–9	1910–19	1920–9
'Old'								
Land	3 (+B 75)	2 (+B 18)	2 (+B 15)	2 (+B 10)	8 (+B 22)	10 (+B 14); 1 Austral. land	10 (+B 14)	18 (+B 6)
Banking/Finance	2; 1 E. India Co	2	7	3	8	13	11	9
Bullion	1 (Gold-smith)	1	1				1 Diamonds	
Insurance	1	1		1	1	2	1	
Stockbrokerage						2	3	
Foreign merchants		2	2	4		1 Carrier	1	2
Warehouses	1	1			1	2		2
Minerals								
Iron master	1	3	3	1	1		3	1
Coal			1		2		2	2
Copper				1			1	1
Textiles								
Cotton	2	1	1	3 (1 sewing thread)	1	3 (2 sewing thread)	6 (5 sewing thread, 1 exporter)	6 (5 sewing thread, 1 spinner)
Worsted				1	1		1	
Woollens	1	1					1 (Hosiery)	2 (Hosiery)
Linen			1					1 (Lace)
Silk			1					4 Silk
'Intermediate'								
Engineering Contractors, Engineers			2	2	2 Chemicals; 1 Machinery; 1 Metal Mfc; 1 Dyer; 1 Eng./Cont.	2 Chemicals; 2 Eng./Cont.	2 Chemicals; 3 Eng./Cont.	2 Machinery; 1 Chemicals; 4 Eng./Cont.
Shipping/Builders	1	1		1	3	2	8	8
Brewers	1	1		4	4	3	3	8
Distillers				1	1 Maltster	2		2

TABLE I (*cont.*)

'*New*'

	1809–58	1858–69	1870–9	1880–9	1890–9	1900–9	1910–19	1920–9
Builder	1			1 Unknown 1 Misc.	1 Newsagent 1 Sugar Mer. 1 Condiments 1 Retail Mer. 1 Misc.	2 Tobacco 1 Biscuits 1 Min. Water 1 Condiments 2 Retail Mer.	3 Tobacco 1 Sweets 1 Miller 1 Starch Mfc. 2 Pat. Medic. 2 Art Dealer 1 Unknown 1 Misc.	4 Tobacco 3 Newspapers 1 Sugar 1 Sweets 1 Jam 2 Soap 3 Retail 1 Book cloth 1 Newsagent 1 Credit 1 Rayon 2 Steel 1 Petrol 1 Misc.

'*Old*'

	1930–9	1940–9	1950–9	1960–9
Land	12	15	10	6
(Foreign land)	—	1	1	3 (& minerals)
Banking	4	7	5	2
Insurance	3	1	2	1
Stockbroker	2		1	1
Foreign Merch.	1			
	1 Jeweller			
Coal	1	1 Currency Printer	1	
		1 Mohair		
Textiles				
Cotton		1	1 Dress Muslin	
Silk	1			
Sewing thread	1			
Woollens	1 (Merch.)			

'Intermediate'				
Contractors/Eng.	2	1	2	2
Machinery			2	1
Chemicals	2 Utilities			1
Shipping	8	11	4	3
Brewers	5	1	2	2
Distillers	2	6	1	1
'New'				
Retail Chains	2	3	2	6
Autos	2	1		3
Food				
Importer	1		1 Miller	1 Custard
Dairy	1	2 Sweets		1 Sweets
Sugar	1			1 Meat Import.
Biscuits	4	3		1
Mustard	1	2		2
	2 Petrol	8 Tobacco	3 Tobacco	1 Elect. Heaters
	1 Travel Agt.	3 Rayon	1 Rayon	1 Wallpaper
	7 Tobacco	1 Celanese	1 Asbestos	1 Hotels
	1 Manf. Chem.	1 Gravel	1 Timber	1 Timber
	1 Lino	2 Newspapers	1 Newspapers	1 Glass
	2 Newspapers	1 Soap	1 Builder	1 Petrol
	1 Book cloth		1 Prop. Dev.	1 Packaging
	1 Pawn		1 Misc.	1 Gravel
	1 *Rentier*		1 *Rentier*	1 Steel
	1 Turbines			1 Newspapers
				6 Property
				2 Unknown

TABLE II. *Half-millionaires' occupations*

	1858–79		1880–99
'Old'		*'Old'*	
Land	15 (+B 150)	Land	14 (+B 50)
Banking	26	Banking	29
Bullion	1	Foreign merchants	10
Insurance	2	Jeweller	1
Stockbrokers	2	Stockbrokers	4
Foreign merchants	9	Warehouses	2
Carrier	1	Cotton spinners	13
Warehouses	2	Thread mfc.	1
Cotton spinners	7	Needle mfc.	1
Cotton exporters	3	Silk	1
Silk	3	Jute	1
Silk merchants	2	Flax	1
Lace mfcs.	2	Woollen mfcs.	5
Woollens	1	Worsteds	1
Ironmasters	11	Ironmasters	5
Iron merchants	3	Iron merchants	1
Copper	2	Lead	1
Colliery	1	Coal merchant	1
		Colliery	6
'Intermediate'		*'Intermediate'*	
Shipping	2	Shipping	7
Machinery mfcs.	1	Chemical mfcs.	4
Engineers/Contractors	1	Machinery mfcs.	5
Brewers	2	Engineers/Contractors	8
		Varnish mfcs.	2
'New'		Gellatine & glue mfc.	1
Builders	2	Brewers	9
Paper mfc.	1	Wine merchants	3
Furniture printer	1	Tea merchant	1
Retailer	1	Hop merchant	2
Guano merchant	1	Pottery mfc.	1
Newpaper	2		
Tobacco	1	*'New'*	
Carpet mfcs.	2	Steel mfc.	1
Miscellaneous:		Glass mfc.	1
Solicitors	4	Guano merchant	1
Cleric	1	Art dealer	1
Unknown	3	Travel agent	1
		Publishers	3
		Newspapers	1
		Patent medicine	1
		Jam mfc.	1
		Mustard mfcs.	3
		Sweets mfc.	2
		Condiment mfcs.	1
		Tobacco	1
		Retailer	1
		Miscellaneous:	
		Accountant	1
		Solicitors	3
		Cleric	1
		Miscellaneous	1
		Unknown	1

TABLE II (*cont.*)

	1925–29		1964–8
'Old'		*'Old'*	
Land	17	Land	13
Banking	8	Foreign land	1
Stockbrokers	2	Bankers	2
Foreign merchants	10	Gold merchant	1
Insurance	3	Insurance	8
Diamonds	1	Stockbrokers	1
Colliery	3	Cotton spinner	1
Metal merchant	1	Cotton merchants	2
Ironmaster	1	Ex-colliery	1
Cloth mfc.	1	Non-ferrous metals	1
Cotton spinner	1	Brass founder	1
Thread mfc.	1	Tea planter	1
Wollen mfc.	2	Rubber planter	1
Worsted mfc.	3		
Jute mfc.	1	*'Intermediate'*	
Cotton merchant	1	Shipping	4
Tea merchant & planter	1	Engineers/Contractors	4
		Screw mfc.	1
'Intermediate'		Brewer	1
Shipping	12	Wine merchant	1
Bleacher	1		
Chemical mfc.	2	*'New'*	
Engineers/Contractors	4	Aeroplane mfc.	1
Brewers	4	Radio mfc.	1
Wine merchant	1	Carpet mfc.	1
Distillers	3	Wholesale clothing mfc.	1
		Collar mfc.	1
'New'		Industrial services mfcs.	2
Asbestos mfc.	1	Rubber-products mfc.	1
Petroleum	1	Surfacing contractor	1
Printer	1	Container mfc.	1
Newspapers	1	Heater mfc.	1
Timber merchant	1	Seed merchant	1
Starch mfc.	1	Food essence mfc.	1
Bottle mfc.	1	Meat merchant	1
Football club owner	1	Retailer	1
Gas works owner	1	Advertising agent	1
Glass mfc.	1	Art dealer	1
Retailers	3	Impressario	1
Mail order merchant	1	Property developers	5
Sugar merchant	2	Builders	3
Tobacco	1	Miscellaneous:	
Biscuit mfc.	1	Architect	1
Vinegar mfc.	1	Solicitor	1
Confectionery mfc.	1	Unknown	10
Millers	2		
Unknown	2		

This shift in the occupational sources of the great fortunes may well be closely related to a second source of change among wealthholders, the disposition of their fortunes at death. Exactly what happens to the fortunes of the wealthy over the generations, and how its disposition may affect the attitudes and performance of its heritors, is surely a question of great importance about which nothing precisely is known. Folk wisdom brings to hand several contradictory points of view. There is, on one hand, the implausible but popular belief in 'shirtsleeves to shirtsleeves in three generations'. Again there is the image of a perpetual movement since the Middle Ages, of trade and commerce into the land, wherein the wealthy merchants of one generation disappear from view, to re-emerge only in some corner of *Burke's Landed Gentry*. Finally there is the view that, since money begets money, the wealthy of one generation simply become wealthier in the next.

The disposition of property from one generation to another according to the wills of the wealthy is therefore a crucial concern here. On the one hand, wealthy businessmen may imitate the aristocracy and leave nearly everything to their eldest son, or they may divide their property equally or nearly equally. Which of these it will be will of course vary with the self-perception of each wealthholder: in the Victorian age, and even later, there are examples of men, such as Lord Overstone the millionaire banker, or James Morrison, who purchased land on a vast scale. Morrison, for example, not only secured 76,000 acres for his eldest son, but respectable estates, ranging from 3,000 to nearly 14,000 acres, for his younger sons. The sum of these choices is almost certainly a crucial factor to the economic development of Britain since the Victorian period, for if equal division rather than primogeniture is the rule, the younger sons of the wealthy, and, indeed, all of their descendants for several generations at least, would be wealthy enough to be idle, and it is most unlikely that, in any substantial number of cases, any descendant would carry on in the entrepreneurial spirit that made the family wealthy. Moreover, the positive inducements to withdraw from the world of business that have always existed in British society – whether to the landed gentry, to London's clubland, or to Imperial service – must in any case have had a profound, and perhaps irresistible effect upon the descendants of the entrepreneur. For information on this point, the wills of about half of the non-landed wealth-holders deceased between 1858 and 1899 – those whose details were published in the weekly 'Wills and Bequests' column of the *Illustrated London News* – were checked for information on this point. In addition, an attempt was made to check as many other non-landed wealthholder wills as was possible, though ultimately the number was limited by the length and illegibility of many wills, or their location in Scotland and Ireland. In all, 123 half-millionaire wills, and 66 millionaire wills, were included in this study. Among millionaires, seven of the 66 left their

estates wholly or primarily to a relative of the same generation as themselves – in six cases, to the wife. Of the fifty-nine whose principal heirs
were of the next generation, 27 left more than half of their fortune to one
descendant, while 32 did not. No fewer than 15 left less than 29 per cent of
their fortune to any one descendant. Among the half-millionaires in this
study, 102 left their fortunes to a member of the next generation, and, of
these, a two-thirds majority left less than half to their principal heir. In
some cases, curiously enough, a younger son received more than an elder,
either because he was more competent, to balance a previous gift to the
elder, or because the elder son received the wealthholder's land – a
remnant of aristocracy-aping.[12]

It is important to test as well whether in fact many younger sons were
or were not men of substantial means, and therefore the probate valuations
of all male descendants of these wealthholders were traced in all cases in
which this was possible. In this study, all male descendants aged 25 or more
were included for non-landed millionaires deceased between 1858 and 1899,
and for non-landed half-millionaires deceased between 1870 and 1884.
These findings, it should be realized, are entirely dependent upon the
vagaries of *Burke's Peerage* and *Landed Gentry* in their various editions,
the source for all family trees but two. A substantial number left no male
issue. In some cases, only one son of a wealthholder is specifically named in
Burke's; in other cases, no date of death is shown. Furthermore, this
sample is strongly skewed in favour of the millionaires. While only eleven
family trees of these millionaires entirely escaped detection, those of forty-
half-millionaires could not be traced. Finally, the limitations of the
probate calendars should be kept in mind, particularly that the younger
sons of wealthholders were likely to be the legatees of settled personalty.
In some cases, therefore, their wealth is understated. Tables III and IV
summarise the results of this exercise. Table IIIa lists the fortunes of the
descendants of millionaires, in those cases in which the millionaire had
more than one son; table IVa lists those cases in which the millionaire had
one son only. Table IIIb and IVb repeat this for half-millionaire descendants. The numbers in brackets refer to those cases in which the descendant in question was killed in a war. In addition to these war deaths, about
a dozen other cases are known for whom no valuation could be found at
Somerset House, indicating they may have had only insignificant estates.
It is not unlikely that there was a considerable amount of *inter vivos* giving
in these cases because of the risk involved.

Among the sons of millionaires, it will be seen that there is a slight
tendency to primogeniture, while there is a more discernible trend among
their grandsons and great-grandsons. For example, six eldest sons of eldest
sons themselves left £500,000 or more, compared with eight among all
other categories. Among the solitary sons of millionaires, there is a clear
tendency toward keeping the fortune intact, with a certain tendency, in the

TABLE IIIa. *Probate valuations of male millionaire descendants: more than one son*

Valuation Sons of millionaires...	I (eldest)	II	III	IV	V	VI or more
Under £1,000	2	1 (+1)	—	2	—	—
Under £10,000	2	1	1	1	1	4
Under £50,000	3	2	3	2	1	—
Under £100,000	2	3	3	—	—	1
Under £200,000	—	3	(1)	2	2	—
Under £300,000	2	2	2	—	—	1
Under £500,000	3	3	4	—	2	2
Under £1 million	5	3	1	—	1	—
Under £2 million		—		—	2	—
Over £2 million	4					

Grandsons ...	Sons of I				Sons of II			Sons of III			Sons of IV		Sons of V			Sons of VI	
	I	II	III	IV or more	I	II	III	I	II	III	I	II	I	II	III	I	II
Under £1,000	—	—	—	—	1	(1)	—	—	—	—	—	—	—	—	—	1	—
Under £10,000	1	—	—	—	1	1	1	2	2	1	—	—	—	1	—	—	—
Under £50,000	1	2	1	—	—	—	1	1	1	1	1	—	2	1	—	1	1
Under £100,000	1	1	1	—	1	2 (+1)	1	1	—	—	1	1	(1)	—	—	1	1
Under £200,000	2	1	1	—	1	—	—	1	—	—	1	—	—	—	—	1	—
Under £300,000	—	1	—	—	2	—	—	—	—	—	—	1	—	—	—	—	—
Under £500,000	1	1	—	—	—	—	—	1	1	—	—	—	—	—	1	—	1
Under £1 million	1	1	1	—	1	—	—	—	1	—	—	—	—	—	—	—	—
Under £2 million	2	—	1	—	2	—	—	—	—	1	—	—	—	—	—	—	—
Over £2 million	3	1	—	—	—	—	—	—	—	—	—	—	—	—	—	—	—

TABLE IIIa (*cont.*)

	Grandsons			
Great-grandsons ...	of I	of II	of III	of IV
Under £1,000	(1)	—	1	—
Under £10,000	(1)	—	1	1
Under £50,000	—	1	1	1
Under £100,000	1	(1)	2	—
Under £200,000	1	—	—	1
Under £300,000	—	1	—	—
Under £500,000	—	—	—	—
Under £1 million	1+(1)	—	—	—
Under £2 million	1	—	—	—
Over £2 million	—	—	—	—

TABLE IIIb. *Probate valuations of half-millionaire male descendants: more than one son*

Valuation Sons of half-millionaires ...	I (eldest)	II	III	IV	V	VI or more
Under £1,000	—	—	—	1	—	—
Under £10,000	—	2	—	—	1	—
Under £50,000	1	1	1	2	1	1
Under £100,000	2	3	1	1	—	2
Under £200,000	7	3	4	1	3	2
Under £300,000	—	1	—	—	1	—
Under £500,000	5	3	4	3	1	—
Under £1 million	4	3	1	—	—	—
Under £2 million	1	—	—	—	—	—
Over £2 million	—	1	1	1	—	—

TABLE IIIb (*cont.*)

Grandsons ...	Sons of I				Sons of II					Sons of III				Sons of IV+		
	I	II	III	IV	I	II	III	IV	V	I	II	III	IV	I	II	III
Under £1,000	2	—	—	—	1	—	(1)	—	—	—	(1)	—	—	—	—	—
Under £10,000	2	1	—	—	1	—	2	(1)	1	1	1	—	—	—	1	(1)
Under £50,000	1	2	1	1	1	3+(1)	—	1	—	3	1	1	1	3	1	—
Under £100,000	1	1	—	—	2	1	—	—	—	2	—	1	1	1	—	—
Under £200,000	1	1	2	1	1	2	1	1	—	—	1	—	—	1	—	—
Under £300,000	3	1	1	—	1+(2)	—	—	—	—	—	—	—	—	—	—	1
Under £500,000	1	1	1	—	1+(1)	1	—	—	—	—	—	—	—	—	—	—
Under £1 million	—	—	—	—	—	—	—	—	—	—	—	—	—	—	—	—
Under £2 million	1	—	—	—	—	—	—	—	—	—	—	—	—	—	—	—
Over £2 million	—	—	—	—	—	—	—	—	—	—	—	—	—	—	—	—

Great-grandsons ...	of Grandsons I	of Grandsons II
Under £1,000	—	(2)
Under £10,000	1+(2)	(1)
Under £50,000	—	2+(1)
Under £100,000	—	2
Under £200,000	—	1
Under £300,000	—	—
Under £500,000	—	—
Under £1 million	—	—
Under £2 million	—	—
Over £2 million	—	—

TABLE IVa. *Probate valuations of male millionaire descendants: one son only*

Valuation					
Under £10,000	2				
Under £200,000	—				
Under £300,000	1				
Under £500,000	2				
Under £1 million	5				
Grandsons ...	I (eldest)	II	III	IV	V
Under £1,000	—	—	—	—	—
Under £10,000	—	—	—	—	—
Under £50,000	1	—	—	—	1
Under £100,000	1	1	—	—	—
Under £200,000	—	—	1	—	—
Under £300,000	—	—	—	—	—
Under £500,000	—	—	—	—	—
Under £1 million	—	1	—	—	—

Great-grandsons (only examples) ...	Of grandson I		Of grandson V
	I	II	I
Under £10,000	—	—	1
Under £50,000	1	1	—

TABLE IVb. *Probate valuations of male half-millionaire descendants: one son only*

Valuation				
Under £10,000	—			
Under £50,000	1			
Under £100,000	1			
Under £200,000	—			
Under £300,000	1			
Under £500,000	2			
Under £1 million	2			
Under £2 million	1			
Grandsons ...	I	II	III	IV
Under £1,000	—	1+(1)	1	1
Under £10,000	1	—	(1)	—
Under £50,000	1	(2)	1	—
Under £100,000	—	—	—	—
Under £200,000	2	—	—	—
Under £300,000	—	—	—	—
Under £500,000	1	1	1	—
Under £1 million	1	—	—	1

Great-grandsons...	Of grandson I	Of grandson II	Of grandson III	Of grandson IV
Under £10,000	—	—	—	—
Under £50,000	—	2	1	—
Under £100,000	1	1	—	1
Under £200,000	1	1	1	—
Under £300,000	1	—	—	—

few cases that are known, toward primogeniture among the grandsons. Among these half-millionaires with more than one son, there are more cases of fourth, fifth, and sixth or later sons leaving smaller fortunes, with no examples of such sons themselves leaving over £500,000. But among the first, second, and third sons there is less to choose, with, indeed, the only examples of sons leaving over £2 million among the second and third sons. They were Sir Everard A. Hambro (1842–1925), and Sir Lucius E. Ralli (1846–1931). Among the grandsons, however, the tendency toward primogeniture is very marked indeed.

Nevertheless, the great majority of even the youngest sons of these wealthholders were hardly penniless. At any time before 1914, or, indeed, before 1939, most of the poorer descendants had ample resources to live in considerable comfort. To live comfortably without working required surprisingly little money. Investments and securities of about £12,000 would yield £500 *per annum* – as great an income as that enjoyed by a country doctor or local newspaper editor. A fortune of £120,000 safely invested would yield £5000 *per annum* – as much as Asquith made in legal practice, so Roy Jenkins tells us, when he was one of England's leading barristers, or as much as a substantial member of the gentry earned from his rentrolls during the Golden Age of agriculture. A doubling of this level of income brings one to the proverbial £10,000 a year: yet nine of the fifteen of the fifth and sixth sons of millionaires were at this level or higher.

The consequence of this spread of wealth is not difficult to foresee. The incentives to continue in the entrepreneurial paths of the founder of the family's wealth would be gone. It is likely that most of these wealthy sons would simply live off their interest, invested unimaginatively in blue chips and consols.[13] When in their turn they came to divide their fortunes, it is not unlikely that most would leave little more than they inherited, which would, because of inflation, be worth that much less. Among the grandsons of wealthholders – admittedly, among a much smaller sample – only three of the thirty-two who were not themselves killed in a war left £500,000 or more. However, even among the third generation, the great majority probably retained enough to live on without working, although at a reduced level. The substantial fortunes of the younger sons of the wealthy may have constituted the precondition for failure among many nineteenth-century business dynasties. This was not a case of shirtsleeves-to-shirtsleeves, but of stately home to villa. The descendants of the nineteenth-century wealthholders are still wealthy, and, by the standards of the average man, very wealthy indeed, but in most cases they are simply not as wealthy as the *paterfamilias*.[14]

Another ray of light is thrown on the wealth elite by an examination of their social origins, and particularly in comparison with the status of their fathers. This has been undertaken previously by Wedgwood in the case of those leaving £200,000 or more in 1924–5, and by Harbury for those leaving

£100,000 or more in 1956–7, by a comparison of the estate left by each wealthholder with that of his father. Such an approach could not, for a variety of reasons, be adopted in this paper.[15] Rather, an attempt was made to determine the occupation/social status of the fathers of all millionaires as well as of the three groups of half-millionaires (in this case, the nineteenth century group of half-millionaires included only those deceased in 1870–84). Aside from standard reference works and *The Times*, biographical information was taken from local newspapers and memoirs in the possession of provincial libraries and record offices – to whom grateful acknowledgement is made – and some correspondence with the firms or relatives of these figures. In the case of those born in England and Wales after 1837, or in Scotland after 1855, it is possible to secure birth certificates which record the name and occupation of the father at that time. This has been adopted only as a last resort, since English birth certificates now cost 75p. each – with no discounts available for scholars – and it is not, I take it, a precondition for writing about millionaires that the author be one himself. For those deceased since the last War, when local newspaper obituaries began to decline greatly in quality, it proved necessary to check a substantial number of such birth certificates.

The results are detailed in Tables V and VII. In addition to the strictly occupational categories used elsewhere in these Tables, any father known to have left £500,000 or more is listed as a 'Wealthholder', while any titled father not leaving £500,000 is classified as such. The great bulk of the fathers classified as 'Established businessmen/landowners' were in the same field as that in which the son became wealthy – about 90 percent of the total. The category of 'Other established' includes those cases in which the father was, e.g., a Justice of the Peace, or listed in Walford's *County Families*, as well as those cases in which a wealthholder attended a fee-paying school, but the precise occupation of the father could not be traced. The 'Professional' category includes military officers and clergymen. In the 'Small businessmen/farmers' are included local shopkeepers, as well as tenant farmers and small 'yeomen'. Among the 'Manual/low clerical' class I have included, besides those cases in which the father's occupation is definitely known, a number of examples in which the wealthholder began working as a teenager or earlier in a manual or low clerical capacity, but who was known not to have been apprenticed, nor related to the firm's principals. The 'Foreign' category includes those born and raised abroad. I am rather certain that an inclusion of the 'Foreign' category would raise the percentage of 'self-made men', as most were impoverished immigrants. It should be reiterated that the *Bateman* land-owning wealthholders are excluded: to include them would substantially lower the 'self-made' percentage for the earlier period. Furthermore, this is simply an objective reckoning of the occupations of the wealthholders'

6

TABLE V. *Occupations/social status of the fathers of millionaires*

Father	Son deceased:											
	1809–58	1858–69	1870–9	1880–9	1890–9	1900–9	1910–19	1920–9	1930–9	1940–9	1950–9	1960–9
Wealthholder	—	1	6	2	2	8	11	36	22	33	9	8
Titled	4	3	5	4	7	9	11	7	7	8	5	5
Established businessman/land owner	3	6	3	9	19	15	25	30	22	13	18	16
Other established	—	—	—	2	—	1	1	—	4	3	2	6
Professional	1	—	1	1	3	2	2	5	2	5	3	1
Small businessman/farmer	1	4	2	5	2	4	3	4	7	4	1	6
Manual/low clerical	1	—	1	1	1	2	4	6	6	2	3	10
Foreign	1	—	1	1	1	7	3	4	1	1	2	1
Unknown	—	—	2	1	4	4	5	6	7	8	4	4
Total British known	10	14	19	24	34	41	57	88	70	68	37	52
Total 'self-made'	2	4	4	6	3	6	7	10	13	6	4	16
Percentage 'self-made' of known British	20	28	21	25	9	15	12	12	19	9	11	31

TABLE VI. *Occupations/social status of the fathers of three half-millionaire groups*

Father	Son deceased: 1870–84	1925–9	1964–8
Wealthholder	8	8	7
Titled	6	12	13
Established business/landowner	42	42	29
Other established	4	7	8
Professional	4	6	4
Small business/farmer	10	5	6
Manual/Low clerical	7	10	5
Foreign	20	15	0
Unknown	4	3	14
Total known	81	90	72
Total 'self made'	17	15	11
Percentage 'self made'	21	17	15

fathers: it does not take into account cases in which wealth 'skipped a generation' or came from more distant kin, nor examples of 'marrying the boss's daughter', nor indeed those occasions when some factor other than sheer merit played a part in the rise to wealth of a poor lad. The two items that will be of most interest here are the extent to which wealth tends to perpetuate itself, and the extent to which new men can rise into the top wrungs of the wealth ladder. Some definite information can be gleaned from these Tables.

The 'self-made' portion of the millionaires, to group together the 'Small businessmen/farmers' and the 'Manual/low clerical' categories, was at a substantially high level during the nineteenth century – as high as 28 per cent for the cohort deceased 1858–69. For the cohorts deceased after 1890, however, there is a decline to a fairly constant level of about 12 percent per decade thereafter. This picture is reinforced if one keeps in mind two important considerations: in the first place, all millionaire landowners inherited their wealth, and a reckoning of the social origins of millionaires in non-landed fields only would substantially increase the percentage of 'self-made men'. Secondly, the large number of unknowns are likely to include a higher portion of self-made men than for millionaires whose origins are known. For all those who came from titled or substantial landed families are known through standard reference works; while men without an identifying middle name are difficult to find precisely among the index of birth certificates, and many of these probably came from humble backgrounds.

Up to the millionaires deceased in 1940–9, a high and increasing percentage were themselves the sons of very rich fathers; thereafter, while this percentage drops, the 'self-made' percentage rises. Among millionaires deceased in the 1960s, nearly one in three were self-made men. It is interesting to note that this trend is not evident from the figures among the half-millionaire groups presented here, and that the 1964–8 group of half-millionaires contained proportionately only half as many self-made men as the 1960–9 millionaire group. The relatively high number of unknowns in this group may be a factor here.[16]

It would not seem implausible to relate the increase in self-made men to the shifts in the occupational patterns of British wealthholders noted above.[17] I do not at this stage of my research desire to offer any precise statistics on this point, but it should hardly seem surprising that the British motor industry, for example, was developed in part by several sons of bicycle mechanics, nor that the modern retail chains were built up by, among others, penniless immigrants. Indeed, it is the spectacular disconfirming example of this process – the Dukes of Bridgewater and Hon. Charles Rollses – who are likely to claim the interest of the historian. It may seem perverse to claim any virtue by which the British entrepreneurs of one generation become the idle rich of the next, but this process at least has the merit of ensuring that many of the basic shifts in the economy – to industrialism in the nineteenth century, to consumerism and personal service in this – will be undertaken by new men. A society in which the rich did not go to ground in this manner could well give considerably less scope for individual opportunity.

Is the British wealth picture a half-filled or half-empty glass? A comparison with the historical wealth picture in America may lend the perspective necessary to answer this question. It must be emphasised that there is no central probate index in America, and any list of putative American millionaires must to a certain extent be guesswork, while any conclusions drawn from studies of business leaders rather than wealthholders is likely to overstate the 'self-made' portion of the economic elite, by excluding all the idle rich.[18] Also, obviously, the lower boundary of the American millionaire class is considerably below the lower boundary of the British millionaire class, and it is presumably easier (but see note 16) to scrape into the lower boundaries of the American millionaire class in the course of a single lifetime than the British. At the risk of stating what may be familiar to some readers, it is worth summarising some of the leading studies of American social mobility:

1. Of 1464 businessmen appearing in the *Dictionary of American Biography*, according to C. Wright Mills, only 10.4 per cent came from lower-class backgrounds, while 25.9 per cent had their origins in the lower-middle class. Mills divided the American business elite into seven generations by date of birth. The generation born 1820–49 contained the highest percentage of both lower- and lower-middle class origins, respectively 13.4 and 28.6 per cent. For the most recent generation in his study, born in 1850–79, these two percentages were, respectively, 11.2 and 18.1.[19]

2. Sorokin's early, and by more recent standards, primitive study of American millionaires and multi-millionaires found that 38.8 per cent of such men deceased between Colonial times and 1925 had 'started life poor', while 29.7 per cent began 'rich'.[20] Turning to then-living American millionaires, Sorokin noted a trend towards 'the wealthy class of the United States... becoming less and less open, and more and more closed, and... tending to be transformed into a caste-like group',[21] as the number beginning in poverty had dropped to 19.6 per cent, while those with wealthy backgrounds had increased to 52.7 per cent. Sorokin's conclusions were more than borne out by his investigation of the occupations of the fathers of his group of millionaires. Of 228 fathers of then-deceased millionaires, only sixteen – 7 per cent – had been workingmen. Of the others, 56 had been farmers, with 119 merchants, bankers, etc. The remainder were professionals. Of 248 fathers of then-living millionaires, only four had been workingmen.[22]

3. Professor Pessen's recent study of top wealthholders in four large eastern cities during the Jacksonian period, as judged by tax returns, concluded that only about two percent had been born poor, while about six percent were of 'middling economic status'.[23] Conversely, 'about ninety-five percent of New York City's one hundred wealthiest persons were born into families of wealth or high status or occupation', and similar percentages were found in Boston and Philadelphia. Pessen also found no difference between the social origins of his top wealthholders and the 'lesser rich' of these cities.[24]

4. William Miller's well-known study of American business leaders of the 1901–10 period found that only five percent of his total of 179 were of 'lower family status' origins.[25] The fathers of only two percent of his group had been workers, while 79 per cent had been businessmen or professionals. Another well-known study of the 'Industrial Elite of the 1870s' found that the fathers of 8 per cent of the total of 194 such men had been workers.[26]

5. For business leaders of the 1920s there is F. W. Taussig and C. S. Joslyn's immense *American Business Leaders*. Collating 8749 replies to a questionnaire among persons listed in *The Registry of Directors* of 1928, they found that 11.1 per cent of the business leaders aged fifty or more, and 10.5 per cent of those younger, were the sons of labourers. The sons of businessmen and professionals amounted to, respectively, 58.6 per cent and 13.4 per cent of those aged fifty and over, and 68.3 per cent and 12.5 per cent of those under fifty.[27]

6. Two recent lists of the very tip of American wealthholding in the contemporary period are found in the *Fortune* magazine surveys of multi-millionaires of 1957 and 1968. The former included all those Americans identified as worth $50 million – 155 in all – and the latter, those worth $150 million or more – a total of 66.[28] Only a minority of these super-rich

were named, and not all of those named could easily be traced, but it appears that about one-fifth of these men had acquired their fortunes in a single lifetime, although some of this fifth had attended college, and would probably not be 'self-made men' by the standards of this paper. It should be noted that the number of wealthy Americans has increased very sharply in recent years, from 27,000, according to one estimate, in 1953, to about 90,000 in 1966.[29] A considerable number of these must at one time have been much poorer.

A substantial recent increase in the percentage of self-made men among millionaires is seemingly reflected by the British statistics, too, and, indeed, this is the most likely outcome of the secular boom that has continued now for nearly thirty years. What would seem surprising, however, is how little the 'self-made' components of millionairedom in Britain and America has differed over the past century, especially when the *caveats* noted above are taken into account. Such a conclusion is surely unexpected, and, indeed, contrary to what is normally believed.

Can the facts of wealth be related to the facts of power? Only, surely, in a limited and tenuous way, and only if our great limitations on what power is, and who wields it, are kept in mind. In this section of the paper, the probate sources will be used to indicate some trends in wealthholding among members of the House of Commons since 1895. As the formal holders of political power, it is to Parliament that any study of power in Britain must initially turn, although it is perfectly clear that important questions about what power really is, as well as the relevance of one's wealth to his political outlook, are thereby begged. If it should indicate no more, at least an increase or decrease in the wealth of successive Parliaments, or within the parties, must be of considerable importance in determining the extent to which two key variables in a successful definition of power in Britain are united in the same group of persons. In Table VII, the Somerset House valuations of the members of the Parliaments of 1895, 1906, 1922, and 1950 (and 1951 in the case of Conservative M.P.s) have been established.[30]

Both the Liberal and the Conservative parties prior to the First World War contained within their ranks a large number of extremely wealthy members. The Liberal Party also contained a substantial number of poorer M.P.s, but it would be nonsense to see the post-Home Rule Bill Liberal party as devoid of men of property. Men like Hudson E. Kearley (Lord Devonport), the grocery chain proprietor; Sir John Brunner; Alfred Mond; Samuel Montagu (Lord Swaythling), the merchant banker; Charles H. Wilson (Lord Nunburnholme), the shipping magnate; Lord Leverhulme; and two of Lord Northcliffe's brothers – millionaires or near-millionaires – sat as Liberal, not Conservative M.P.s, even after the Budget of 1909. The 1895 Parliament contained thirty-one men who died as millionaires, in addition to a considerable number who left settled land

TABLE VII. *The wealth of Parliaments*

Valuation	1895			1906				1922			1950		
	Conservative	Lib. Unionist	Liberal	Con.	Lib. Un.	Lib.	Labour	Con.	Lib.	Lab.	Con.[1]	Lib.	Lab.
Under £1,000	9	2	4	3	1	8	2	3	1	20	0	—	5
Under £10,000	24	2	21	9	2	51	16	34	20	55	7	—	42
Under £50,000	78	7	33	26	4	82	3	69	25	13	10	2	18
Under £100,000	47	11	31	23	5	68	—	38	11	4	5	—	5
Under £200,000	49	12	17	16	6	36	—	44	10	0	11	—	—
Under £300,000	24	3	9	8	1	13	—	24	5	1	3	—	—
Under £500,000	23	5	3	10	1	16	—	10	4	—	3	—	—
Under £1 million	17	5	7	7	1	15	—	10	1	—	2	—	—
Under £2 million	8	5	7	5	1	9	—	6	1	—	0	—	—
Over £2 million	6	2	3	2	2	3	—	4	—	—	0	—	—
Total known	285	54	141	109	23	301	21 Unk.	247	78	93	41	2	70
Unknown	47	6	36	21	2	79	22 Still living	91	34	51	—	—	—
Percentage of known above £500,000	11	20	12	13	15	9	—	8	3	—	5	—	—
Percentage of known between £100,000 and £500,000	32	38	23	31	31	22	—	31	23	—	40	—	—
	43	58	35	44	46	31	—	39	26	—	45	—	—

47% above £100,000 (1895); 44% (1906)

[1] Includes 1951 Parliament (Conservatives only).

worth as much. Since there were probably at that time two hundred living millionaires in Britain, many of whom were members of the House of Lords, it seems likely that any state opening of Parliament during the period saw a greater concentration of Britain's economic wealth in one place at one time than ever in British history, and possibly in the annals of any legislature anywhere. Many of these men had lifelong associations with the constituencies they represented, and it was common, especially in small and middle-sized boroughs, for the town to send its richest man – and largest employer – to Westminster. One could easily cite fifty examples of this. Both Brunner and Mond were M.P.s for Cheshire constituencies near their alkali works; Spencer Charrington did not think it beneath him to represent Mile End, Stepney, where his great brewery stood; Mr Harland sat for Belfast North, and Mr Wolff, not to be outdone, for Belfast East. The position held by so many of these wealthy men in their towns during this period, so reminiscent of the landlord *vis-à-vis* his tenants, is, it seems to me, a theme in nineteenth-century history that has been unduly neglected. Most of these M.P.s were, it should be noted, the merest lobby fodder. Probably the only millionaire M.P. to matter politically during this period was Walter Runciman. The coming of the ballot in 1872 made no difference to this state of affairs: indeed, as an explanatory variable, it made less than no difference, since there were probably more wealthy M.P.s after 1872 than before, and it was not until the rise of the Labour party that this feature of political life was altered fundamentally. Since the rise of Labour eliminated most of the safe working class seats, for the Liberal party this symbiotic relationship was no longer possible after the First World War. After 1918, if the probate figures are any guide, the Conservative party became slightly poorer – which should be read in light of Keynes's remark about hard-faced men. The Labour Party from its appearance was overwhelmingly a party of the poor, and a large fraction of its members left trifling estates or none at all. Four Labour M.P.s in the 1922 Parliament left £50,000 or more: Noel Buxton (£233,000), A. V. Alexander, Sidney Webb, and Josiah Wedgwood.

Based on the limited data for post-World War Two M.P.s, it seems probable that there are far fewer wealthy members of the House of Commons than previously. None of the forty-one Conservative M.P.s whose estates were traced were millionaires, and only two left over £500,000. Since the total number of very wealthy men has increased markedly in Britain since 1895, the connection between wealth and Parliamentary service is even more tenuous. On the other hand, there has been a levelling-up of the fortunes of Labour M.P.s, with the very poorest section declining markedly. This would probably indicate that it is now possible to save something from one's Parliamentary pay (which would enrich Tories as well as Labourites): this was not, of course, a factor for back-benchers until 1912.[31]

The most important, or at least the most obvious, reason for this decline in the wealth of M.P.s probably lies in the professionalism of Parliament, which has most strikingly affected the process of candidacy selection. In a nutshell, there are simply too many good candidates for the wealthy to have any special advantage as such. It is now fairly common for there to be 200 or more prospective candidates for any reasonably safe seat, a far cry from the situation in 1885, for example, when the Hackney Central Conservative Association had so much difficulty in finding a candidate that it had to turn to Conservative Central Office to suggest a nominee. At the time Central Hackney was regularly Conservative.[32]

The withdrawal of the wealthy from participation in national politics is perhaps one facet of a trend that is manifest in business itself. The wealthy are not to be found in such commanding positions among the largest industrial companies as formerly – not as chairmen, nor even as directors. Whereas those on my list of wealthholders were either chairmen or principals of eleven of the fifteen largest industrial companies in 1905, and of seven of the ten largest industrial units by profits in 1908–10, it is unlikely that wealthholders deceased during the past ten years have been as prominently connected with today's leading companies.[33] Even more marked, perhaps, is the withdrawal of the wealthy from leadership in their communities and towns since the earlier part of the century. Taken together, this might be said to mark a systemic breakdown in the function of the very wealthy in British society, and undoubtedly places them in a more precarious position than previously, especially in view of the increased attention paid by many within the Labour party to wealth distribution and to a replacement of estate duties by a more realistic wealth tax. Some future Tocqueville may well be documenting the breakdown of the *ancien régime* of wealth in terms of the withdrawal of the wealthy from their old public functions.

R. K. KELSALL

9 Recruitment to the higher civil service: how has the pattern changed?

This paper presents the results of comparing recruitment data (concentrating particularly on social and educational backgrounds) in a study originally published in 1955 under the title *Higher Civil Servants in Britain from 1870 to the Present Day* with corresponding data, relating to the period since then, that have now become available. It is, in fact, concerned with the changing pattern of recruitment to a particular occupational elite, mainly over the period since 1929. It might be as well to begin, however, by discussing the virtues and the failings of studies of occupational elite recruitment generally.

What useful purpose is served by this kind of enquiry? The main justification clearly lies in the light that an investigation of this type can throw on the degree of openness of a particular society at a given point in time, and the extent to which this has changed over a period. For though it is true that a study of recruitment to a single occupational elite cannot of itself tell us how open the particular society may be, nevertheless if we have the results of a number of such studies we ought to be able to make a broad assessment of the position. When people want to give a tentative answer to the question as to how far Britain is, or is not, a society of equal access to occupational opportunity, the results of research into the recruitment of high ranking army officers, bishops, higher civil servants or other occupational elites are clearly highly relevant, even though they may show a considerable measure of diversity amongst these and other high status professions.

A closely related question which may well be asked is as to how beneficial to society it would be to have an occupational elite (or occupational elites generally) which is (or are) broadly representative in terms of social background, sex and ethnic origin of the eligible population from which recruitment takes place. Two reasons at once suggest themselves. First, if the society concerned is one where it is popularly supposed to be the case that there is equality of access to important and interesting jobs as between those, regardless of their origins, who have the qualifications to undertake such work, then it is obviously desirable that the facts of the actual situation should not belie the principle that is supposed to be operative to too great an extent. It can serve little useful purpose to anyone if in the course of their socialisation young people internalise a belief that theirs is a society of equality of opportunity, only to find when they read the results of research into the recruitment of occupational elites that this belief has been unfounded.

A second and equally obvious reason for trying to ensure some measure of representativeness in occupational elites is that of making full use of the talents available in society. Where high status jobs are not in practice open to able people of low status origin, they may be less well performed than could be the case, and society suffers. Or again, where people of lowly origin but high ability are denied access to posts in which they could utilise their talents effectively, and have therefore to engage in work which fails to 'stretch' them or stimulate them, there is a clear waste of potential human resources for society, and frustration for the individuals concerned.

There are certain claims, however, which should clearly *not* be made when trying to show the usefulness of studies of occupational elite recruitment. One of these is the claim that, if the top people in a particular service or profession are properly representative in social-origin terms of the population at large, then they will, in their decision-making and their policy generally, behave in ways which reflect the interests and needs of the population as a whole. By contrast, it is sometimes claimed, an occupational elite recruited from a narrow social band will tend to pay regard only to the interests of that particular band instead of those of society in general. Such claims cannot, of course, be substantiated on the kind of evidence commonly obtainable in social research; and there is an inherent improbability in the assumption of a direct linkage between social origin and subsequent behaviour in high office. There are too many examples of aristocrats who, as politicians or statesmen, fought for the interests of the underprivileged, and also of people of humble social origin who, on obtaining high positions, seem bent on destroying the ladder up which they themselves have climbed. It is, therefore, not unreasonable to ask what difference it makes if the top people in key occupations are predominantly of one kind of social origin rather than another? And the honest answer to such a question must be that the attitudes and behaviour of such a group would not necessarily be altered in any predictable direction by a change in the social background of the office-holders.

So although occupational elite recruitment studies have value, they also have their limitations, and one would freely admit that research concerning itself purely with the type of person who reaches high office in an occupation, and how he gets there, ought ideally to be supplemented by the much more difficult investigation of how he behaves when he has reached the top. It should be noted also that the study with which we are here concerned relates to the people who held certain ranks in the Service at various dates, and the Service and outside populations from which they were drawn. We cannot be sure that some people of lower rank, or whose offices were advisory, technical or professional rather than administrative, may not on occasion have taken or influenced key decisions to a greater extent than some of those whom we are studying. Perhaps with inside knowledge of events at a particular point in time an *ad hoc* group of those associated with decisions of central importance could have been identified. If we are to throw light on the changes that have taken place over a stated period, however, we have no such choice; we have to compare those of specified ranks at different dates, and to hope that broadly speaking we have caught in our net most of the important fish, and have not caught too many whose real power is very much less than the office they hold would lead one to expect.

There is a need, then, to bring later material in for comparison with that originally presented in 1955, and to give some account of the extent to which the social and educational background of higher civil servants, and of the new recruits coming forward, has changed in the period since then. A number of important developments have taken place in these two decades.

(*a*) Method II in the Open Competition for administrative class posts, which only accounted for less than a third of the Open Competition entry in 1949–52, has now completely replaced Method I. It should be explained that Method I is the traditional type of competition, where a candidate undergoes a rigorous written examination in subjects of his own choice and is also (since the 1920s) given a mark for his performance at an interview, his position in the final order of merit depending on the aggregation of these two sets of marks. Method II was introduced after the Second World War, and is closely modelled on the techniques then used for the selection of army officers; it is more of the nature of a greatly extended interview. As will be shown later (see Table 4), the two Methods have tended to attract rather different fields of applicants, and to produce rather different groups of successful candidates, in terms of social and educational origin.

(*b*) A major, if hastily-mounted, study of a sample of civil servants was undertaken at the request of the Fulton Committee by Halsey and Crewe, and together with much new information furnished by the Civil Service Commission is reported in volume 3 (1) of the *Evidence*.

(*c*) The implementation of the Fulton recommendation for the abolition of classes in the Service (including the administrative class) has meant that, from 1971 onwards, the recruitment we have to consider has been to a much wider range of posts than was previously the case. On many counts, therefore, stocktaking is clearly called for.

We may begin by looking at the data in Table 1 comparing the characteristics of the upper grades of the administrative class in the Halsey–Crewe 1967 sample (those of under secretary and higher rank) with those of virtually the same grade (above assistant secretary rank) in 1929, 1939 and 1950. In terms of social origin, the proportion with fathers in routine non-manual or in manual work has increased from 12 per cent in 1929 to

TABLE 1. *Social and educational background data for higher civil servants and open competition entrants to the administrative class 1921–70*

Percentage	In post — Above assistant secretary rank (Open competition entrants / All) 1929 (1)	1939 (1)	1950 (1)	Upper grades 1967 (sample) Men (2)	1967 Both sexes (2)	New recruits by open competition 1921–32 (1)	1933–9 (1)	1949–52 Method I (1)	1949–52 Method II (1)	1949–52 Both methods (1)	1948–50 Method I (2)	1948–50 Method II (2)	1951–5 Method I (2)	1951–5 Method II (2)	1956–60 Method I (2)	1956–60 Method II (2)	1961–5 Method I (2)	1961–5 Method II (2)	1966–7 Method I (2)	1966–7 Method II (2)	1968–70 both methods Men (3)	1968–70 Both sexes (3)	Graduates of 1960 as a whole (excluding medicine and dentistry) Men (4)	Both sexes (4)
(a) With fathers in routine white collar or manual work	7	12	15	33	31	—	—	—	—	27	51	44	48	21	43	14	25	18	31	23	—	—	40	29
(b) With manual working fathers	—	7	9	19	17	—	—	—	—	19	—	—	—	—	—	—	—	—	—	—	—	—	26	18
(c) With fathers in semi- or unskilled manual work	0	2	3	6	6	—	—	—	—	2	16	10	19	3	12	4	5	3	3	5	5	—	7	4
(d) Whose last school was administered (post-1939) by L.E.A.	6	14	16	36	35	20	19	29	18	26	43	22	39	21	47	26	25	29	34	35	34	38	56	57
(e) Who had been at Oxbridge	90	70	81	41	51	84	89	74	76	74	65	74	75	89	77	93	81	80	78	64	64	59	30	25
N	71	121	113	211	261	160	333	152	71	223	127	50	140	123	157	93	125	327	37	226	162	230	9404	12986

— = data not available.

Adapted from data in:
(1) R. K. Kelsall, *Higher Civil Servants in Britain* (1955).
(2) Committee on the Civil Service, *Evidence*, vol. 3 (1) (1969).
(3) Civil Service Commission, *Reports* for 1968, 1969, 1970.
(4) R. K. Kelsall, A. Kuhn and A. Poole, *Six Years After* (1970) and *Graduates: The Sociology of an Elite* (1972). (The totals have been 'grossed up' as explained in the text.)

TABLE 2. *Original routes of entry to the administrative class of higher civil servants 1929, 1939, 1950, 1967 and of new recruits to the principal and assistant principal grades 1949–53 and 1961–5*

	Upper grades in post				New recruits to principal and assistant principal grades	
Route of entry to the administrative class	1929 (1) (%)	1939 (1) (%)	1950 (1) (%)	1967 (sample) (2) (%)	1949–53 (1) (%)	1961–5 (2) (%)
Open competition	59	63	63	57	50 ⎫	63
Other direct entry	17	13	9 ⎤		0 ⎭	
Transfer	12	8	4 ⎬	43	7 ⎫	37
Promotion from the ranks	12	16	24 ⎦		43 ⎭	
	100	100	100	100	100	100
N	121	179	332	261	447	586

Adapted from data in:
(1) R. K. Kelsall, *Higher Civil Servants in Britain* (1955).
(2) Committee on the Civil Service, *Evidence*, vol. 3 (1) (1969).

18, 27 and 31 per cent in 1939, 1950 and 1967 respectively. If we confine our attention to manual work alone, the proportions become 7, 9, 20 and 17 per cent at the four dates, the drop between 1950 and 1967 being at first sight surprising. And if only semi-skilled and unskilled manual work is taken into account the figures are nil, 3, 3 and 6 per cent. In about a fifth of the 1950 cases the last school attended was one administered by the local education authority; this proportion had risen by 1967 to over a third. The percentage who had been to Oxbridge was 70 in 1929, and fell to 66, 60 and 51 at the three later dates.

Though all this suggests a certain, if not spectacular, broadening of the band of types of social and educational background from which top civil servants were drawn over this period of nearly 40 years, we have to ask how much of this was due to the changing importance of the different routes of entry to the administrative class of these people at these four dates. Up to 1950 the position is reasonably clear. If we adopt the manual-working father as the index, the proportion of these high-ranking civil servants who had entered the administrative class by routes other than promotion from the ranks, and who came from such families, rose from around 4 per cent in 1929 to 9 per cent in 1950 (i.e. it a little more than doubled). The proportion of high-ranking civil servants *generally* with this manual-working family background rose during the same period from 7 to 20 per cent (i.e. it nearly trebled). The difference in the two cases is mainly to be explained by the doubling of the importance of promotion from the ranks, from 12 to 24 per cent (see Table 2). For we know that of the 77 promotees in the 1950 higher ranks, 31 (or 40 per cent) were the children of manual workers, but for whose presence there would have been much less difference in the social background profile of top civil servants in that twenty-year period.

As we lack comparable information regarding the routes of entry (and the social and educational history of those who came in by the various routes) of the 1967 high-ranking group, this not being an issue on which data were collected in the Halsey–Crewe survey, we cannot say whether the overall *decline* in the proportion with manual-working fathers compared with 1950 arose from a decline in the importance of promotion from the ranks, or from those so promoted being less working-class in origin than their predecessors, or from other factors. It is at least clear, however, that one contributory factor must have been the much higher proportion of *women* in the later group (19 per cent as against less than 2 per cent); for if we confine our attention to the men in the sample, the actual decline in the importance of manual-working fathers largely disappears. One possible line of explanation that is ruled out, incidentally, is an increase in the open competition entry component, for this accounted for *fewer* of the 1967 group than it had done for the 1950 one (57 instead of 63 per cent). It may well be, however, that other forms of direct entry (such as the post-war establishment of wartime temporary civil servants) brought into the higher ranks of 1967 significant numbers of people of somewhat similar social background to the traditional open competition entrant, and so helped to maintain the predominantly middle-class character of the group even during a 17-year period when some further social leavening might have been expected.

Having looked at the changing social origin distribution of the population of top-ranking civil servants for this 40-year period, we can make a similar examination of the new recruits to the administrative class by the only route for which reasonably complete information is available over most of an even longer time span, the half century or so from 1921 to 1970. This route is, of course, open competition, always the most important source from which the upper grades of the Service were drawn, and accounting for 59, 63, 63 and 57 per cent of them in 1929, 1939, 1950 and 1967 respectively.

We lack *direct* evidence regarding the social background of such entrants in the period 1921–39. If, however, the high-ranking civil servants of 1950 who originally entered by open competition are taken as representative of all such entrants in the competitions of the 1920s, then around 18 per cent of these entrants probably had fathers in routine non-manual or manual work. Looking again at Table 1, and confining our attention for the moment to Method I, we can see that by 1948–50 this proportion had risen spectacularly to 51 per cent, but fell back to 48, 43 and 25 in the early 1950s, late 1950s and early 1960s, finally rising a little to 31 per cent in 1966–7, the last occasion for which such information is available.

TABLE 3. *Extent to which entrants by open competitions 1909–70 came from certain specified British public schools, compared with the male graduate population of 1960*

	Eton		Harrow		Win-chester		Rugby		Any of the nine Clarendon schools		All schools	
	No.	%	No.	%	No.	%	No.	%	No.	%	No.	%
Open competition entrants												
1909–14 (men) (1)	8	4.3	1	0.5	15	8.1	8	4.3	50	26.9	186	100.0
1921–32 (1)	6	3.8	1	0.6	6	3.8	4	2.5	24	15.0	160	100.0
1933–9 (1)	9	2.7	5	1.5	11	3.3	10	3.0	62	18.6	333	100.0
1949–52 (1)	5	2.2	1	0.4	3	1.3	0	0	19	8.5	223	100.0
1968–70 (men) (2)	1	0.6	1	0.6	3	1.8	1	0.6	14	8.6	162	100.0
Graduates of 1960 (men) (3)	40	0.4	14	0.1	52	0.5	58	0.6	354	3.8	9404	100.0

Adapted from data in:
(1) R. K. Kelsall, *Higher Civil Servants in Britain* (1955).
(2) Civil Service Commission, *Reports* for 1968, 1969, 1970.
(3) Unpublished figures from the survey.

We may turn now to some data concerning the changing pattern of last schools attended by open competition entrants. Taking first of all attendance at certain famous English public schools, Table 3 shows that whereas over a quarter of those who entered by open competition in the years preceding 1914 had been at one of the nine Clarendon schools, less than a tenth of their counterparts in 1968–70 were in this position. Over the same period Wykehamists had declined in importance from 8 to under 2 per cent. By comparison with the general population of graduates of British universities, however (excluding medicine, veterinary science and dentistry), the proportion of open competition entrants with this kind of school background was still, even in recent years, substantially higher – the Clarendon proportion was more than twice as large, and the Winchester proportion was three times as great.

If we take another school index, the proportion whose secondary school was administered by the local education authority, Table 1 shows that a pre-war percentage of around 20 rises to 29 in 1949–52 (though the Civil Service Commission's figure for 1948–50 is 43 and for 1951–5, 39), rises urther to 47 in the late 1950s, falls back to only 25 in the early 1960s and rises again to 44 in 1966–7. The proportion of Oxbridge open competition entrants, which stood at between 85 and 90 per cent pre-war, remained fairly steady over most of the post-war period (for Method I entrants) at around 75 per cent, showing a slight rise to 81 in the early 1960s and a slight falling back to 78 in 1966–7.

In the meantime, of course, Method II had become much the more usual mode of open competition entry, and in 1970 replaced Method I entirely. In the early post-war years it was pointed out in *Higher Civil Servants in Britain* that Method II would by its very nature be expected to give even more of an advantage to candidates from independent schools and from Oxbridge than was the case with Method I, and the figures quoted there for 1949–52 (only 18 per cent of the entrants coming from local education authority schools as compared with 29 per cent of those entering by the traditional method) strongly suggested that these fears were well grounded. Now that later figures are available they confirm this in a very striking way. For over nearly the whole of the period 1948 to 1967 it can be seen that entrants by the new method were, as a group, drawn to a greater extent (and often to a very much greater extent) from the upper reaches of the social hierarchy, from independent schools and from Oxbridge, than was the case with entrants by the traditional method.

Given that Method II (or something closely modelled on it) has now become the *only* mode of open competition entry, what is the extent of unrepresentativeness socially and educationally of those recruited by this means over the post-war period 1948–67 taken as a whole? A useful yardstick in this connection is provided by data from following-up a very large national sample of those who completed first degrees at British universities (in subjects other than medicine, dentistry and veterinary science) in 1960. Some 29 per cent of these graduates came from families where the father was in routine non-manual or manual work. The corresponding percentage for Method II entrants is 20 (and for those coming in by Method I, 41). If we only include fathers in semi-skilled or unskilled manual work, the 1960 graduate percentage is 4 and for Method II is also 4 (for Method I, 13).

Measured in this way, the graduate open competition entrants to the administrative class seem to have been as representative (or, in the case of Method I, more representative) of the lower social strata as (or than) the general population of those graduating. When we use as our index the proportion whose last school attended was administered by the local education authority, however, they seem substantially less representative, in that the Method II percentage is 30, that for Method I is 39, while for the general population of those graduating it is 57. In this case we can also provide a percentage for the open competition entrants of the three years 1968–70 (the vast majority of whom came in by Method II), and it is 38. And, as we have already seen, the open competition entrants with a Clarendon school background formed more than twice as great a proportion by comparison with graduates in general. The Oxbridge proportion also shows the post-war open competition entrants to have been drawn predominantly from a relatively narrow range of universities, the percentage being 79 for Method II, 76 for Method I, 59 for the entrants in the three years 1968–70, and 25 for our 1960 graduates as a whole.

How does all this compare with other graduate-recruiting occupations? One difficulty always tending to arise when attempting to make such comparisons is that of ensuring that the age and sex structure of the two populations being compared are the same. Fortunately the nature of our national survey of graduates of 1960 enables us to compare like with like. Confining our attention to men, and looking only at the proportion with fathers in routine non-manual or manual work, it is clear that entrants to the legal profession in the 1960s, only 22 per cent of whom came from such families, were somewhat narrower in their social background band than the corresponding graduates entering the administrative class, where the percentage was 28; but that entrants to 'general management' were similar in social origin to these civil service entrants, while entrants to university teaching (41 per cent) or to school teaching (51 per cent) were drawn to a marked extent from families of origin lower down the social scale.

The very varying occupational aspirations of those with different types of family background and from different types of university clearly have an important bearing on all this. We asked our graduate respondents about their occupational plans on graduation, and of those men with a manual-work background who had an occupation in mind at that time, only 11 per cent said they had been thinking of administrative or managerial types of work. The proportion was double this (22 per cent), however, for those of the same social origin at Oxbridge.

The Civil Service Commissioners have, of course, for a long time past expressed regret that those presenting themselves for the open competition were not representative of a wider range of school and university types. The extent to which this has, in the post-war period, been a limiting factor in providing a more balanced intake is shown in Table 4. Several points are clear. First, both for Method I and Method II, the successes in these competitions have come from a narrower range of social background, and school and university types than a random sampling of the candidates would have brought about. This could be, of course, because the proportion of *suitable* candidates was different in the various social and educational strata. It could also, however, be because the nature of both methods of selection gave an advantage to applicants from certain types of school and university. This is a point to which we shall have to return. Secondly, over most of the post-war period, the differences in social origin and school and university type as between candidates and successes seem to have been greater in the case of Method II than in that of Method I. Thirdly, particularly in the earlier post-war period, candidates for Method I seem to have been less unrepresentative of graduates as a whole, in social and educational background terms, than candidates for Method II. This naturally makes one wonder whether this reflected a realisation on the part of candidates of certain types of social and educational origin that their chances of success varied as between the two methods of selection.

TABLE 4. *Social and educational background of candidates as a whole compared with successful candidates in open competitions for entry to the administrative class, 1948–67*

| Percentage | 1948–56 | | | | 1957–63 | | | | 1964–7 | | | | Graduates of 1960 as a whole (excluding medicine and dentistry) (2) |
| | Method I | | Method II | | Method I | | Method II | | Method I | | Method II | | |
	Candidates (1)	Successes (1)	Candidates (1)	Successes (1)	Candidates (1)	Successes (1)	Candidates (1)	Successes (1)	Candidates (1)	Successes (1)	Candidates (1)	Successes (1)	
(a) With fathers in routine white collar or manual work	31	26	24	16	24	19	21	13	28	18	27	22	29
(b) Whose last school was administered by L.E.A.	57	49	47	31	40	36	33	26	46	26	46	32	57
(c) Who had been at Oxbridge	48	72	58	86	56	80	67	88	51	78	56	76	25
N	1720	319	2746	208	941	169	2649	294	806	93	2199	364	12986

Adapted from data in:
(1) Committee on the Civil Service, *Evidence*, vol. 3 (1) (1969).
(2) R. K. Kelsall, A. Kuhn and A. Poole, *Six Years After* (1970) and *Graduates: The Sociology of an Elite* (1972).

Fourthly, as measured against the yardstick of our national sample of graduates of 1960, the *candidates* for the open competition do not seem to have been very different in social origin, though they did tend somewhat to under-represent local education authority secondary schools, and to a much greater extent to under-represent universities other than Oxbridge (and also to a fairly marked degree those other than the Scottish universities).

We may now examine the difficult issues raised in the last paragraph as to how far the actual selection procedures could be shown, from a field of candidates of known and roughly equal ability in one respect, to favour those who appeared to demonstrate ability in another respect and who also happened to have come from higher social strata than their less successful peers. Because special permission was given to the present writer to have access to marks awarded and educational and social background data for both unsuccessful *and* successful candidates for the open competition in one pre-war year, 1938, an analysis of a rather special kind was for the first and only time undertaken to throw light on this type of issue. Ability in one respect was measured by the marks awarded in the rigorous examinations forming the backbone of the traditional open competition ever since the 1870s. Ability in another respect was indicated by marks awarded for the interview (this component having only been brought in as an integral part of the competition in the 1920s). It emerged that the effect of the interview marks was to eliminate 24 per cent of the original successful group, whose marks in the written part of the examination would have brought them the offer of a post in the administrative class, and to replace them by an equal number of candidates with slightly poorer results in the written examination but with better interview marks. These two groups of 18 men, one of which changed places with the other as a result of the interview, were found to be very different in social origin, type of school, and university. And though we cannot say which would have brought greater credit to the administrative class, we can say that the effect of an interview of the pre-war unstructured type, given the relative marks for the different parts of the competition, was (whether intended or not) to replace nearly a quarter of those who would on the written examination alone have been offered admission, by an equivalent number of less successful examinees but who were more successful at their interviews, and in the course of doing so significantly to modify in a particular direction the social and educational origin distribution of entrants.

The absence, in the Method II type of open competition which has now become the only mode of selection by this route, of any rigorous testing of intellectual ability in which the identity of candidates is unknown to the examiners, unfortunately makes it difficult if not impossible to replicate the 1938 analysis of the whole field of candidates in such a way as to identify the components in the *present* selection process responsible for weeding out some candidates of probably greater intellectual merit than their socially superior replacements.

It may be noted that, partly because of the disturbing data relating to candidates and successes commented on in the Halsey–Crewe report, an investigation of Method II was set in motion. Predictably, however, the Davies Committee of Inquiry into the Method II System of Selection (Cmnd. 4156 of 1969) could find no acceptable evidence of social bias in any of the selection procedures. History has, in a sense, repeated itself. For just as it was not felt necessary to modify the Method I unstructured interview following the publication of the results of the analysis of all 1938 candidates in *Higher Civil Servants in Britain* in 1955, neither do any serious doubts seem to have arisen since then in official circles concerning the possible side-effects, in modifying the social 'mix' of entrants, arising from retaining the Final Interview Board for Method II. On this latter point it can, of course, be argued that, in a mode of selection where face-to-face situations predominate, there would be no point in singling out one of these as more potentially unfair than others to candidates of less favoured social and educational background.

Before discussing the future, it may be appropriate to list some of the more important features of the social pattern of recruitment to the British higher civil service.

(1) The inequalities of educational opportunity inherent in our arrangements in the present and the recent past undoubtedly preclude some young men and women who probably possess the qualities needed for success in this occupation from entering it, as they do in the case of other high-status types of employment. The extent to which this is so can be very roughly estimated by comparing the social profile of the adult population with that of higher civil servants in post.

(2) The under-representation of certain types of school and university in the field of graduate candidates for entry to what until recently has been known as the administrative class, is clearly partly to be explained in terms of a culture in the under-represented schools and universities unfavourable to the development of aspirations to enter this field of employment. This can be illustrated by the quite wide variations in the stated aspirations at the point of graduation of graduates of similar social background from different types of university.

(3) A further line of explanation of the under-representation of certain types of school and university and the over-representation of others in the field of open competition competitors lies in the awareness of potential candidates of the relative chances of success associated with different types of social and educational background. The appraisal of such chances represented particularly by the educational characteristics of the field of candidates presenting themselves seems on the evidence to be broadly realistic.

(4) Current methods of selection in the open competition undoubtedly produce a socially and educationally biassed sub-sample of successful candidates from the sample of competitors. Whether or to what extent this is justified by the differential distribution of the qualities needed for success in the administrative class (or groups) amongst the social and educational strata represented in the field of competitors it is, of course, difficult to say.

(5) In the past the social origin 'mix' of higher civil servants as a group has been made much less unrepresentative of that found in the wider society than would otherwise have been the case by the admission of a substantial component of promotees, many of whom were of humble social origin and had joined the civil service comparatively young and often without the benefit of either secondary or higher education. There is some evidence (*a*) of a decline in the extent of such promotion from the ranks and (*b*) of those who are so promoted now being more middle-class than their predecessors and having had more formal education.

(6) In common with other highly-paid occupations, and with the field of administration and management generally, there has been a marked under-representation of women. As we have seen, women formed only two per cent of the higher ranks in 1950, though when this rose to 19 per cent in 1967 it had the side-effect of altering the social 'mix' of that group in an upward direction, because of the well-known circumstance that highly-educated women tend to come more from the higher social strata than do their male counterparts. The proportion of open competition entrants to the administrative class in the three years 1968–70 who were women was 30 per cent, and that for all candidates for administrative group open competitions was 32 per cent. These proportions suggest, therefore, that both candidates for, and new recruits to the administrative class by that route now broadly reflect the sex ratio in the relevant graduate population as a whole.

The issue of whether the band of types of social and educational background from which higher civil servants were being drawn was too narrow, and if so what should be done about it, did not form a major preoccupation of the Fulton Committee. At a very late hour, however, a hastily-summoned working party (of which the present writer was a member) did plan a major survey of a sample of civil servants then in post. The Halsey–Crewe report on this survey and on other relevant information supplied by the Civil Service Commission, the Treasury and others, formed volume 3(1) of the *Evidence*, and this has proved invaluable in the preparation of the present paper. It could hardly, however, prove equally invaluable to the Fulton Committee, since the results could not be made available in time substantially to influence their recommendations. Their recommendations were, of course, far-reaching; and though none was specifically designed to influence the social 'mix' of higher civil servants, this does not preclude the possibility that some of them might, if implemented in particular ways, in fact do so. It is of some importance, therefore, to speculate (and it can at this stage be little more than that) on the possible effects of the main recruitment and related changes actually introduced or decided on and in process of being introduced.

The merging of the old administrative, executive and clerical classes from the beginning of 1971 into a single Administrative Group inevitably involved changes in recruitment arrangements. One feature of these has been that something closely modelled on previous Method II recruitment to Assistant Principal posts (involving a qualifying examination, two-day tests and interviews at the Civil Service Selection Board, and interview by a Final Selection Board) is to be used for the direct recruitment from outside of graduates to fill a much wider range of posts – aiming, amongst other things, to strengthen the Service's so-called 'middle management' – but also for the upgrading of suitable existing staff. One important decision has been that the Final Selection Board will grade successful candidates, and that these candidates (and the departments in which they serve) will be told their grading. They will then become Administrative Trainees (of whom there are expected to be around 175 directly-recruited graduates each year, and perhaps 75 to 125 upgraded serving civil servants). After from two to four years they will be 'streamed' on the basis of a combination of their initial F.S.B. grading plus their Service performance to date. Those in the Fast Stream will, of course, if all goes well, form the new recruits to the group of higher civil servants at the appropriate time.

This is admittedly an inadequate summary of a complex set of arrangements. What the overall effect may be on the social and educational background from which the future higher civil service is drawn will depend on the answers to a number of questions on which at present little light can be shed. (1) Will the new competitions for a much wider range of ultimate, and a much larger number of immediate posts, attract a field of graduate candidates significantly different in calibre and in social and educational background from those who previously competed by Method II? (2) Will the relative competition success-rates of those from different school and university types continue to discourage non-Oxbridge, local-education-authority-educated candidates from applying? (3) Will the publicity and importance attached to the Final Selection Board grading, and the extent to which it helps to determine allocation after a few years to a Fast Stream, mean that for the favoured few, new Administrative Trainee (with an F.S.B. grade A) will merely be old Assistant Principal writ large? (4) What will be the effect of the new arrangements on promotion from the ranks? On the face of it, the figures of proposed annual intake by the revised procedures would seem to imply an open competition intake (to a wider range) of between 58 and 70 per cent, which would mean promotion-by-way-of-competition contributing between 30 and 42 per cent. This is not, however, the exact equivalent of promotion to the old administrative class (whether by limited competition or otherwise). One suspects (and it can be no more than a suspicion) that confusion resulting from the merging of the old classes, together with official enthusiasm for the new competition, may result in the proportion of likely future higher civil servants recruited by open competition rising (as the data in Table 2 would suggest was already happening in the 1960s). If so, the social leaven that promotion used to provide will be very much less effective, particularly if, as seems inevitable, tomorrow's promotees come from higher social strata and have been in a better position to grasp secondary and higher education opportunities than their predecessors were. So although the position remains very uncertain one would guess that the higher civil service of the future might well be significantly more homogeneous in social and educational background than was the case in, say, 1950 or 1967, with all that this implies. At least, however, it may be expected to include a higher proportion of women than it has done hitherto.

10 Universities and the study of elites

The degree of integration of the contemporary university with both the polity and the economy remains problematic and constantly subject to renegotiation. The university stands as vulnerable and highly visible in both arenas. Beyond this, a university's opportunities for articulation with the various elite groups are considerably enlarged in a changing social and economic context, and there is the need for systematic examination of how policies in higher education are created, resurrected, effected or dropped, and of whether, and in what way, a university's policy-making and development is influenced by such connections and relationships as have been established with local and national elite groups. Senate and perhaps Council are often assumed to make nearly all the effective decisions for their universities, but there is always the possibility that they, as one Vice-Chancellor put it, 'simply approve in quick time, decisions made elsewhere perhaps by some group which has no statutory warrant for existence'.[1] Little is known about the distribution of power or about the process of decision-making in universities or, for that matter, about the external constraints posed, for instance, by the Department of Education and Science, by the University Grants Committee or the various Research Councils.

We recognise the extraordinary difficulties in embodying in any research programme speculations about *present* trends and movements discerned as likely agents for change. The observations offered in this paper and the speculated trends to which we have alluded should be read only as preliminary generalisations. At the outset this paper focuses on some of the shared features of certain delineated elite groups, including academic leaders, noting in some instances that they have overlapping, if not circulating, personnel. We indicate sets of people in prominent positions in public life who share certain social and educational characteristics not only with each other but also with certain wealthy individuals and with titled aristocrats. We indicate also that, for certain of these sets of people, the experience of a university education and in particular an Oxbridge collegiate education is characteristic. The documentation of trends in the recruitment of the Cabinet and other senior posts along such lines is quite familiar now, as is the predominance of Oxbridge graduates among those listed in *Who's Who* and among those entering the Administrative Class in the Civil Service and Foreign Service.[2] The two ancient foundations have been and apparently remain pre-eminent in providing the higher education of several generations of members of various elite groups. In our analysis Vice Chancellors emerge as a distinct cluster, of greater significance as universities are *de facto* hierarchical.[3] As yet, however, we can only speculate on the relationship between the power structures within the university sector and those power structures operating in the society at large, and on the contributions to the reproduction of the latter made by the higher education system.

Certain values and normative criteria underlie the British university system; Halsey and Trow have supplemented the ideas of 'high culture', 'purity' and recruitment, socialisation and certification of the elite with others: national rather than local recruitment of students, ancient origins or at least associations, selectivity, small-scale preferably residential community life, individual tuition and the government of the institution by a 'democracy' of its own members.[4] Mainly because of historical contingencies universities are differently placed to respond to 'popular' and 'service' demands. Not surprisingly, they do respond differently, particularly those universities whose resources and relationships with both the polity and the economy reflect a very different degree of internal quality-determination from Oxbridge. The documentation here of some of the carefully forged links between universities and government and industry in particular will no doubt be criticised as 'a travesty of the state of affairs in British universities'.[5] Certainly it is indisputable that in many cases universities have implacably opposed the erosion of what Raymond Aron refers to as the moral code of liberalism. But vague, multiple and changing goals prevail at any one time among different members of the university, who are concerned with individual decisions rather than patterns or trends. There are situations in which there is apparently quasi-resolution of conflict in the university, where a series of goals, perhaps sub-goals, in actual or potential conflict are contended according to circumstances. The second focus of this paper is thus on what seems to us an increasing involvement, particularly significant for the newer foundations, in 'popular' or 'service' functions rather than traditionally stressed 'autonomous' functions.[6]

As yet scant empirical data substantiates the various identifications of dominant groups in Britain, though several research projects are in progress.[7] The published data is variable in quality and incomplete; prevailing methodological issues and ambiguity in conceptual assumptions present considerable problems. The social ties apparently most significant for such a study may neither be sought by the compilers of directories nor exhibited by their contributors.[8] Discussion of such data as is available typically indicates that members of certain delineated elite groups share links through kinship, marriage, common schooling at a small number of prestige schools, common membership of a few colleges at the two ancient English universities and of a small number of exclusive London clubs and a range of other channels of everyday association. But studies in this field have generally been limited to the examination of a single link at a time – for instance the proportions of various elite groups who have attended the same school, attended the same university or were members of the same club. Thus it has been difficult to distinguish the contribution made by each – a crucial issue when such factors are interactive.[9] The development of a new technique for seeking out clusters among a large number of individuals and using a number of attributes simultaneously provided us with the opportunity to examine which individuals in the 'elite' population considered here share various selected educational and social characteristics to the greatest degree.[10]

We use Bottomore's definition of the term elite: 'functional, mainly occupational, groups which have high status (for whatever reasons) in a society'.[11] As Giddens has emphasised, until some working definitions of the term have been measured in systematic research against sociological realities, the decision to include or exclude positions is rather arbitrary. We included the top wealth-holders, the upper stratum of the aristocracy and life peers and, like Giddens, we cast the net wide. Twenty-one categories of people considered representative of those prominent in public life were selected for the study, people who, it might generally be agreed, were in a position to be exercising considerable political and economic influence in Britain. Using available published sources their membership was listed and details recorded of date of birth, social background, kinship links, education, club membership and current affiliations. Lack of information reduced the categories to eighteen.

The importance of higher education at Oxford and Cambridge emerged at once. While thirteen per cent of elite positions were held by Old Etonians and another fourteen per cent by past pupils of a further five elite schools, over half were held by graduates of Oxford or Cambridge, many of whom were contemporaries.

Within the elite population even more striking relationships emerged. The clustering indicated seven prominent groupings within the population being analysed, four of them centering on common occupation and three on educational characteristics. Of the first three only the '*Life Peers*' cluster showed heterogeneous educational background. It was the only cluster to have less than half of its members with higher education. Of the other three, '*The Military*', made up almost entirely of 67 senior army officers, had generally attended one of the two military academies (now amalgamated), '*The Vice Chancellors*,' Oxbridge and frequently other universities, and '*The Judiciary*,' a major public school followed by Oxford.

The most prominent attribute of the other clusters was a common educational background. One cluster was almost entirely composed of Old Etonians who had attended Oxford (or, to a much lesser extent,

TABLE 1. *Eighteen selected elite groups, 1971*

	Number in group	Number included in study
The Cabinet	40	40
Senior Civil Servants (Permanent Secretaries and Permanent Under Secretaries with salary at least £9,000 per annum)	19	17
The wealthiest businessmen[a]	41	29
The chairmen of the fifty largest industrial companies (from *The Times* 1000, 1970–1)[b]	50	32
Board members of the major nationalised industries (BEA, BOAC, National Coal Board, Electricity and Gas Councils, Railways Board, Steel Corporation and the Post Office)	70	59
Senior officers in the armed forces		
(i) *Army* – (Field Marshalls, Lieutenant Generals and Major Generals)	124	106
(ii) *Navy* – (Admirals of the Fleet, Vice and Rear Admirals)	80	46
(iii) *Air Force* – (Marshals, Air Chief Marshals and Air Marshals)	31	28
Directors of the Bank of England	19	19
Directors of the 'Big Four' clearing banks (Barclays, Lloyds, Midland and National Westminster)	113	90
Directors of the four major British insurance companies (Prudential Assurance, Royal Insurance, Legal and General, Commercial Union)	67	40
The Monopolies Commission	18	15
Bishops of the Church of England	37	35
University Vice-Chancellors and Principals[c]	120	103
Controllers of the media (Governors of the BBC, Members of the Independent Television Authority and the proprietors of the seven major national daily newspapers)	33	26
High Court judges	91	81
Top aristocracy (Dukes and Royal Dukes)	21	18
Life peers	167	150
Total	1,141	934

NOTES:

  [a] Details for 1971 of group published in *The Times* 15 December 1967 as 'The £400m League'.

  [b] *The Times* 1000: *Leading Companies in Britain and Overseas*, Times Newspapers, London 1971.

  [c] This included principals of Oxbridge colleges. For exact definition see P. Collison and J. Millen, 'University Chancellors, Vice Chancellors and College Principals', *Sociology*, Vol. 3, No. 1, 1969. See also A. H. Halsey and M. A. Trow, *The British Academics*, Faber, London, 1971, pp. 160ff.

Cambridge). Many of the group are now prominent members of the Cabinet or directors of the Big Four clearing banks, but the cluster also contributed to the membership of all except four of the elite groups that made up the original population. The second were public school boys who had been at Cambridge, a large cluster with 155 members who contributed

TABLE 2. *Higher education of those holding elite positions*

	No.	%
Cambridge University	243	26
Oxford University	228	24
London University	67	7
Other English university	47	5
Other university in Great Britain	69	7
(including Trinity College, Dublin)		
University abroad	28	3
Military academy (Sandhurst or Woolwich)	68	7
Dartmouth College	23	3
Cranwell	9	1
No higher education	186	20
Technical College	29	3

NOTES:

(1) Some attended more than one institution. Figures indicate attendance and do not necessarily indicate that a degree or other qualification was obtained.

(2) The analysis throughout is of *holders of the positions* in the eighteen groups and therefore those who occur as members of more than one category appear more than once in the total group. The 934 positions were in fact held by 793 individuals.

to all eighteen groups, particularly numerous among Bishops of the Church of England. The final cluster, the '*Grammar School*' cluster, contained a majority with non-Oxbridge university education.

The data available and the number and composition of the categories chosen for an analysis of this kind clearly has a considerable effect on the results, and different ways of categorising schools or universities would no doubt produce somewhat different clusters. However the figures in Table 3 suggest that if we look at those prominent in the public life of 1971, the contribution of Oxford and Cambridge together is even greater than the crude overall percentage suggests and that links clearly exist between the two ancient universities and various schools (or categories of school), various elite groups and potentially significant clusters. For instance their contribution to the recruitment of members of the two clusters based on Vice Chancellors and the High Court Judges is considerable; their contribution to the 'Military' cluster, however, is small.

An examination of the three clusters based on educational background and the contribution they make to the eighteen categories of the 'elite' (Table 4) shows the particularly close connections the ancient universities have with the Cabinet, the Directors of the 'Big Four' clearing banks, the four major insurance companies and the aristocracy (at least as represented by dukes). In addition, ex-public-school and Cambridge men in one cluster make up nearly one third of the Bishops of the Church of England and high proportions of the wealthiest businessmen, senior civil servants, Directors of the Bank of England and High Court Judges.

TABLE 3. *The contribution of institutions of higher education to the elite clusters*

Cluster	Named (according to the most prominent characteristic)	No. in cluster	Higher education									No higher education	Technical College
			Cambridge	Oxford	London	Other English university	Other university in Great Britain	Abroad	Military	Dartmouth	Cranwell		
1	'The Vice Chancellors'	90	19	35	11	11	24	5	0	0	0	0	0
2	'The Military'	70	5	4	2	3	1	0	52	0	0	6	0
3	'The Judiciary'	85	13	71	3	2	3	5	0	0	0	0	0
4	'Life Peers'	99	11	4	7	6	4	6	4	4	1	49	8
5	'Eton and Oxford'	89	17	60	0	0	0	1	8	0	0	6	0
6	'Public boarding school and Cambridge' (1)	155	123	5	4	0	0	3	0	0	1	23	1
7	'Grammar School'	109	17	10	16	10	19	2	0	1	1	33	9
	Total in the seven clusters	697	205	189	43	32	51	22	64	5	3	117	18
	Total in study	934	243	228	67	47	69	28	68	23	9	186	29
	Percentage of those included in study	75	84	83	64	68	74	79	94	22	33	63	62

NOTE: (1) 'Public boarding school' included all 76 independent boarding schools in England and Wales with the headmaster a member of the Headmasters' Conference and which have at least a third, and at least 200 boarders, but *excluding* both (i) Eton, and (ii) Winchester, Harrow, Rugby, Charterhouse and Marlborough, which were classified separately.

TABLE 4. *The contribution of clusters 5, 6 and 7 to the eighteen elite categories*

	Cluster 5 Eton and Oxford	Cluster 6 P.B.S. and Cambridge	Cluster 7 Grammar School	Total in study
Wealthiest businessmen	2	7	5	29
Cabinet	13	13	2	40
Senior Civil Servants	—	4	6	17
Directors of Bank of England	—	7	—	19
Directors of 'Big Four' banks	23	27	5	90
Directors of four largest insurance companies	10	9	6	40
Church of England bishops	1	14	5	35
High Court judges	4	15	5	81
Controllers of media	3	4	11	26
Aristocracy	6	2	—	18
Monopolies Commission	—	1	—	15
Senior Army officers	5	12	6	106
Senior Air Force officers	1	4	5	28
Senior Naval officers	—	4	8	46
Board members of nationalised industries	2	8	30	59
University Vice Chancellors	3	5	—	103
Life peers	13	13	6	150
Chairmen of fifty largest industrial companies	3	6	5	32

In our study 88 of the 103 Vice Chancellors and Principals appear in the 'Vice Chancellorial' cluster as, on the whole, a 'meritocratic' grouping with distinctive careers. The proportion with an Oxbridge education is high, whereas the proportion with a major public school education is relatively small; most had been either to a minor public, private or direct grant school, or to a grammar school. Unlike members of other elite groups, over half had some experience as students at other universities. This cluster also exhibits the familiar vice-chancellorial predilection for the Athenaeum; we can only speculate whether membership of that institution enhances the chance of selection or merely follows as a concomitant of appointment. If it is plausible that the major sources of advice and pressure for the academic world are 'probably the civil service, parliament official advisory committees and business leaders'[12] then shared backgrounds and career experience between individuals in such positions and academic leaders are significant. We have no data to present here on the extent of circulating personnel; Collison and Millen cite Lord Franks as an example of an individual who has held positions, either simultaneously or successively, in more than one sector of national life: 'academic civil servant, ambassador, bank chairman and academic leader once more'.[13]

At the national level Vice Chancellors chair Royal Commissions, are members of specialist committees, research councils and boards of trustees and at least one has been appointed to the Board of Directors of an international organisation. Locally they are often members of organisations such as regional planning councils, governing bodies of private and direct grant schools and local charities. Many regularly appear at local 'elite' gatherings. As Collison and Millen point out, the role of the Vice Chancellor forms part of every piece of the administrative machinery which has any consequence and enables him to direct the business of the university and shape its policy.[14] In new universities in particular the distinguished people who take on the chancellorships and pro-chancellorships are also in a position to exert considerable influence. There are also interesting procedures in the awarding of honorary degrees.

The names of people prominent in local and national elites appear among the lay membership of university courts and councils and equivalent bodies, and some are reportedly frequent visitors to the campus and guests at university functions,[15] but there are no systematic studies of the social composition and connections of governing bodies of British universities comparable to those undertaken by Beck and by Hartnett in America.[16] Nor are there British studies which examine the extent to which the participation of members of the university (and their wives) in a range of social and leisure activities, including charitable and other voluntary work in the local and national community, can be linked with the maintenance of control and influence. From a study in Chicago, Hoffman has concluded that participation in such activities 'far from being an innocuous frill or mere outlet for conspicuous display, is a vital part of that elite matrix which includes the corporation, the law firm, and the executive branch of the federal government'.[17]

A consistency was evident in the two randomly selected halves of the elite population isolated and examined in our analysis. This consistency lends qualified support to the suggestion that within the upper levels of British public life there are sets of individuals who, it could be maintained, in terms of educational experience and current social and occupational links, but particularly in a common education at Oxbridge, appear to display at least a potential for a degree of similarity of outlook or of 'life-space'. It seems plausible to suggest that those who have experienced an Oxbridge education, including the thriving range of extra-curricular activities, where the traditional priority is on 'knowledge as process', may share to some extent certain curriculum values, particularly in so far as their experience can be said to amount to an intense process of socialisation and cognitive development within the contrived environment of the university.[18] But we echo Bernstein's question 'How are forms of experience, identity and relation evoked, maintained and changed by the formal transmission of educational knowledge and sensitivities?',[19] or for that matter by extra-curricular activities such as the Oxford Union or the Cambridge

Footlights? Even were we broadly to postulate that similar, common or contemporaneous experiences within a university facilitate the establishment and maintenance of inter-relationships between the universities and elite groups, this does not in any way specify what would be the crucial *decisions* on which any degree of accord is likely among elite groups, or the manner in which such accord might be reached. One potential for cohesive action by elite groups, of course, is to influence appointments to top positions: only in the last two years have some universities begun to advertise for candidates for the post of Vice Chancellor.

The external constraints and pressures exerted on universities come from a variety of sources, their extent being modified by the interpretation and reception given to them by academics and university authorities. Some, such as those from students, are resisted and selectively channelled into acceptable forms and, exceptionally, legitimised as in the NUS-Committee of Vice Chancellors *concordat* of 1968. To others, universities succumb with or without recognising them. Research activities are now almost entirely financed from sources of funds not subject to university control; in the last decade at least, priorities among their research activities have been in most cases made for them, by bodies such as research councils, with special reference to 'national needs'. The influence of government on the decisions of these bodies is large and looks likely to increase.[20] The creation and expansion of new courses are influenced in some instances by local and national government – for example in the creation of departments specialising in the study of particular foreign countries, war studies (currently with lectureships at five universities directly sponsored by the Ministry of Defence), and social work training. Few universities press forward with courses which professional bodies have not recognised for the purpose of exemption from part of their own certificating procedure. Indeed in many subjects the professional bodies are intimately involved in the design and detailed content of the majority of a students' courses. Some actually provide the initial impetus for a department by endowing the new chair.[21]

Although universities may resist some of these pressures – as Oxford and Cambridge have resisted the moves to establish accountancy – resistance to the increasingly specific 'Memoranda of Guidance' from the UGC, and to their offers to support development in specified areas, is more difficult. The UGC have stated clearly the basis for 'guidance':

> The Committee, in framing their advice to universities, have to try to meet the needs of the country as a whole, while taking account of any requirements laid down by the government of the day.

In their earlier memorandum of 1968 they reminded universities:

> It would be in accordance with generally accepted convention that the Committee be consulted before any major new developments outside the framework set by the universities' quinquennial sub-

missions and the guidance contained in this memorandum, are undertaken.[22]

The penalty for contravention of such conventions is considerable, as a pro Vice Chancellor has pointed out:

> ...if we deliberately started things which [the UGC] said should not be done (a new school of law, for instance, or a new school of architecture, or a proliferation of new small language departments) we should be likely to find our bid for cash for 1977–82 cut by at least the amount which we showed ourselves to be spending on these developments....[23]

However one less discussed and little documented constraint on universities in this country involves the activity of industry and commerce. While at the turn of the century industry was closely involved in the creation of the new redbrick universities, Sanderson has suggested that an increasing involvement of the university with industry over the last century has been 'perhaps the most important single development in the history of the British universities'.[24] The Robbins Report, in laying the foundations for the development of the 'modern' university system in Great Britain, made a point of urging closer co-operation with industry[25] (one activity that the UGC has stated that it is particularly anxious to sponsor in the current quinquennium). In fact the bulk of expansion in the 1960s was provided by the older civic universities and, as their founders intended, their links with local industry were already close. Similarly the ex-CATs had developed in close association with industry and commerce.[26] But it was less predictable that the *newly* founded institutions, most of which were not sited adjacent to large industrial centres, would also do so. Keele, despite the wishes of its founders, had been little involved with the affairs of the locality; but the rest of the new universities did not emulate Keele. Most of them, particularly Essex, Lancaster and Warwick, despite only recent origin and still relatively small-scale operations, developed close relations with industry locally and nationally.[27] The Essex Vice Chancellor broadcast his view in the Reith lectures that 'universities...should work more closely with industry', and by the end of the 1960s Sanderson can cite from the Docksey Report that two thirds of universities had specifically 'close links' with industry, that only nine per cent of large companies had 'no contact' with universities and that eighty-one per cent of those using university consultants found them 'useful and effective'.[28]

These developments have been accompanied by a considerable number of appointments to university posts of senior industrialists and, as recommended in the Robbins Report, of senior management and research directors as visiting, honorary or part-time professors, and by the use of 'industrial tutors' to supervise the work of postgraduate students. Business subjects have been introduced, subjects such as Operational Research, Systems Engineering, Marketing and Financial Control pioneered in certain universities and traditional subject-areas modified to produce new, more 'relevant', foci such as Environmental Science and Educational Research. Lines of development were proposed by some universities, and by individual departments within them, explicitly because they contributed to industrial firms with plant in the locality.[29] The research facilities and expertise of certain universities have publicly been placed at the disposal of companies operating in the locality and in some instances it is indicated that new academic staff will be encouraged to undertake industrial consultancies and to function generally as 'available experts'.[30]

As individuals many university staff act as advisors or consultants particularly for government and industrial concerns. The academic is faced with the difficulty of deciding whether the problem his sponsor confronts him with is researchable, particularly within a given time-limit and with underlying pressures for 'acceptable' answers.[31] How should the question to be answered be framed, and how can possible manipulation, misinterpretation and mis-use of 'answers' be avoided? Even when the requirements of the sponsor are apparently reconciled with the scholarly pursuit of 'pure' knowledge and canons of science, the source of the knowledge, quite apart from the knowledge itself, gives power to the sponsor – the lesson of Project Camelot and a lesson American anthropologists are relearning in South East Asia.

When research is undertaken for the government, as it has been pointed out, research strategies and priorities are in government control, though this may mean *de facto* control by senior civil servants. 'It is in the interests of an established government', Halsey suggests, 'to define the social sciences as apolitical and organized social science as, in effect, an extension of the Civil Service. On such a view the problems are essentially technical.' Beyond this, as Halsey points out, there are 'political as well as scientific determinants of the localities chosen' by governments for their sponsored projects. Nor do donors seem to favour universities with well publicised 'troubles' – a point with all kinds of sociological implications.[32]

The universities' dependence on state funds is now overwhelming.[33] In most cases the actual financial contribution to university funds from other sources is only a small part of their total budget and it would be very difficult to examine how the financial and contractual relationships with, for instance, industry actually affect university policies and development decisions. But the effect of accepting such funds is considerably greater than would appear from their contribution to the annual accounts. Gifts and endowments, as the Robbins Report stressed, provide a certain flexibility and freedom which has been used in recent years to provide for activities not at the time favoured by the UGC.[34] They undoubtedly involve, however, distinct though often unspecified limitations. Grants are often given on the understanding that the university contributes a similar sum from its own funds, undertakes to develop particular specialisms or provide accommodation and equipment and to take over the development in the next quinquennium, and staff for such developments are frequently assured that their employment will continue beyond the expiry of the particular contract. The normal expectation is that Senate will later sanction the continuation and further expansion of 'successful' ventures, this time out of UGC funds.

Unless one equates social need and market demand or sets out with the democratic-pluralist assumption that power in Britain is diffuse and competitive – in Dahl's terms that 'all the active and legitimate groups in the population can make themselves heard at some crucial stage in the process of decision'[35] – there remains the probability that certain social and economic interests are more likely to be 'serviced' by some British universities than others, and the possibility also that these interests might be those of individuals, groups or organisations who are in a position to provide the universities with the means to do so. We are not aware for instance of *any* studies in this country of the factors that enter into the decision of organisations, from the Bank of England to quite small industrial companies, to respond positively to the universities' appeals for funds, or any examination of how such relationships evolve.[36] *Why* is money offered, by whom, and, perhaps more significantly, when and why is it refused?

Clark Kerr's notion of the 'multiversity' has been interpreted as a 'pragmatic' substitute for a solution to an impasse reached in America between elite and so-called vulgar conceptions of higher education, between scholarship and service.[37] Fundamental to the idea of the multiversity is the assumption that it is possible to accommodate many varied and conflicting external demands (and their concomitant structural relations) by internal differentiation within an institution of higher education, so as to maximise the service given to the society which supports it. Kerr frequently mentions the importance of the multiversity's responsiveness to national needs. But as Wolff points out in a sceptical account of the notion as an ideal for the modern university, by 'systematically confusing the concepts of need and demand, Clark Kerr begs all the major political questions of the day'.[38] Kerr's emphasis on the multiversity's role as an *instrument* of national purpose circumscribes, if not precludes entirely, its role of providing a sustained critique of 'national purpose'. Nisbet's pleas for the phasing out of most sponsored research programmes in universities, for the depoliticization of the university, the elevation of the teaching function and the restoration of a system of recognised authority, are as unconvincing as is his idealised picture of the pre-war American university, but his basic point echoes Galbraith and Miliband and Wolff, all from their different perspectives, and is fundamental: to what extent are universities confirmed critics of all aspects of their society? Is it a cherished value that they should be? Those universities already closely allied to traditional elite groups have the resources to nurture and transmit to their students 'high culture', the scholarly pursuit of 'pure' knowledge and fundamental scientific enquiry, and the conservation of accumulated knowledge and experience 'uninhibited and unfettered by any extraneous considerations whatsoever' (Mountford's 'cardinal premise'), whether social, political or dogmatic. Several writers have noted the strength of what Shils refers to as the 'London–Oxford–Cambridge Axis'.[39] Other universities whose resources and relationships with both the polity and the economy reflect a very different degree of internal quality determination, are faced with a real dilemma: should they primarily strive to emulate the elite universities or should they rather adopt an alternative model along the lines perhaps of Perkin's and Armytage's concept of 'community service stations',[40] staffed by and recruiting, socialising and certificating for a 'service class'?[41] What influences the decisions a university makes in the face of this dilemma, and what effects will its resolution have on the future of higher education in Britain?

KENNETH THOMPSON

11 Church of England bishops as an elite

Introduction

Most studies of elites have tended to concentrate on the dimension of *recruitment* rather than on the dimensions of organization and *structure* or the distribution *of power* as exercised by those in elite positions.[1] This is particularly so with British studies, which have often been envisaged as case studies in the broader discussion of social mobility. It is probably also due to the greater possibilities for finding hard statistical data to support hypotheses about recruitment, whereas evidence on structure and power tends to be more impressionistic, although the hypotheses here are often of more interest theoretically. This paper will not deviate much from that established pattern, but some effort will be made to show how changes in recruitment have significance for the structure and power dimensions.

Recruitment

There have been frequent examinations of the social and educational backgrounds of Church of England bishops. It has now reached the point where it seems to be required etiquette to preface any remarks on the subject with an apology for adding to their 'over-exposure'. The most appropriate apology is that which incorporates Paul Ferris' remark:

> Everything conspires to cut the bishops off. They must be one of the most annotated bodies of men in the world, providing copy for any writer who cares to spend an hour with *Who's Who*, *Crockford's Clerical Directory* and *Whitaker's*. Their high average age and the large number who went to public schools are the most commonly quoted statistics...[2]

The facts about age of recruitment, schooling, university and family background are usually stated in order to suggest they ought to be otherwise – on the grounds that they reduce efficiency, frustrate democracy, or simply because they are in some sense invidiously unrepresentative. An hour with the directories is well spent for this purpose. It can produce a crisp letter to *The Times* about the need for younger bishops:

> ...Since the beginning of 1970 there have been 12 appointments of new diocesan bishops at an average of age $53\frac{1}{2}$ years. In fact, seven of the 12 were over 55 and none was under 45.

When one takes account of the bench as a whole, it can be seen that their average age on first diocesan appointment was just over 51…At first sight, therefore, it seems that recent appointments are if anything being made at a rather older age than was the case in the 1950s.[3]

What is more difficult to decide (and takes more hours with directories to arrive at an answer) is whether such figures indicate a trend that is sociologically significant as well as being polemically useful. In this case of figures relating to the age of bishops, there is no trend discernible. The mean average age of bishops on first appointment to a diocese has remained fairly constant over the last century (e.g. 1880, 52.5 years; 1900, 53.1 years; 1920, 51.7 years; 1940, 52.4 years; 1960, 51.2 years).[4] However, what might be sociologically significant as far as the study of elites is concerned, is that this constancy is in marked contrast to changes occurring in the composition of the parochial clergy. Here, with the exception of a brief period at the beginning of the 1960s, the Church has experienced great difficulty in covering its losses in manpower, throughout the post-war period. Over the last decade the decline in numbers of entrants to the ministry has been acute (see Table 1) and in 1969 the Church took the step of agreeing to the idea of a part-time, auxiliary parochial ministry. Thus, the seriously understaffed parochial ministry is now being supplemented by two categories of auxiliary ministry:

(*a*) self-supporting priests who earn their own living; and

(*b*) a 'post-retirement' ministry (also self-supporting) of older men, who retired from another career and are ordained for a period of service as auxiliary parochial priests.

A similar point can be made about the educational background of bishops. On the whole, the high proportion of bishops who went to Oxford or Cambridge for their University education has remained fairly constant. In 1969–70, for example, 38 (88 %) of the 43 diocesan bishops had had an 'Oxbridge' education. This is not greatly different from the periods 1880–99 and 1920–39 when the figure was 90 %. It is in marked contrast, however, with the decline in the number of parochial clergy who attended *any* university. Leslie Paul noted in his 1964 report on *The Deployment and Payment of the Clergy* that of those ordained between 1953 and 1962 less than 50 % were graduates and that since 1960 the number of graduates appeared to be falling as a percentage of ordinands. He added:

A radical transformation of the ministry may be under way. The trend is unmistakable, and at least one part of it can be attributed to the efforts of the Church in post-war years to make provision for those whose vocation is unquestioned and gifts of personality high, but who have proved educational casualties…(in part because it was forced to by falling recruitment).[5]

TABLE 1. *Ordinations in the Church of England, 1962–72*

	1962	1963	1964	1965	1966	1967	1968	1969	1970	1971	1972*
Total ordinations	633	636	605	592	576	496	478	436	437	393	361†
Over 40 years of age	140	110	110	149	148	110	104	94	88	66	61
Graduates‡	270	304	230	249	197	190	181	161	185	166	149

NOTES:

* Provisional figures as of 19 March 1973.
† This figure includes 21 ordained to a part-time auxiliary pastoral ministry.
‡ The decline in the number of graduates entering the ministry should be viewed in the context of a rise in the number of students graduating from universities in Great Britain over the same period from 24,700 in 1961–2 to 47,400 in 1968–9.[7] (Figures supplied by the Advisory Council for the Church's Ministry.)

The proportion of non-graduates being ordained has fallen slightly recently, but it is still a fact that without the reversal of all its previous policies which insisted on graduate qualifications, the Church would have been facing an even more severe manpower crisis (see Table 1).[6]

Over the recent period therefore, the significant sociological point with regard to recruitment to the elite is that in some respects it has remained remarkably unchanged in contrast with the important changes in the composition of the rest of the clergy. Whereas the main trend in recruitment to the clergy has been one of increasing variety with regard to their backgrounds, i.e. a move towards recruiting older men, non-graduates with experience of other occupations, this trend has not yet made an impact on the episcopal elite. Of course, there is bound to be a certain time lag even if the trend does spread, for the simple reason that the episcopate is recruited from the more senior sections of the clergy. But this still means that in recent years there has been a trend (however temporary it may turn out to be) towards increasing divergence in the composition of the two groups – episcopal elite and parochial clergy.

The possibility of there being a divergent trend with respect to the composition of the two groups has not been publically discussed within the Church. On the whole the prevailing ideology has been one of optimism about a continuing reduction in the degree of social distance between the elite and non-elite. And changes in the composition of each of the groups have tended to be discussed separately rather than in relation to each other.

In the case of bishops the long-term changes most often discussed are those concerning family background – the decline in landed and peerage connections, and the shift in terms of parental occupation from old landed ruling class to a more professional background (especially worthy of note being the increase in the number of bishops whose fathers were themselves clergymen). This change has been depicted as a shift from a situation where the episcopate was part of a broader social elite to one where it is a more narrowly defined ecclesiastical elite (see Table 2).[8]

TABLE 2. *English diocesan bishops, 1860–1960: summary table of family backgrounds*[9]

Year/period*	No. of bishops in each period	Fathers clergy† (%)	Fathers professions‡ (%)	Fathers ruling class§ (%)	Bishops married (%)	Father-in-law clergy† (%)	Fathers-in-law professions‡ (%)	Fathers-in-law ruling class§ (%)	Landed peerage connections‖
1860–79	27	18	61	33	96	24	62	33	112·5
1880–99	29	23	59	17	93	16	58	30	96.3
1900–19	42	45	73	10	88	33	64	22	87.1
1920–39	47	51	74	6	83	24	58	20	68.4
1940–59	58	48	63	2	86	27	63	2	51.2
1960–	43	54	70	2	91	31	56	2	34.9
Total‖	222	42	65	9	88	26	60	16	67.0

NOTES:

  * Data relate to bishops in twenty year periods or for single years when shown in italics.

  † Number of fathers who were clergymen as percentage of total number of occupations recorded.

  ‡ Including clergymen, armed services, parliament, doctors, solicitors etc.

  § Roughly, those with landed or peerage connections where that is *all* that is known about them, plus those M.P.s with aristocratic connections or holding important office. Also archbishops.

  ‖ Total number of known peerage/landed connections by birth and by marriage as percentage of total number of bishops. For single years only.

  ¶ Totals take account of the fact that bishops may occupy dioceses in two of our periods.

With regard to family background, therefore, it might seem that the bishops have drawn closer to the rest of the clergy. But in educational terms the most recent period has seen a divergence in the composition of the diocesan episcopate and the lower clergy. Whilst there has been a marked trend towards a non-graduate clergy, the episcopate has remained overwhelmingly 'Oxbridge'. If we add to this the fact that in 1960–2, even before the recent shift to non-graduates really got underway, only 27.34 % of the candidates accepted for the ministry were public school educated, compared with 85 % of the bishops, the educational cleavage is clear.[10] And in so far as public school education serves to create and perpetuate a distinct social stratum, the schooling of the bishops also sets them apart socially from the majority of the clergy.

Two other factors distinguish the bishops from the general body of clergy. The first, as we have noted previously, is that bishops are increasingly recruited from clergy who themselves come from clergy families. Thus, in 1960, 54 % of the bishops were sons of clergymen, whereas, out of a sample of Anglican ordinands in theological colleges in 1962, only 8 % were clergymen's sons.[11] Secondly, bishops are drawn predominantly from clergy who have been trained at one or other of a handful of elite theological colleges. Whereas Coxon's *Ordinand's Survey* in 1962 found a fairly even distribution of ordinands training in more than 30 colleges, 31 of the 43 bishops in 1960 came from only four colleges (Wells, Cuddesdon, Ridley and Westcott).

To summarise the most discussed findings on recruitment: on the one hand, recruits from the clergy are being drawn from a wider variety of backgrounds, whilst bishops, on the other hand, remain a fairly narrow elite group (although the situation of that group has shifted slightly from being part of a broader social elite to one where it is more clearly an elite within a profession).

What light does this discussion of *recruitment* throw on the other dimensions – *structure* and *power* – of the ecclesiastical elite?

Structure

Giddens has emphasised that in analysing the structure of elite groups we should be concerned with their level of both 'social' and 'moral' integration.

> 'Moral' integration refers to the degree to which those in elite positions share common ideas and a common moral ethos; and to how far they are conscious of an overall solidarity. 'Social' integration concerns the frequency and nature of the social contacts and relationships between elite groups...We can normally expect social and moral integration to vary directly with each other, and hence can conflate them and speak of the degree of 'integration' of elite groups.[12]

Anglican bishops would clearly rank as highly integrated compared with most other elite groups – particularly with regard to moral integration. Not only do they subscribe to the same religious beliefs, most of them also received the same kind of schooling – one in which the religion taught and imbibed was of a particular type. The religious element in public school ideology has been frequently depicted as a traditional faith bound up with classical learning and stressing the responsibilities of leadership and service. It is the religion of the 'healthy' mind – not a crisis religion or one given to extremism or strong emotional expression. This type of religion fits smoothly into an ideology which stresses traditional leadership, and a process of education which is concerned with role allocation among the upper classes, i.e. an education which is diffuse or liberal as opposed to specific or technical. Even theological colleges, which might have been expected to introduce more of a technical element into the education of the clergy and so lay the ground for a democratisation process in the recruitment of bishops, have had the unintended consequence of perpetuating the elite. The theological colleges were intended to raise the standard of ordinands and to create uniform criteria of acceptance for the ministry. In fact, they have had the unintended consequence of widening the gap between the bishops and the rest of the clergy, because a handful of the minority of theological colleges in the vicinity of Oxford and Cambridge have become the main source of future bishops.

Over the last century, therefore, despite changes such as the introduction of theological colleges and the decline in the aristocratic connections of bishops, it is probably true to say that the trend has been for bishops to belong to a more clearly delimited social group. And this may have increased their moral integration. A. M. Ramsey, the future Archbishop of Canterbury, found in them a

> tendency to be 'of a type' – lacking in marked differences and clash of individuality which, in a period a little earlier, assisted the Church's vigour of mind and appeal to the community.[13]

In general, however, evidence for the close moral integration of the episcopate is hardly surprising. After all, religious groups are supposed to be morally integrated – relatively speaking! It is perhaps more enlightening to discuss the question of the degree of organisational or 'social' integration of the episcopate at different times.

It is at this point that our discussion of the divergent trends regarding recruitment of clergy and bishops becomes significant. It might not be too paradoxical to suggest that a trend towards greater variety among subordinates in an organisation can proceed hand in hand with a trend towards closer integration among superordinates who have to exercise overall control. This is not the place to discuss in detail the organisational conflicts that have occurred in the Church over the last hundred years as it has sought to adapt its structure in response to social changes,[14] and we will turn to questions of power and authority in the next section of this paper. Nevertheless, it is relevant here to note that both a trend towards heterogeneity of clergy backgrounds and a trend towards greater homogeneity in the episcopate can be related to a more general organisational trend – increasing professionalisation *and* bureaucratisation.

The increasing professionalisation of the ministry can be seen in the growth of specialised training institutions (theological colleges) and the development of more formalised methods of recruitment and examination. It is also evident in the dropping of the traditional non-religious rights and duties which had been attached to the clergyman by virtue of his status as a 'gentleman' or 'squarson'. The profession of clergyman has become more clearly differentiated, but it has continued to rest on very diffuse qualities rather than specific skills. For this latter reason (among others) it has been possible for the Church to cast its recruiting net more widely in its search for candidates when absolutely forced to do so by the recent shortage of more traditional recruits.

Bureaucratisation has been particularly evident in the financial administration of the Church. Max Weber suggested that an essential condition for the development of a rational bureaucratic form of organisation from a traditional type is an increased command over monetary funds, both in the means of administration and in remuneration. The bureaucratic official normally receives a fixed salary paid in money, instead of being dependent on sources of income which are privately appropriated and which can be called benefices. Benefices typically involve payments in kind, and the receipt of a benefice implies the appropriation of opportunities for collecting dues. The significance of this for organisational developments can be seen in the sale of glebe-land formerly attached to benefices, the decline of private sources of clerical income, and the commutation of tithe, which created a need for supplementation from central funds, and so of central organisation and control. This threatened the independent professional status of the clergy by virtue of the change from local and private sources of income to central monetary payments (salaries, pensions, grants for maintenance and dilapidations), all of which seemed to be in the direction of reducing the clergy to salaried, dependent status, and increasing executive roles at the centre.

As far as the bishops were concerned, the effect of these changes was to increase their executive and administrative responsibilities at the diocesan level and in the central organisation of the Church. The attitude of the lower clergy towards the bishops, and towards the new organisation, has been one of ambivalence. The bishops are seen as being both a part of the new bureaucratic organisation, but also (in terms of their more traditional authority) as a possible buffer between the dependent clergymen and the bureaucratic organisation.[15]

The bishops, in turn, have been torn between their different roles in relation to the clergy and to the central organisation. Frequently, over the last century, especially when major organisational changes have produced conflict in the Church, the bishops have reasserted their own organisational integration as a group in the private and 'informal' organisation of the Bishops Meeting. This was particularly evident during the period of the biggest innovation in the Chirch's organisation – the setting up of the Church Assembly in 1919.[16] The Bishops Meeting itself is not really part of the 'formal' organisation. It is private and has no legal standing in the Church. Consequently, its agenda and discussions are not made public. However, the range of its business can be discerned in the letters and papers of archbishops and bishops, as in the case of Archbishop Davidson's correspondence before and immediately after the creation of the Church Assembly. Its business tends to be concerned with issues of the middle range of policy – not the detailed business carried out by offices of the formal organisation, nor great issues concerning the relation of the Church to society. A former Bishop of Sheffield commented in 1966 that he had attended more than a hundred meetings of diocesan bishops:

> Some of the subjects discussed were of urgent passing importance; others of recurring importance. But I cannot recall many occasions when we really faced the revolution in English society since the Book of Common Prayer was promulgated in 1662, or the radical change in thought and belief and in the pattern of life since the industrial and scientific revolutions; and in the light of these changes, the need for a new policy of engagement and penetration.[17]

Perhaps the main function of these meetings except in periods of organisational crisis, is revealed in Hunter's prior statement about such meetings, that they had left 'a happy memory of friendly association'. The social integration of the bishops as an elite group is maintained by such informal organisation in the face of the more impersonal, bureaucratic formal organisation.

Power

It was stated earlier that the clergy have an ambivalent attitude towards the bishops' position in the Church's organisation. Sometimes they associate the bishops with the controlling organisation that seems to threaten their own independence and professional status. At other times they regard the bishops as the locus of a separate, traditional authority which can act as a buffer between the clergymen and the impersonal rational–legal authority of the bureaucracy. The bishops legitimise their power by just such an appeal:

> But when the worst has been said of us and allowed, let it never be forgotten that the diocesan bishop in our English inheritance is the

safeguard against a centralised bureaucracy and oligarchy, and a protection from the dictatorship of a *curia* from which the Vatican Council is trying to release the Roman Church.[18]

The bishops, therefore, have an interest in maintaining the traditional (and institutionalised charismatic) bases of legitimation of their authority and role. This places limitations on the extent to which organisational changes and demands can push them towards a purely rational–legal authority and narrowly professional role. Compared with bishops in the middle of the nineteenth century, present-day bishops are certainly more 'professional' in the sense of having to be much more fully involved in internal church administration. This role change is reflected in the changed character of the episcopate as an elite group – a shift from being a central part of a social elite to a situation where it is first and foremost an internal ecclesiastical elite.

But, as we have stressed throughout this paper, in contrast with changes elsewhere in the Church (especially in the composition of the clergy) the episcopate has continued to be drawn overwhelmingly from a narrow, traditional section of the available population. Clergy family – public schools – Oxbridge – elite theological colleges, this is the favoured route for recruitment to a diocesan bishopric. In fact, this preference for recruits from a traditional background is closely related to the changes occurring elsewhere. For the more uncertainty there is about the Church's goals, the clergy's tasks, the necessary qualifications for the clergy, the legitimacy of new powers vested in offices of the formal organisation, the more there is likely to be dependence on leaders who have been presocialised in an established tradition. The alternative would be to develop new agencies of socialisation of future leaders; for example, to recruit specialists for particular tasks and to be prepared for the episcopate to become much more heterogeneous. Thus, a letter to *The Times* in response to the correspondent who complained of the trend towards recruiting older bishops, suggested that, 'Greater use could be made of fixed term appointments together with specified objectives'.[19] But this would be a development in the direction of adopting rational–instrumental criteria in recruitment and in defining the role of a bishop. This might undermine the traditional authority of episcopal office, which has been an important element in the Church's effort to maintain its stability in a period of disturbing change.

Conclusion

I have suggested elsewhere that the Church of England's response to social change over the past century has been mainly a defensive attempt to preserve its own identity:

> The desire to maintain the Church of England's basic identity as an *ecclesia*, which incorporated diverse elements in one religious

establishment, limited the extent to which it developed an autonomous administrative and governmental system along the lines found to be typical in the denominations, which are sometimes described as the appropriate form of religious organization in modern societies, where institutional domains are highly differentiated. The Church of England has developed a certain degree of autonomy, and is inclined to accept some of the implications of denominational pluralism, but it still prizes its own comprehensiveness and internal diversity, which it preserves by following a *via media* with regard to doctrine, principles of authority, and organization. This is the crucial limiting factor on any development in its organization towards the 'ideal types' of denomination and bureaucracy.[20]

The position of the bishops in this 'balancing act' has been to a large extent one of providing a counterbalance to changes elsewhere. Changes in the formal organisation in a bureaucratic direction, with an assertion of rational–legal bases of authority, have been counterbalanced by a re-assertion of the traditional authority of the bishops. To a lesser extent there has also been a reassertion of the institutionalised charismatic (sacred, priestly) bases of authority of the ministry, including the bishops. But this too has had to be balanced by a reassertion of the separate traditional bases of episcopal authority, because not all parties in the Church accept a high sacerdotal doctrine of episcopacy.

Changes in the status and composition of the lower clergy, which weaken their traditional character and background, have been justified in terms of rational–legal and institutionalised charismatic criteria, e.g. the need for specialised ministries, or the claim that the priestly office sheds its light on the occupant irrespective of his social background.

What is significant is that neither of these latter considerations has been applied to the episcopate. The bishops provide the traditional counterbalance. If the Church of England is to maintain its *ecclesia* identity, then the bishops are likely to remain a mainly traditional and homogeneous elite.

12 Capitalism, elites and the ruling class

Giddens has suggested that, although they have been produced for a variety of intellectual, ideological and political reasons, elite theories could be used to direct empirical studies of stratification in Britain in relatively undeveloped and more profitable directions. The research project which has been undertaken in the Department of Applied Economics at Cambridge is seen as doing this.[1] This paper reviews some of the theoretical issues raised in a symposium organised in connection with this project, and argues that elite studies need to be located within a theory of capitalism and the ruling class, albeit a complex and specific one, if they are to be of value.

Quite clearly Giddens' approach to elite studies is a critical one, and he makes a number of suggestions as to how the concept should be modified if it is to be used effectively. In the first place it must be rid of the anti-Marxist, and, indeed, anti-democratic, overtones which the work of Pareto, Mosca and Michels attached to it. But, given that this is done, elite studies in Britain might do much to correct an overemphasis in stratification studies on the working class, and raise crucial questions about power which such studies avoid. The specific orientation of the Cambridge study is then seen as a critique of the 'decomposition hypothesis' which argues that 'there is no longer a distinctive "upper class", still less a "ruling class" in contemporary Britain; and that "Elites are no longer cohered by the common social and moral ties which were once created by the gentlemenly ethos of the Clarendon schools and the ancient universities"'.[2]

This may at first be somewhat confusing, for Giddens refers in his account of the hypothesis which he wishes to refute to three different things, the existence or non-existence of a ruling *class*, the coherence of elites, and the ethos of privileged educational institutions. It is to be hoped, therefore, that his subsequent analytic breakdown of the elite concept might have the effect of clarifying some of these confusions. What we seek to do here is to look at Giddens' analysis and, while partially accepting its insights, to argue that it would be worthwhile following through some of his insights more completely than he does himself.

Giddens distinguishes between the process of recruitment to elite positions, elite structure, 'which refers to the level of social and moral solidarity between members of elite groups in different institutional settings' and the question of the distribution of power, which includes on the one hand 'the institutional mediation of power' and 'the mediation of control'. The first of these last two sub-headings 'refers to the general framework of state and economy within which elite groups are recruited and structured', the second to 'the power of policy-formation and decision making'.[3]

It is quite true that the preoccupation of British political intellectuals and sociologists has been with the question of recruitment, partly because this lends itself to easy measurement (e.g. in terms of percentages with Clarendon or Oxbridge education) but partly also because of a continuing sense of resentment on the part of the industrial classes at their exclusion from positions of privilege in a society which never fully rid itself of its aristocracy. Studies of structure have also focussed on the analysis of exclusive organisations and institutions, often using the methods of the anthropologist and the novelist to delineate the means by which exclusion is achieved. But most of the contributions to this book are also focussed on these problems. We learn of the social background of company chairmen, of directors, of bishops, civil servants and M.P.s. Here again we have accounts of the anti-egalitarian trend of wealth distribution and of the capacity for collective action of capitalist directors. Only one slightly idiosyncratic contribution deals with the question of policy-formation[4] and decision making, and only in a contribution from Pahl and Winkler[5] is there much immediate reference to the larger socio-economic system in which elites may make decisions or rule.

It is to be hoped that the issues raised by Pahl and Winkler as well as those raised in the present paper are followed through, because it would appear to be at least a good starting point to ask whether the socio-economic system of which we are talking is basically a capitalist one. This is by no means to suggest that we should adopt some simplistic model of capitalist society. But it is to suggest that the institutions which provide the framework for our social political and economic action are to some extent and in some way interconnected, so that the question of whether those who occupy the command posts in these institutions 'cohere' is not simply a matter of direct empirical observation of attributes. It depends upon the goals which men seek and the institutional means and personnel which they use to achieve their goals.

Now, as a matter of fact, the most influential study using the concept 'elite' in recent years, that of C. Wright Mills,[6] is actually primarily concerned with the question of the functional interrelationship between one institution and another, and it is primarily because he finds it necessary to call into question the dominance and leading role of the capitalist corporation taken by itself that Mills also finds it necessary to become a Marxist revisionist. But he does this by one of the traditional routes, namely the rejection of the concept of class in favour of the concept of elite, when what is really called for is a re-assessment of the concept of class in relation to a variety of complex socio-economic formations. We may readily dispose of Mills' notion of an elite which is distinguishable by the fact that members all exercise power. But having disposed of this notion the real problem remains. If in the U.S.A. a sociologist of a generally Marxist persuasion finds that productive institutions are not the sole leading ones in social change, might it not be the case that something analogous, although not directly similar, is also the case in other societies?

Of course Mills has been criticised for his notion of some kind of structured ruling group whose main distinguishing attribute and *raison d'être* was the possession of power. This is a trap in which all elite theorists are likely to be caught. For the fact of the matter is that power cannot be understood simply as a generalised means, regardless of the end to which it is applied, whether it is defined as the power to command the actions of another or power to reach decisions. Mills' three command centres in the economy, in politics and in the military are only cohesive because they work towards shared goals or in alliance to compatible ones. The proof of the power is in the pay-off and comes in a currency other than power. Parsons is therefore wrong in criticising Mills for having a zero-sum conception of power. Mills certainly would have had such a conception if he had retained the notion of a class pursing its goals by compelling the actions of another class. But as soon as he attempted to define his elite in terms of the possession of power regardless of the ends for which it was used, he moved to a position very similar to that of Parsons, holding power to be a generalised resource, even though, unlike Parsons, Mills thought that the resource had been usurped by a ruling group who could then run the system and other mens' lives for their purposes.

The difficulty which Mills and other modern sociologists have had in using the term class really derives from the fact that, whereas the notion of class assumes the existence of a close functional relationship between different institutions, so that what the decision makers in one institution do has direct implications in means–ends terms for those in another, the looseness of functional fit which sociologists like Mills (and, for that matter, Dahrendorf)[7] see between one institutional area and another, raises the possibility that the decision makers in each institution operate independently. Hence, it is argued, one may speak of a class or an elite for each separate institutional area, using the former term if one thinks that those in command enhance their own life-chances, or the latter if one notes only their power to direct policy and make decisions. It is perhaps also worth noting that similar problems arise in Marxist sociology, where the notion of looseness of functional fit becomes replaced by that of contradictions, though, of course, most Marxists would assert that in the last analysis the leading role of productive institutions asserts itself.[8]

Mills, of course, is significantly more of a Marxist sociologist than

Dahrendorf could ever be *precisely on this issue*, for while he shares with the latter the notion that different institutional hierarchies are relatively independent of each other, he posits united action by those who occupy the three leading sets of command posts. His modified Marxism simply asserts that the understanding of 'power', or what we here would call class rule, involves the recognition of a complexity of interests and a coalition of forces rather than unitary class domination from the productive centre. The question to which we should address ourselves, and in terms of which we can examine Giddens' problem of 'the general framework of state and economy within which elite groups are recruited and structured' is whether it is the case in Britain that there is a significant looseness of fit between institutional areas. Is there any reason to modify the 'economic determinism' (using the term here simply as a shorthand phrase) of Marxist models, by recognising some other leading institution or jointly leading institution? Or can we safely assume that at least 'in the last analysis' a Marxist model is applicable?

The curious thing when one comes to this point in the debate is that very few non-Marxist sociologists in Britain have ever really given definite affirmative answers to the first two of these three questions. There is some suggestion made by pluralists amongst political scientists that politicians act relatively independently of their own economic interests and of those who elected them, but apart from this no definitive claim is made for the total independence of any institution from the ultimate need to keep the economy running and profitable. We have no serious claim made for example that the military are poised to take over and direct the overall social system in their own interests, and, though we hear occasional complaints of the Civil Service acting autonomously of politicians, it would surely have to be agreed that they are subject to economic constraints. And, if no great looseness of fit is claimed, there does not appear to be any strong case made that the society is governed from several different command posts whose incumbents act in coalition. Yet there *is* a British peculiarity, and this is the curious insistence of popular sociologists and political intellectuals that the society is governed by something called the 'Establishment', which is occasionally likened to Mills 'power elite'. What sociological sense can we make of this notion?

One possible interpretation is that there is a set of professionalised roles, whose dynamic and whose ethics are dictated by the moral and political education imparted by elite educational institutions.[9] In some sense this seems to be accepted by many elite and stratification theorists for there is a stress upon the importance of elite educational background in nearly all British sociology, and this shows quite clearly in this volume, even though its editor and inspirer insists on the importance of moving attention away from recruitment. Moreover there is considerable evidence, which we shall be discussing later, that the role of elite education is resented. This could either be because educational institutions are dominated by groups pursuing their own aims, or it could be because they are the instrument of the purposes of some other group which remains independent of the entrepreneurial industrial class.

The actual claim which is made here is by no means clear. There is very little reference made to an aristocracy in this volume and, when Stanworth and Giddens,[10] for example, refer to 'upper class' background, they define this as including 'industrialists, landowners and others who possess substantial property and wealth', merging it with a discussion of the *educational* background of the various elite categories to which they refer. In so doing, they seem to reflect a widely held British political notion, namely that there is a ruling class which is partly merged with the industrial bourgeoisie, but has its own distinct interests and way of life, which it perpetuates by ensuring that those who go on to important positions of authority in government, industry and the professions are thoroughly indoctrinated via the public schools and the traditional universities. But it is doubtful whether this could be accommodated by a 'looseness of institutional fit' hypothesis or one which posits an independent institutional realm, like that of Mills' warlords. It would in fact make far more sense to posit the continued existence within the framework of bourgeois society of some of the institutions of a pre-capitalist economic formation. If this were the case, one might expect (*a*) some kind of accommodation between the old ruling class and the new entrepreneurial one or (*b*) that the ruling class from the older order would move in, accepting the new institutions, and incorporating them to its own profit within its way of life. In either case the social system would deviate in macrosociological terms from a 'capitalist' ideal type.

Before we go on to explore the implications for elite theory of a pure capitalist model and of an aristocratic ruling class model it might be as well to rule out one possible logical variant of the latter theory. This is the notion that such a class, with its own separate aims, is simply a land-owning class, defined in terms of its relation to the means of production. In a country where agriculture plays as small a role as in Britain it would not be possible for a purely land-owning class to survive as a significant historical agent. What might be the case, however, is that it has continued to exist as a collectivity, or status group, while finding new means of enhancing its life-chances. The central problem, if this were so, would be an educational one. Individual descendants of land-owning families might go 'into trade', and some from trade might even be co-opted to this class, but both the renegades and the new entrants would be held to the true faith and to proper goals through educational indoctrination.

On this point it is surely of some interest to notice that, while Max Weber could find a place for market-classes akin to Marx's classes in themselves (and probably also for classes for themselves), he also retained the notion that status groups could be hegemonic collectivities imposing their way of life on a whole community through domination of the educational system.[11] This is a notion which has been fruitfully explored by Michalina Clifford Vaughan and Margaret Scotford Archer in their pioneering work on the comparative sociology of education.[12]

We shall shortly be considering the relationship between all that we have been saying and the notion of elites, but it may perhaps be asked, at this point, whether much of the discussion of elites (rather than classes) does not arise mistakenly from an awareness of the relative inadequacy of Marxist models of capitalist society, and of the relative importance of this other notion of a ruling status group which imposes its social, cultural and political, if not its economic, sway on society as a whole. The reason why we have placed so much emphasis on this part of the discussion is precisely to *separate it out* from the real problem of elites, i.e. the problem of those who actually exercise power of command, *given* the existence of class interests of one kind or another which are being defended.

Let us now posit a simple model of a capitalist society of a Marxist kind. In the first place such a model must assume at its heart that there are two different types of participant actor, one, who joins in, or individually initiates, enterprises with a view to profit, and who treats labour, along with raw materials, and machinery, as a productive resource; and the other, who is compelled, because he has no other alternative, to sell his labour in order to live. This may seem obvious to Marxists and it is certainly obvious to everyone who has lived in a family where the daily bread depended upon the sale of labour. It is, however, a point worth making, because it was a point which was disputed by at least one social scientist at the symposium where these papers were first discussed. Given the existence of this kind of class relation in industry and in employment, it would follow in the Marxist model that other institutions would have to be so managed as to sustain the power of the entrepreneurs to treat labour in this way. It would be necessary, on the one hand, to use political means to ensure that labour never got into a position of market power which enabled it to produce conditions of total economic crisis that might end the system and, on the other, to allow as much regulation as was necessary, but no more than was necessary, to ensure that crises and contradictions within the system were ironed out as they arose. So far as the use of violence is concerned, the military and the police must at least be treated as separate from the working class in pursuit of its interests, although it might only be in conditions of crisis that these agencies would actually be invoked for the entrepreneurial class against the workers.

In fact no-one would claim that the British socio-economic order has had to be perpetually sustained in this way, and naked violence, the use of bullets and prisons, has on the whole not been seen as necessary elements in this model of British capitalism. What is far more important is the role of moral, legal, religious and educational institutions in relation to the masses. In this sphere our Marxist model would lead us to expect that judges, bishops, teachers and intellectuals would have a role to play in maintaining through their words and actions a belief in the legitimacy of the existing system of property on which the subjection of labour depends. Moreover one would expect that given the vast increase in the importance of mass communications but a whole world-view embodied in stories, news and various forms of entertainment would be created which would help to sustain the existing order of things.

Now it is not suggested that this 'pure' Marxist model ever existed in reality. But when this is said it is often forgotten that it does represent an exaggeration of an *actual* social reality. There *is* a profit motive at the heart of industry, industrial relations *are* based on collective bargaining, there *are* political parties representative of 'both sides of industry', the Conservative Party, supported by at least some industrialists, *has* in recent years sought to invoke the law against trade unions, the police and the military do *not* show signs of disaffection, and Bishops, Judges, Vice-Chancellors and media pundits *do* continually work to sustain a morality which is at least not inimical to the needs of capitalism. Moreover, finally, it can be argued that the whole system of 'Establishment' education has been used to ensure a common mind on the legitimacy of the existing order of things among those who have to occupy positions of power and decision, particularly at the highest, but also at the middle levels of power.

It is not of very great relevance here to elaborate an ideal type of a purely aristocratic ruling class operating in an industrial society. What is important is the model of a ruling class, the origins of whose power and influence lie in the possession of wealth and titles, which has to adjust to living in an industrial society. In this society continuing power and influence depend upon large scale participation in entrepreneurial activity. This means that the members of the ruling class must gain entry to the board room themselves and that they must win the support of non-ruling class entrepreneurs for the ruling class way of life. There is considerable scope in a new capitalist industrial society for the maintenance of the position of an earlier governing class, however, quite apart from entry into the board room, for those who are set on making things and making money have little time for anything else, least of all for the arts of government and moral education. It is here that the older class has something to offer. From a German perspective Max Weber noticed how much more successful the British aristocracy had been in this sphere than the Prussian Junkers, and from a French point of view Durkheim saw that in a society like his own, where the aristocracy had been destroyed and the Church deprived of its educational influence, a huge gap existed which he as a moral teacher felt called upon to fill.

It is not to be expected, however, in this model, that there will be totally smooth co-operation between those who provide the skills of government, and the new rich and men of power in industry. In the Conservative Party those who have a prime moral commitment to aristocratic values may find themselves in conflict with those whose prime commitment is to the value system of the entrepreneurs. In fact this conflict has been quite severe in recent years and has been expressed in struggles for the leadership.

So far as the use of the means of violence is concerned, this is a skill which a class whose origins lie in feudal times has deeply engrained in its culture. The culture and forms of organisation on which the police and the military depend are almost entirely its own, and the latter at least still provides one of the main careers for its sons. Equally it has lived long with the established Church and has seen the rise and fall of the non-conforming churches of the business classes; and, last but by no means least, it has retained very considerable influence over the content of the law, of legal education, and of the actual personnel of the legal profession. It is not surprising that when British generals, bishops and judges make moral and political pronouncements that they have a splendidly archaic ring. It can surely be said that the kinds of inequality and injustice which they defend are far more severe and far reaching than is necessary in a bourgeois society. Very often as one reads what they have to say one recalls that most neglected but most open and honest of the founding fathers of sociology, Joseph de Maistre.[13] From a bourgeois point of view they seem to be practising a kind of moral and ideological overkill, which is convenient, because it makes necessary bourgeois morality seem quite liberal. But in fact the true explanation may not be in terms of the functional contribution which they make to the survival of the bourgeoisie. It may be simply that they do represent the full-blooded philosophy of an archaic ruling class. One could see a case here from bourgeois as well as from a working-class point of view for a cultural revolution.

One thing which is clear is that the maintenance of the old ruling class as a sociological entity depends upon the preservation of a separate form of education where that class's values can be fostered and maintained. Not merely must the actual office-holders within the various institutions be educated and indoctrinated; so also must a wider class, who will constitute a kind of reservoir from which new supplies of suitably trained talent can flow in the future, but who serve also to give the existing 'Establishment' officers a sense of legitimacy and support. It is surely a remarkable fact that a privileged educational system such as exists in the British public schools and Oxford and Cambridge could have survived all the economic and social upheavals of the past two centuries. Indeed it is one which is probably quite insufficiently explained by the thesis that it is a convenience for the entrepreneurial class to have this kind of support. As we have said already, it is so important a factor in British life that most sociologists turn naturally to the question of type of educational background, when they are diagnosing the source of inequality. It is hard to accept that they all dwell in a world of false consciousness.

But what then of the elites problem? Does the Cambridge study really wish simply to stop at the point at which our argument has arrived? From the point of view of the present writer, one would hope not, for *within* the context we have outlined, the question of the recruitment and structure of office-holding groups, and of the efficiency which they display in the performance of their roles is an important question: given all that has been said, if all those who exercise command in crucial social and cultural areas are so recruited and educated that they share the same loyalties, the same way of life, and have with this a sense of belonging together, then their hegemony over society will be the more strongly founded.

It is not, of course, an important question to answer whether there is sufficiently open recruitment to the sorts of position which the Cambridge research discusses. This is actually a petty question. For, even if there were completely open competition for commanding positions in capitalist industry, the system would not change in its essentials and what sociologists call the role behaviour of capitalists would be no different. And, even if new men were to find their way into the Judiciary, the Army and the Church, by the time they got there, they would be trained to behave in the appropriate way and say the appropriate things. But it is important to the working of the class system that, given the existence of elite positions, those who occupy them should have a sense of eliteness bestowed on them by their education and their shared culture, and that there should be a further 'reservoir' of class members who share this culture and recognise the legitimacy of their positions.

One type of problem which comes under the heading of this chapter, but which seems to have been relatively neglected by the Cambridge Elites Project, concerns the institutional and ideological means whereby the elites relate themselves and the classes which they represent to those over whom they exercise hegemony. Three phenomena of importance here would appear to be the political labour movement, the non-elite institutions of higher education and the media. The central process here is the incorporation into or co-option of the leading figures in these spheres into the elite world. So far as the labour movement is concerned the process of co-option operates on two levels, firstly within the trade-union infrastructure of the movement and secondly, as Michels saw, amongst Parliamentary representatives. The first of these processes is in some ways the more striking, precisely because a kind of elite status is bestowed on a group of men, the vast majority of whom have not been indoctrinated into the shared elite culture. It is certainly, however, a striking fact of contemporary British social life that as a result of the establishment of joint negotiating committees and joint consultative committees, local capitalist elites and their political equivalents become used to entertaining, talking with, and seeking the co-operation and support of union officials. Naturally, therefore, some of these men are allowed to share in performing the symbolic functions which are central to the local community, especially in such offices as that of mayor. Privately, 'true' members of the local elite may mock the mayor, who, despite his morning coat and top hat contrives to look every inch a miner, a docker or a steelworker, but in terms of political reality they know that he must be reassured and cosseted. There are after all proper elite clubs to retreat into and relax after the mayoral reception with its dropped aitches is over.

The take-over of the political wing of the labour movement, however, has been a smoother process, and, when what politics is conceived to be about is the relative share of labour and capital against a background of shared assumptions about limited planning, collective bargaining, moderately full employment and the welfare state, it is perfectly possible for some of those who have been through the elite educational institutions to look to the Labour Party as the means by which they will further their parliamentary careers, and for others who emerge, either in the universities or outside, to be put through an appropriate process of socialisation. As a consequence the necessity of having second-class meeting places to deal with labour leaders disappears, for the labour leaders tend themselves to be more and more members of the club.

The result of this situation for the labour movement is that the class struggle, which for many rank and file members is the *raison d'être* of the movement tends to be replaced by an argument about different ruling class options. Thus one might note that, once Gaitskell and his intellectual mentor Anthony Crosland[14] had established that the Labour Party was no longer concerned with changing the system, but with getting fairer shares within it, Harold Wilson specifically based his campaign, not on an appeal to the working class, but to the man in the white coat as against the man from the grouse moor. The crux of Labour Parliamentary politics thus became the decision as to which of the class options within the Conservative Party it supported!

The management of non-elite education, particularly higher education, was a problem for which the ruling class and the ruling elite were ill-prepared. Clearly the crucial role of the provincial university vice-chancellor is one which was reserved basically for those with an elite education but it is probably the case that, in retrospect, if some of those who took on these roles had known what difficulties they were likely to present, they would have preferred the chairmanship of a brewery. The vice-chancellor, in fact, has a very difficult role indeed. He comes from a background in which the class assumptions of his culture are fairly well concealed and he probably hardly begins to understand them, but he has to come directly to terms with the businessmen on his foundation committee, as well as with students who have no faith in the capacity of the system to offer them rewards even in the middle ranges of power. Eventually a body of somewhat weary men apply the old trade union techniques of joint consultation and co-option with the recalcitrant students and buy off the local business men with honorary degrees and other symbolic rewards. On the whole they stumble into these decisions rather than planning them, but in the process have done yeomen service in maintaining the foundations of the system in an ideologically sensitive area. It remains to be seen whether the engineers and scientists who have been put in charge of the polytechnic part of the binary system will have the necessary background and skills even to stumble in the right direction. One may expect them to display their true technological and bourgeois virility with open days in the labs for the local population, but they may lack the necessary political sagacity to succeed in their tasks, and it may well be that in the long run the class system is not able to contain the consequences of the expansion of the system of higher education.

A more direct confrontation with the people at large confronts the media. Here a twin approach is likely. On the one hand there will be education and indoctrination of an upper stratum of the population. On the other there will be trivialisation and mass entertainment. Generally speaking the B.B.C. and the so-called quality press represent the first option and I.T.V. and the popular press the second. Until recently this also meant that the quality media were dominated and controlled by men trained in the true Oxbridge tradition and that the popular media were more open to men who worked in terms of journalistic values, i.e. who were intuitively sensitive to what the public wants and what will increase circulation. A system of controls had therefore to be worked out in the first place to check as well as to educate the popular media men. It may well be, however, that what we are now witnessing is a two-fold process of education whereby the popular media men learn to play a more civilising role, while their 'quality' colleagues learn the arts of tittivation. This may corrupt the 'Establishment' in terms of cultural standards, but it will not endanger it, for what the popular journalist stands for is not some kind of counter-culture, but essentially for journalistic values. The command positions in this area are, like those in higher education, still ill-defined, but as these new institutions are assimilated into the system and class rule becomes perfected, those who occupy them will have to be found places either in the club or at least in some ante-room such as is kept open for the union bosses. A recent move in this sphere is interesting. A vice-chancellor was appointed as chairman of the B.B.C. Board of Governors, and almost immediately criticised his studio audience for not attaining the standards normally expected in civilised discourse. Clearly he had not yet understood the specificity of his new role when he said this.[15]

We may now, finally, sum up and clarify the main points which have been made. We are saying that Britain is a country characterised by a form of class rule and that there is a good prima facie case to be made out both that the class which rules, when it comes to the crunch, is the bourgeoisie, and that there survives a more historic aristocratic class. In either case the capacity to rule must depend upon the control of significant economic power, but there is room for argument as to how much looseness of functional fit there is between one institution and another and how far some other institutions rather than economic ones might play a distinct leading role in the system. A case could be made that the elite educational institutions play this role, or have at least taken on a life of their own *within* the overall system. Our inclination, however, would be to say that they play a crucial functional role within an overall system of class rule in which an aristocratic element plays at least some part. The question of elites, however, is in the last analysis a different question from that of class-rule. It may well be the case that within the overall class system there are quite specific roles to be filled and jobs to be done. Those who fill these roles and do these jobs are bound to be brought into contact with each other and to varying degrees to share a sense of corporate solidarity. This, however, does not make them the ultimate arbiters of the society's destiny. They are not even a ruling status group in the sense that Weber's Confucian literati were. The crucial difference is that the Confucian literati had no class power to contend with. As we have pointed out, it is the surviving aristocratic class which, adapting itself to capitalism, has more of the attributes of a ruling status group. What certainly is the case is that elite members do have a tendency towards corporate identity, that they do practice techniques of selection and exclusion against potential entrants and that they share a sense of exercising, not merely power as do Mills' three elites, but authority which rests upon cultural legitimations.

What then is the purpose of elite research? Taken by itself its significance might be limited. It might appeal to the discontents of those who have not secured preferment within the Establishment but, if this discontent got out of hand and the intra-elite selection system were destroyed, there might result a moral anomie that would entail resort to a more marked and brutal form of class rule. What, however, elite research might show is how the command posts in a class-ruled society are integrated with one another and for what ends they operate at all. If this is done and if future studies concentrate not simply on recruitment and structure or on decision-making but upon 'the general framework of state and economy within which elite groups are structured and recruited', they may lead to a far more profound and undogmatic understanding of the class system of British society than we possess at present.

Notes

Preface

1 A notable exception is to be found in the case of the political elite, which has received a good deal of scholarly attention. Otherwise, the literature is sparse indeed. G. D. H. Cole's *Studies in Class Structure* (London, 1955) includes an article entitled 'Elites in British Society'; a recent relevant collection is to be found in J. Wakeford and J. Urry: *Power in British Society*, London, 1973. There are, however, numerous biographical sources, studies of the public schools, etc. which contain valuable documentation. (See note 1, chapter 1.)

2 T. B. Bottomore: *Elites and Society*. London, 1966, p. 44.

3 *The Class Structure of the Advanced Societies*. London, 1973, pp. 99–112 and *passim*.

4 P. Bachrach and M. Baraz: 'Two faces of power', *American Political Science Review*, Vol. 56, 1962.

5 Mills himself gave the following reason for adopting the notion of 'power elite' rather than 'ruling class': '"Ruling class" is a badly loaded phrase. "Class" is an economic term; "rule" a political one. The phrase "ruling class" thus contains the theory that an economic class rules politically. That short-cut theory may or may not at times be true, but we do not want to carry that one rather simple theory about in the terms that we use to define our problems; we wish to state the theories explicitly, using terms of more precise and unilateral meaning.' C. Wright Mills: *The Power Elite*. London, 1959, p. 277.

1. A. GIDDENS: Elites in the British class structure

1 The outstanding exception is W. L. Guttsman: *The British Political Elite*, MacGibbon and Kee, London, (rev. edn.), 1968. A wide range of information is contained in the various editions of Anthony Sampson's *Anatomy of Britain*. (Latest edition: *The New Anatomy of Britain*, Hodder and Stoughton, London, 1971.) Other relevant studies include Sam Aaronovitch: *Monopoly*, Lawrence and Wishart, London, 1955; and *idem*: *The Ruling Class*, Lawrence and Wishart, London, 1961; Ralph Miliband: *The State in Capitalist Society*, Weidenfeld and Nicholson, London, 1969; and Michael Barratt-Brown: 'The Controllers', *Universities and Left Review*, No. 5, 1959. Zapf notes in the Introduction to his study of the German elite that 'Die oberschichten sind weit weniger bekannt als andere soziale Gruppen...' (Wolfgang Zapf: *Wandlungen der deutschen Elite*, Fischer, Munich, 1965, p. 12.)

2 John Goldthorpe *et al.*: *The Affluent Worker* (In three vols.), Cambridge U.P., 1968–9.

3 C. A. R. Crosland: *The Future of Socialism*, Jonathan Cape, London, 1956, p. 35.

4 The original German term (*herrschende Klasse*), although conventionally translated as 'ruling class', can also be interpreted, somewhat more broadly, to mean 'dominant class'.

5 'In all societies...two classes of people appear – a class that rules and a class that is ruled. The first class, always the less numerous, performs all

political functions, monopolises power and enjoys the advantages that power brings, whereas the second, the more numerous class, is directed and controlled by the first...' (G. Mosca: *The Ruling Class*, McGraw Hill, New York, 1939, p. 50.) A useful survey of different usages of the term 'elite' is given in Hans Peter Dreitzel: *Elitebegriff und Sozialstruktur*, Ferdinand Enke, Stuttgart, 1962.

6 Cf. James R. Meisel: *The Myth of the Ruling Class*, Michigan U.P., Ann Arbor, 1962, pp. 36–7.

7 Ralf Dahrendorf: *Class and Class Conflict in Industrial Society*, Stanford U.P., Stanford, 1957, pp. 165ff.

8 Max Weber: *Economy and Society*, Bedminster Press, New York, 1968, Vol. i, pp. 302–7; Vol. ii, pp. 926–40.

9 See, however, Raymond Aron: 'Social Structure and the Ruling Class', *British Journal of Sociology*, Vol. i, 1950; and *idem*: 'Social Class, Political Class, Ruling Class', *Archives européennes de sociologie*, Vol. i, 1960. The scheme offered in the present article, however, departs from that set out by Aron.

10 Suzanne Keller: *Beyond the Ruling Class*, Random House, N.Y., 1963.

11 As C. Wright Mills says, some institutions or organisations 'shape modern life', whereas others have to 'adapt to it'. (C. Wright Mills: *The Power Elite*, Oxford U.P., London, 1959, p. 6.)

12 Dahrendorf: *op. cit.*, p. 46. 'Capitalists' here are those who found and control their own enterprises; 'heirs' are those who are born to such a position.

13 *Ibid.*, p. 46.

14 Cf. the various writings of Adolf A. Berle: *The Twentieth Century Capitalist Revolution*, Macmillan, London, 1955; *Power Without Property*, Sidgwick and Jackson, London, 1960; etc. Also W. H. Whyte: *The Organisation Man*, Simon and Schuster, New York, 1956.

15 Nichols has remarked: 'we still severely lack studies of the relationship between the manager's personal motivations and beliefs and the interests of shareholders...It follows from the absence of such empirical data...that, for the most part, *all* participants in the ownership–control controversy have been forced to rely upon *inferences* drawn from industrial and social structure'. (Theo Nichols: *Ownership, Control and Ideology*, Allen and Unwin, London, 1969, p. 62.)

16 Cf. J. Blondel: *Voters, Parties and Leaders*, Penguin, Harmondsworth, 1963.

17 H. F. Lydall and D. G. Tipping: 'The Distribution of Personal Wealth in Britain', *Bulletin of the Oxford University Institute of Statistics*, Vol. xxiii, 1961; J. E. Meade: *Efficiency, Equality and the Ownership of Property*, Allen and Unwin, London, 1964; Jack Revell: 'Changes in the Social Distribution of Property in Britain During the Twentieth Century', *Actes du Troisième Congrès International d'Histoire Economique*, Vol. i, Munich, 1965; and G. E. Routh: *Occupation and Pay in Great Britain*, Cambridge U.P., 1965.

18 See T. H. Marshall: *Citizenship and Social Class*, Cambridge U.P., 1950.

19 Karl Marx: 'The Crisis in England and the British Constitution', in Marx and Engels: *On Britain*, Moscow State Publishing House, 1953, pp. 410–11.

20 For a useful collection of contemporary documents, see W. L. Guttsman: *The English Ruling Class*, Weidenfeld and Nicholson, London, 1969.

21 Bendix has noted: 'the changes of social stratification in the course of industrialisation do not present the simple picture of a declining aristocracy and a rising bourgeoisie. In most European countries the social and political pre-eminence of pre-industrial ruling groups continued even when their economic fortunes declined, and the subordinate social and political role of the "middle classes" continued even when their economic fortunes rose' ('Tradition and Modernity Reconsidered', in *Embattled Reason, Essays on Social Knowledge*, Oxford U.P., New York, 1970, p. 302).

22 Floyd Hunter: *Community Power Structure*, Anchor Books, New York, 1963.
23 Cf. R. A. Dahl: *Who Governs?*, Yale U.P., New Haven, 1961.
24 See R. A. Dahl: 'A Critique of the Ruling Elite Model', *American Political Science Review*, Vol. LII, 1958.
25 For a classification of these positions see *The Army List.*, H.M.S.O., London, 1971.
26 For a recent analysis, see Peter Blau and Otis Dudley Duncan: *The American Occupational Structure*, John Wiley, New York, 1967.
27 That is to say, the characteristics of 'group traits', e.g. the 'moral ethics of the public school', cannot be directly inferred from observations which pertain to individuals. Two individuals who have attended the same school may have had quite divergent experiences in it and reactions to it.
28 A numerical classification appears in Guttsman: *op. cit.*, 1968, p. 328. Any such broad classification as this necessarily oversimplifies. Thus, to take just one example, in the armed forces, 'rank' is not always the same as 'post': two men who have the same rank may differ significantly in terms of the positions of authority they actually hold. The classification offered here also neglects the important 'overlapping' structures linking elite groups (such as the Defence Council, Church Commissioners, etc.). The hundred 'largest' firms identified will vary according to which of the various criteria which may be used to make such a determination are in fact employed.
29 Blau and Duncan: *op. cit.*
30 For a relevant analysis of the Cabinet, see Richard Rose: 'The Making of Cabinet Ministers', *British Journal of Political Science*, Vol. I, 1971. Rose emphasises: 'The very substantial literature about the social origins and career patterns of men in ministerial office tells the reader much more about where ministers come from than it does about what they do once they get into office' (p. 393). For another useful discussion, see J. P. Nettl: 'Consensus or Elite Domination: The Case of Business', *Political Studies*, Vol. XIII, 1965.
31 See, for example, Barratt-Brown: *op. cit.*; cf., however, the critique of this in Anthony Crosland: *The Conservative Enemy*, Allen and Unwin, London, 1962, pp. 68–96.
32 Cf. Nichols: *op. cit.*, pp. 62ff.
33 For instance, Robert A. Dahl: 'The Concept of Power', *Behavioural Science*, Vol. II, 1957; Talcott Parsons: 'On the Concept of Political Power', *Proceedings of the American Philosophical Society*, Vol. CVII, 1963; idem: 'Some Reflections on the Place of Force in the Social Process', in Harry Eckstein: *Internal War*, Free Press, Glencoe, 1964; and idem: 'On the Concept of Influence', *Public Opinion Quarterly*, Vol. XXVII, 1963; P. H. Partridge: 'Some Notes on the Concept of Power', *Political Studies*, Vol. XI, 1963; and Arnold M. Rose: *The Power Structure*, Oxford U.P., New York, 1967, pp. 1–86.
34 Weber: *op. cit.*, Vol. I, p. 53.
35 Rose: *op. cit.*, pp. 43–4.
36 Cf. Albert Salomon: 'Max Weber's Methodology', *Social Research*, Vol. I, 1934.
37 See Parsons: *op. cit.*, 1963.
38 See my 'Power in the Recent Writings of Talcott Parsons', *Sociology*, Vol. II, 1968.
39 Cf. Dahl: *op. cit.*, 1957.
40 The most comprehensive example of such an analysis is probably John Porter: *The Vertical Mosaic*, Toronto U.P., Toronto, 1966.
41 Dahl: *op. cit.*, 1958.
42 David Lockwood: Comment on P. M. Worsley's 'The Distribution of Power in Industrial Society', *Sociological Review Monograph*, No. 8, 1964,

p. 35. On this point see also P. Bachrach and M. Baratz: 'Two Faces of Power', *American Political Science Review*, Vol. LVI, 1962.

43 It should also be pointed out that the reaching of a policy decision is not the same as its *implementation*; power may also be manifest in the capacity to resist or prevent the actualisation of a policy which has been formally agreed to.

44 Cf. Arnold Rose: *op. cit.*, pp. 89–127.

45 Crossman argues that what Bagehot called 'the efficient secret of the English constitution' – the dominant role of the Cabinet in Parliament – has itself now become a 'respectable legend'; power no longer resides primarily in the Cabinet, but in 'the secret links that connect the Cabinet with the party on the one side and with the civil service on the other... As Parliament has been reduced to a new and more submissive role by the modern party machine, so the powers of the Cabinet have been eroded by the growing ascendancy of Whitehall'. Richard Crossman, Introduction to Walter Bagehot: *The English Constitution*, C. A. Watts, London, 1964, pp. 38–9, and 47.

46 It should be stressed that this article does not claim to deal in any direct sense with the overall problem of the changing nature of so-called 'post-capitalist' society. *None* of the categories of elite formation and power structure developed in this paper prejudice the existence of 'capitalism'. However, it is one of the failures of most past discussions (both Marxist and non-Marxist) of the 'ruling class', to have assumed too close a connection between what I call the *institutional mediation of power* (the general form of state and economy) on the one hand, and the *mediation of control* (types of elite formation and decision-making processes) on the other.

2. W. L. GUTTSMAN: The British political elite and the class structure

1 Introduction to D. Brunton and D. H. Pennington, *Members of the Long Parliament*, 1954, p. xi.

2 For English 'local government', i.e. the rule of the Justices of the Peace, see F. W. Maitland, 'The Shallows and Silences of Real Life', (1888) in his *Collected Papers*, I, pp. 468–77.

3 The size of the House of Commons has been as follows: eighteenth century: 558; after 1801: 658; 1885: 670; 1918: 707; 1920: 615; 1945: 640; 1970: 630.

4 Generally too little attention has been paid to the geographical distribution of the electorate as distinct from the qualification attached to the franchise, but until the introduction of a comparatively wide franchise combined with comparatively equal electoral districts the composition of the House of Commons was not a little affected by this. Thus the First Reform Act still left political power largely in the hands of the electors in the small boroughs (or their *de facto* patrons) whose population, numbering less than 2.5 millions, returned 293 of the 658 members of the House of Commons. The Second Reform Act redistributed in favour of the large towns but still left the counties under-represented.

5 L. B. Namier, *The structure of politics at the Accession of George III*, 1957, p. 1. Namier based this assertion on a study of the Newcastle papers, the largest extant collection of papers relating to electoral matters in the eighteenth century.

6 *Ibid.*, p. 29.

7 In *The British Political Elite*, 1963, I tried to quantify such movements between elite groups and illustrate it as a series of diagrams. These, however, were only in the nature of approximations and they also lacked in sophistication because they did not distinguish between those affiliations which were anteceding, contemporaneous or consequential on political office.

8 On career patterns leading into the Cabinet see F. M. G. Wilson, 'Entry into Cabinets, 1959–1968', *Political Studies*, 1970. Wilson appointed only two outsiders into Cabinet Office – one to the Lord Chancellorship, a common move – and Heath only one. Of the Conservative Cabinet Ministers of the Eden–Macmillian–Home era only six left politics for high positions outside politics, and of Mr Wilson's ministers only two did so.

9 Cf. Namier, *op. cit.*, pp. 142–50. The extent of patronage increased rather than declined for some time, partly due to the inclusion of Ireland. Oldfield, at the beginning of the nineteenth century, connected 300 seats with 144 Peers as patrons and 123 Commoners with 187 seats.

10 Cf. J. G. P. Judd, *Members of Parliament, 1734–1832*, 1955, pp. 30–5.

11 Calculated from J. Bateman, *The great landowners of Great Britain*, 4th ed., 1883; see also H. J. Hanham, *Elections and party management*, 1955, p. xv.

12 *Op. cit.*, p. 31. Allowance must, of course, be made for those who entered Parliament as sons of Peers, many of whom will have succeeded to a Peerage, as well as an unstated number of heirs to Baronetcies or Peerages.

13 There are no adequate statistics about the fluctuations of Membership of the House of Commons, let alone detailed data about the *cursus honorum* to permit more than approximations. For some relevant statistics for the period 1885–1905 and 1950–66, see respectively J. P. Cornford, 'The Parliamentary foundations of the Hotel Cecil' in R. Robson, (ed.) *Ideas and institutions of the Victorians*, 1967, and M. Rush, *The selection of Parliamentary Candidates*, 1969.

14 But see, for the period post 1900, G. Routh, *Occupation and pay in Great Britain, 1906–1960*, 1965.

15 C. Hill, 'The English Revolution' in Hill (ed.), *The English Revolution of 1640*, 1940, pp. 29–30 and 25–6.

16 Brunton and Pennington, *Members of the Long Parliament*, p. 179. But S. D. Antler in a re-analysis of M. F. Keeler's *The Long Parliament, 1640–1641* (1954) has produced some evidence that Parliamentarians counted among their ranks a much larger percentage of the economically upwards mobile than Royalists and the reverse trend is apparent in respect of downwards mobility. Cf. his *Communication* in *Past and Present*, 56, August, 1972.

17 For a successful use of this see J. P. Cornford, *loc. cit.*

18 As late as 1914 we find 53 Conservative M.P.s (of 289) whose fathers had also been in Parliament. Cf. J. M. MacEwan, 'The General Election of 1918', *Journal of Modern History*, 1962, p. 294.

19 *The House of Commons, 1832–1901; a study of its economic and functional character*, 1939.

20 Cf. David Spring, *The Landed Estate in the Nineteenth Century*, 1963 and F. M. L. Thompson, *Landed society in the Nineteenth Century*, 1963.

21 Cf. John Vincent, *The formation of the Liberal Party*, 1969.

22 Cf. Cornford, *loc. cit.*

23 Cf. MacEwan, *loc. cit.*

24 The comparable figure for the increase of the electorate for 1832 was 49 % and for 1884 67 %.

25 Hansard, 3rd series, 188, 1532.

26 Cf. R. Alford, *Party and Society*, 1963.

27 Data about the family background of M.P.s are, of course, notably deficient and we are usually forced to infer from occupational data.

28 Trade Union M.P.s who until recently were almost exclusively recruited from the group of workers and officials in individual industries belong in this group because of their original affiliation.

29 Conservative M.P.s still include owners of sizeable holdings of agricultural land. The acreage, according to A. Roth, *Business background of M.P.s* (1972) was 642,430 in 1962 and 372,161 in 1972. (Quoted with permission from R. W. Johnson's 'The British Political Elite, 1955–1972', *European Journal of Sociology*, Summer 1973.)

30 F. M. G. Wilson, *loc. cit.*
31 Cf. Agatha Ramm (ed.), *The political correspondence of Gladstone and Granville*, 2 vols, 1952.
32 Cf. J. P. Cornford, 'The transformation of Conservatism in the late 19th century', *Victorian Studies*, 1963.
33 For the not insignificant amount of electoral corruption and 'influence' which remained even after 1868 see Hanham, *op. cit.*
34 J. Vincent, *The formation of the Liberal Party*, 1966, p. 88.
35 *Ibid.*, p. 95.
36 Cf. G. M. Rush, *The selection of parliamentary candidates*, 1969. The fact that those who proceed from contesting non-incumbent seats to the contest of incumbent ones are more 'middle class' in character than those who do not seems proof that we are concerned with a process of social selection. (*Ibid.*, p. 59.)
37 It must, however, be borne in mind that we have no data about the character of the applicants for different types of seats.
38 Rush (*op. cit.*) found that of the union sponsored candidates only 28.6 % had received elementary education only. 3.6 % had been to public schools and 13.2 % were graduates.
39 Cf. Johnson, *loc. cit.*
40 Cf. Z. Bauman, *Between class and elite* (1973), p. 321.
41 The latter development is not purely restricted to Britain; it can be observed in the evolution of the political leadership of, e.g., socialist parties throughout Western Europe. For a comparison of developments in Britain and Germany see the author's paper, 'Elite recruitment and political leadership in Britain and Germany since 1950' in Ivor Crewe (ed.), *British Political Sociology Yearbook*, Vol. I (1974).
42 Cf. S. F. Nadel, 'The concept of social elites', *International Social Science Bulletin*, Vol. VIII, p. 418.
43 Of a sample of 100 peerage families in which the title had descended un-interruptedly between 1800 and 1900 the title holders in 31 families had never been politically active while in the case of 34 families *two-thirds* or more of the peers had been politically active. Cf. *The British political elite*, p. 162.
44 On this see the report of the *Committee on 'Top Salaries'* under the Chairmanship of Sir Edward Boyle which gives the findings of a public opinion survey on M.P.s salaries. (Cmnd. 5002, 1972.)
45 L. Stone, 'Social mobility in England, 1500–1700', *Past and Present*, no. 33, p. 54.
46 Namier, *op. cit.*, p. 150. It seems plausible to argue that in a period when conduct was less defined in moral terms than in the Victorian era the parvenu was more readily accepted and assimilated.
47 L. B. Namier, *The structure of politics at the Accession of George III*, p. 134. In the terms of Namier's concept of politics, elections and party political rhetoric are a mere ritual obscuring the original and primary purpose of politics – the acquisition of seats. 'The Tibetans are not the only people to employ praying wheels...'.
48 But for a somewhat different interpretation see D. C. Moore, 'The sociological premises of the First Reform Act', *Historical Journal*, 1966, pp. 39–59.
49 Cf. John Vincent, *op. cit.* and also his *Pollbooks*, 1967. D. C. Moore, *loc. cit.*, and also his 'Social structure, political structure and public opinion in mid-Victorian England in R. Robson (ed.), *op. cit.* and also, tangentially, J. P. Cornford's essay in the same volume (see above, note 13) and his 'Transformation of Conservatism'. (See note 32 above.)
50 Cf. D. C. Moore, 'Social structure', p. 47.
51 J. B. Vincent, 'The electoral sociology of Rochdale', *Economic History Review*, 1963, p. 90.

52 Birch, *op. cit.*, p. 51.
53 Cf. Vincent, *Pollbooks*, p. 28.
54 On the grass-roots politics of the period between the two Reform Acts see T. J. Nossiter's 'Aspects of electoral behaviour in English Constituencies, 1832–68' in E. Allardt and S. Rokkan (eds.), *Mass Parties*, 1970.
55 Cornford, *loc. cit.*, note 32, p. 45.
56 Of the newly elected Conservative M.P.s, the non-Public School element accounted for over 60 %.
57 64% of the Conservative M.P.s elected for the first time in 1950 had been educated in Public Schools.
58 Quoted by G. D. H. Cole in *British working class politics*, 1941, p. 72. (Fifteen candidates entered the field of whom only two were successful thanks to the absence of Liberal opposition.)
59 Quoted in H. Clegg and A. Fox, *History of the T.U.C.*, i, p. 52.
60 Henry Pelling (*Social geography of British elections, 1885–1910*) has suggested that some of the most homogeneous working class constituencies remained long in Liberal and in some cases (e.g. West Midlands, Sheffield) Conservative hands.
61 R. Rose uses the comparatively large number of Grammar School products among contemporary Labour M.P.s as evidence of such a process ('Class and Party', *Sociology*, Vol. II, 1968, pp. 129–62 at p. 155).
62 Cf. *The Affluent Worker: Political attitudes and Behaviour*, 1969, pp. 73–82.

3. C. J. HEWITT: Elites and the distribution of power in British society

1 Hans Evers: *Case Studies in Social Power*, E. J. Brill, Leiden, 1969, p. 129.
2 Also excluded from consideration in this paper is the effect of the exercise of organizational power upon *non-members*, such as the effect of business upon consumers or community residents involved in marketing policies or plant relocation policies. The 'cultural hegemony' argument in which elites are seen as creating or reinforcing social values is also ignored.
3 Gerhard Lenski: *Power and Privilege*, McGraw Hill, New York, 1966, p. 325.
4 Norman Crockett: *The Power Elite in America*, D. C. Heath, Lexington, 1970, p. vii.
5 Floyd Hunter: *Top Leadership USA*, University of N. Carolina Press, 1959, p. 7.
6 C. Wright Mills: *The Power Elite*, Oxford University Press, New York, 1956, p. 18.
7 William Domhoff: *The Higher Circles*, Random House, New York, 1970, pp. 105–6, 157.
8 Sam Aaronovitch: *The Ruling Class*, Lawrence and Wishart, London, 1961, pp. 134, 160–1.
9 Ralph Miliband: *The State in Capitalist Society*, Weidenfeld and Nicolson, London, 1969, pp. 22, 55.
10 Domhoff: *op. cit.*, pp. 107–8; Miliband, *op. cit.*, p. 3.
11 Robert Dahl: *Social Science Research on Business*, Columbia University Press, New York, 1959, p. 36.
12 Aaronovitch: *op. cit.*, p. 146.
13 Anthony Crosland: *The Future of Socialism*, Jonathan Cape, London, 1961.
14 John Strachey: *Contemporary Capitalism*, Gollancz, London, 1956, pp. 260–1. For Strachey at least this involved a rather striking conversion from his pre-war position in *The Coming Struggle for Power*, Modern Library Press, New York, 1935.
15 John Galbraith: *American Capitalism*, Hamilton, London, 1952, pp. 178–9.
16 Suzanne Keller: *Beyond the Ruling Class*, Random House, New York, 1963.

17 Arnold Rose: *The Power Structure*, Oxford University Press, New York, 1967, p. 3.
18 David Riesman: *The Lonely Crowd*, Yale University Press, New Haven, 1950, pp. 177, 252.
19 My evidence for this thesis is primarily based upon the quotations previously cited and similar passages in the rest of their work. Miliband, however, seems to cast this argument in a negative form relying more upon the *lack* of genuinely anti-capitalist policies or upon what he thinks would be the response to militant socialist demands.
20 Thus Aaronovitch attacks Mills elitist conception *op. cit.*, p. 73 and Domhoff considers that the military are not part of the ruling elite *op. cit.*, p. 138. Mills' argument is that ' "Ruling Class" is a badly loaded phrase. "Class" is an economic term; "rule" a political one.' However, he sees the elite as part of an interacting social group, *op. cit.*, pp. 11, 13, 15, and most 'class' theorists define the activities of particular elites as an indicator of upper class organization.
21 Miliband, *op. cit.*, p. 48. Also Aaronovitch: *op. cit.*, pp. 146–7.
22 For a full discussion of these methodologies see Rose: *op. cit.*, pp. 255–80.
23 The reputational method involves asking a panel of 'knowledgeables' to list the powerful individuals. The only national study using this method was Hunter: *op. cit.* For a criticism of this see Rose: *op. cit.*, pp. 10–15.
24 Mills does cite five decisions to illustrate his thesis, but Daniel Bell: *The End of Ideology*, Collier, New York, 1960, criticizes his account of these as inaccurate. Domhoff: *op. cit.*, pp. 174, also lists various issues in which business organizations were involved, and Aaronovitch uses two issues to support his position.
25 On the problems and disadvantages of the issue method see Rose: *op. cit.*, pp. 277–8, Domhoff: *Who Rules America?*, *op. cit.*, pp. 6–7, 144–6.
26 For a fuller description of the panel method, data sources and other methodological questions see the author's 'Policymaking in postwar Britain', *British Journal of Political Science*, April, 1974. The distribution of issues between Labour and Conservative regimes is somewhat arbitrary given that issues overlapped sometimes between regimes, particularly in social policy. These were some of the main sources: James Christoph: *Capital Punishment and British Politics*, Allen and Unwin, London, 1962. H. H. Wilson: *Pressure Group*, Secker and Warburg, London, 1961. David Steel: *No Entry*, Gollancz, London, 1969. Harry Eckstein: *The English Health Service*, Harvard University Press, 1958. Janet Beveridge: *Beveridge and his plan*, Hodder and Stoughton, London, 1954. H. C. Dent: *The Education Act*, Routledge and Kegan Paul, London, 1944. Michael Parkinson: *The Labour Party and Secondary Education*, Routledge, London, 1970. Andreas Kazamias: *Politics, Society and Secondary Education in England*, University of Pennsylvania Press, Philadelphia, 1966. Malcolm Barnett: *The Politics of Legislation*, Weidenfeld and Nicolson, London, 1969. George Ross: *The Nationalization of Steel*, MacGibbon and Kee, London, 1965. Lord Windlesham: *Communication and Political Power*, Cape, London, 1966. Keith Waltz: *Foreign Policy and Democratic Politics*, Little-Brown, Boston, 1967. Ronald Butt: *The Power of Parliament*, Constable, London, 1967. Leon Epstein: *British Politics in the Suez Crisis*, Pall Mall, London, 1964. Laurence Martin: 'The Market for Strategic Ideas in Britain: The Sandys Era', *American Political Science Review*, 1962, pp. 23–41. William Snyder: *The Politics of British Defense Policy, 1945–62*, Ohio State University Press, 1964. Robert Lieber: *British Politics and European Unity*, University of California Press, 1970. A. W. Ford: *The Anglo-Iranian Oil Dispute*, University of California Press, Los Angeles, 1954. David Goldsworthy: *Colonial Issues in British Politics*, Clarendon Press, Oxford, 1971.
27 The low degree of continuity overall does not mean that particular pairs of

issues may not have a large number of organizations in common. Eleven common organizations were involved in the Motorways and Road Haulage issues, and there were significant overlaps between the two educational policy issues, and the two issues concerned with housing and property development.

28 Slightly less than a third of the involvements by promotional organizations were by left-of-centre groups.

29 William Kornhauser: *The Politics of Mass Society*, Free Press, Glencoe (Illinois), 1959.

30 In order the sources are: Epstein: *op. cit.*, pp. 141–5, Richard Rose: *Influencing Voters*, Faber, London, 1967, p. 184. *Gallup Political Index* (October 1962, April 1963, July 1964, August 1964). *Gallup Political Index* (January 1964, February 1964, March 1964, June 1964). Windlesham: *op. cit.*, p. 158. Eckstein: *op. cit.*, p. 144. Barnett: *op. cit.*, p. 116. Christoph: *op. cit.*, p. 117. Burton Paulu: *British Broadcasting*, University of Minnesota Press, 1956, pp. 375–80. Charles Hanser: *Guide to Decision*, Bedminster Press, Totowa, 1965, p. 103. *Gallup Political Index* (November 1961, December 1961).

31 Hadley Cantril: *Public Opinion 1935–46*, Princeton University Press, p. 187.

32 *Ibid.*, p. 327.

33 *Ibid.*, p. 399.

34 Beveridge: *op. cit.*

35 Cantril: *op. cit.*, p. 362.

36 John Sanderson: 'The National Smoke Abatement Society and the Clean Air Act', *Political Studies*, July 1961.

37 *Gallup Political Index* (January 1960, February 1960, June 1960).

38 See Parkinson: *op. cit.*, p. 81. Snyder: *op. cit.*, pp. 52–62. Cantril: *op. cit.*, p. 276. Tom Harrison: 'British Opinion moves toward a New Synthesis', *Public Opinion Quarterly*, 1947–8, pp. 327–41. No data could be found on the Central African Federation, Road Haulage, American Loan or Abadan Issues.

39 Cf. Nora Beloff: *The General says No*, Penguin, Harmsworth, 1963.

40 Peter Bachrach and Morton Baratz: 'Two Faces of Power', *American Political Review*, 1962, pp. 947–52.

41 See Mathew Crenson: *The unpolitics of pollution*, Johns Hopkins University Press, Baltimore, 1971, for one attempt to study non-decision making.

42 William Domhoff: *Who Rules America?*, Prentice Hall, Englewood, 1967, p. 144.

43 Samuel Finer: 'The Political Power of Private Capital', *Sociological Review*, 1955, pp. 279–94, 1956, 5–30.

44 Anthony Sampson: *The New Anatomy of Britain*, Hodder and Stoughton, London, 1971, pp. 117–18.

45 Finer: *op. cit.* p. 15.

46 W. Guttsman: *The British Political Elite*, MacGibbon and Kee, London, 1963. See also Domhoff: *op. cit.*, and Andrew Roth: *The M.P.s Chart*, Parliamentary Profile Services Ltd., 1965.

47 'A Governing class is a social upper class which...contributes a disproportionate number of its members to the controlling institutions and key decision-making groups of the country'; Domhoff: *Who Rules America?*, *op. cit.*, p. 5.
   'There exists today in Britain a ruling class if we mean by it a group which provides the majority of those who occupy positions of power and who, in their turn, can materially assist their sons to reach similar positions'. Guttsman: *op. cit.*, p. 356. Guttsman is talking about political and non-political elites.

48 Domhoff: *op. cit.*, pp. 143–4. Guttsman specifically denies that 'a socially broadly based representation is either a symptom or a precondition of an

effective democratic system', *op. cit.*, p. 373, but seems to believe that in practice upper class occupants of political positions cannot or will not adequately represent the interests and desires of other groups. 'This distance (i.e. the social gap between M.P.s and electors) will in turn affect the quality of the dialogue between the ordinary men and their elected representatives and act as a barrier to democracy'. He thinks that the membership of advisory bodies 'should be much more broadly based and that those who sit around the polished horseshoe tables should be *genuinely* representative of thought and feelings of wide sections of the population'.

49 Glennerster in his essay on 'Democracy and Class' cites figures on the declining proportion of 'working class' M.P.s in the Parliamentary Labour Party, after a discussion in which he has been comparing the political attitudes of the 'Working Class' with the 'Middle Class' of whom he says that 'the characteristic which most clearly distinguishes the middle class from the rest is the presumption that they will be listened to by those in authority. This is partly because of their education, partly wealth, *having one's own solicitor to fall back on*' Brian Lapping: *More Power to the People*, Longman, London, 1968. Clearly there is a large proportion of non-manual individuals without their 'own solicitor' who disappear without trace in this ambiguous taxonomy of social class.

50 Frank Parkin: *Middle Class Radicalism*, Manchester University Press, Manchester, 1968, pp. 178–80. There is evidence that M.P.s from this background do hold much more 'liberal' opinions than the rest of the middle class, and in fact are even more progressive than working class M.P.s. Finer shows that Labour M.P.s from 'miscellaneous occupations' (which includes journalists, welfare workers, local government officers and lecturers) are generally the most leftist in the Early Day motions they sign. *Backbench Opinion in the House of Commons*, Pergamon, New York, 1961, pp. 27, 28, 40, 74.

51 Categories include the following occupations: Bourgeois (Company directors, company executives, 'private means'), Petit Bourgeois (small business, middle and lower managerial and clerical), 'Commercial' professions (Barristers, solicitors, civil engineers, accountants, doctors and architects), 'Service' professions (civil servants, teachers, ministers of religion, journalists, etc.).

This follows Parkin basically except that architects and doctors are counted as commercial professions (not out of any desire to deny their creativity or desire to serve the community, but because they are highly paid and work for fees, or profit making organisations, and hence might be expected to have 'capitalist' attitudes, as in fact their professional associations generally appear to do).

A handful of miscellaneous occupations, and third party M.P.s have not been included in the table. These account for about 30 M.P.s in each parliament.

The Sources are David Butler: *The British General Election of 1951*, Macmillan, London, 1952, *The British General Election of 1955*, Macmillan, London, 1955, *The British General Election of 1959*, Macmillan, London, 1960.

4. R. WHITLEY: The City and Industry: the directors of large companies, their characteristics and connections

1 See T. B. Bottomore, *Elites and Society*, Watts, London, 1964.
G. Parry, *Political Elites*, Allen and Unwin, London, 1969, pp. 31–3.

2 W. G. Domhoff, *Who Rules America?*, Prentice Hall, Englewood Cliffs, N.J., 1967. W. G. Domhoff, *The Higher Circles*, Random House, New York, 1970.

3 T. Lupton and C. S. Wilson, 'The social background and connections of
  top decision makers', *Manchester School*, Vol. XXVII, pp. 30–51.
4 M. Barratt Brown, 'The controllers of British industry', in K. Coates (ed.),
  Can the workers run industry?, Sphere, London, 1968.
5 R. Whitley, 'Commonalities and connections among directors of large
  financial institutions', *Sociological Review*, Vol. XXI, Nov. 1973, pp. 613–32.
6 See Theo Nichols, *Ownership, Control and Ideology*, Allen and Unwin,
  London, 1968. R. E. Pahl and J. T. Winkler, 'The economic elite',
  chapter 6 in this volume.
7 Brown: *op. cit.*
8 These were: *Who's Who 1971, Who's Who in Finance 1972, International
  Businessman's Who's Who 1970, Burke's Peerage 1970, Burke's Landed
  Gentry 1965, 1969, 1972, The Business Who's Who 1972.*
9 P. Doreian, *Mathematics and the study of social relations*, Weidenfeld and
  Nicholson, London, 1970.
10 P. Bonacich, 'Technique for analysing overlapping membership', in
   L. H. Costner (ed.) *Sociological Methodology 1972*, Jossey-Bass, San
   Francisco, 1972.
11 This index refers to the minimal number of connections necessary to link
   any two members of the network. This minimal number is then summed
   over all possible pairs to give the total sum of minimal distances in the
   network. To normalise this sum two further sums are required, the
   maximum possible sum of minimal distances for a symmetrical network of
   the given size and the minimum possible sum of minimal distances for such
   a network. The former is arrived at by calculating the sum of minimal
   distances for network with the same number of elements but in the form of
   a chain and the latter similarly calculated assuming every point is directly
   connected to all other points. The integration score is then arrived at by
   subtracting the actual sum from the maximum possible sum and dividing
   that by the difference between the maximum possible and the minimum
   possible sums. This index ranges from 0 to 1 and can be used for comparing
   the degree of structure in networks of different size.
     An example may help to clarify this measure. If a six element network
   was connected as:

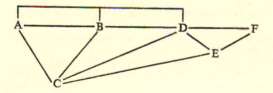

then the sums of minimal distances from

A
B
C   to the other five elements would be
D
E
F

$1+1+1+2+2 = 7$ and for
$1+1+1+2+2 = 7$ and for
$1+1+1+1+2 = 6$ and for
$1+1+1+1+1 = 5$ and for
$1+1+1+2+2 = 7$ and for
$1+1+2+2+2 = 8$

and so the total sum of minimal distances would be: 40

If the six elements were arranged so as to maximise this sum of minimal
distances the network would resemble a chain: A–B–C–D–E–F and so the
minimal distance for

$$
\left.\begin{array}{c} A \\ B \\ C \\ D \\ E \\ F \end{array}\right\} \text{ would be } \left\{\begin{array}{l} 1+2+3+4+5 = 15 \\ 1+1+2+3+4 = 11 \\ 1+1+2+2+3 = 9 \\ 1+1+2+2+3 = 9 \\ 1+1+2+3+4 = 11 \\ 1+2+3+4+5 = 15 \end{array}\right. \text{ and for}
$$

and so the total maximum sum
of minimal distances for a
6 element network is: 70

The minimum sum of minimal distances occurs when every element is connected to every other and so all minimal distances are 1.
Thus that total $= 6 \times 5 = 30$.

Therefore the Integration Score $= \dfrac{\text{Max } \Sigma \text{ Min Distances} - \text{Actual } \Sigma \text{ Min Distances}}{\text{Max } \Sigma \text{ Min Distances} - \text{Min } \Sigma \text{ Min Distances}}$

$= 70 - 40/70 - 30$
$= 30/40$
$= 0.75$ for this particular network.

The main disadvantage of this indicator is that it does not take into account the number of elements in the network as a proportion of those which could be connected. In other words it could indicate a very high degree of integration for a small number of elements but would not take into account the elements not included but which are in the total system. It also ignores other networks which are part of the system but not connected to the one being measured. To partially overcome these difficulties the proportion of firms in the network will be given and where there is more than one network this will be made clear.

12 R. Heller, 'Britain's boardroom anatomy', *Management Today*, May 1973, pp. 81–3.
13 C. Graves, *Leather Armchairs: the Chivas Regal book of London clubs*, Cassell, London, 1963.
14 A. Lejeune, 'Can the clubs survive?', *Daily Telegraph Magazine*, 18 July 1969.
15 R. Matthews, 'The quiet crisis in Clubland', *Financial Times*, 23 February, 1971.
16 A. Sampson, *The New Anatomy of Britain*, Hodder and Stoughton, London, 1971.
17 R. Speigelberg, *The City: power without accountability*, Blond and Briggs, London, 1973, pp. 33–90.
18 Cf. J. Moyle, *The pattern of ordinary share ownership, 1957–1971*, Cambridge University Press, 1971. R. Stone, J. Revell and J. Moyle, *The owners of ordinary quoted shares*, Chapman and Hall, London, 1966.
19 J. W. M. Crawford, *Directory of City Connections*, Crawford Publications, London, 1973.
20 Speigelberg: *op. cit.*, cf. the role of Hambros in the S.I.H.–Vlasov merger, November 1973.
21 Brown: *op. cit.*
22 Cf. H. Radice, 'Control type, profitability and growth in large firms: an empirical study', *Economic Journal*, Vol. LXXXI, 1973, pp. 547–62.

5. P. STANWORTH and A. GIDDENS: An economic elite: a demographic profile of company chairmen

* This paper was prepared in conjunction with a research project in the Department of Applied Economics, Cambridge, financed by the Social Science Research Council.

1 Some relevant studies of directors include G. H. Copeman, *Leaders of British Industry*, London, 1955. D. G. Clark, *The Industrial Manager: His background and career pattern*, London, 1966. R. Heller, 'Britain's Top Directors', *Management Today*, March 1967.

2 The list of companies was compiled from various sources. For a list of the 50 largest companies in Britain in 1905 see P. L. Payne, 'The Emergence of Large Scale Companies in Britain 1870–1914', *Econ. Hist. Review*, Vol. xx, 1967. The list for 1926 was concocted from the Stock Exchange Yearbook by selecting the 50 companies with the largest net assets. The top 50 for 1948 and 53 were gleaned from *Company Income and Finance 1949–53* National Institute of Economic and Social Research, London, 1956. The top 50 for 1966 and 1971 were obtained from the appropriate editions of *The Times '500'* and *The Times '1000'*.

3 The names of chairmen were included only if the company in question was, in the case of miscellaneous manufacturers, retail, breweries, shipping, iron and steel and oil, among the largest 50. Thus when a company 'declined' (that is dropped out of the top 50), was taken over, or nationalised, the names of the chairmen were no longer included. In the case of clearing banks we again selected the largest at particular points in the century, the list being dominated since the twenties by the 'Big Five' (Westminster, Midland, National Provincial, Lloyds, and Barclays), now, of course, the 'Big Four'. The merchant banks were selected by taking the 17 members of the Accepting Houses Committee in January 1971 and including any major merchant bank that any one of them had taken over or merged with in the past. There has, of course, been a dramatic change in industrial concentration (for present purposes the proportion of total industrial assets controlled by the largest companies) during the course of the present century. Between 1885 and 1939 there was a gradual increase in industrial concentration, but this was reversed during the Second World War and the Draconian peace that followed. Since 1954 there has been a strong trend toward increasing concentration such that a relatively small number of companies account for the majority of assets in the private sector. In 1957 the top 80 companies by asset size accounted for 53 % of the total net assets of industrial assets, and the top 320 79 %. By 1967 the figures for the top 80 and top 320 were 62 % and 87 % respectively. The major factor in the growth of top companies appears to have been merger and takeover activity rather than internally generated growth. Clearly the chairmen of top companies in the 1970s preside over enterprises which have far greater significance and power in the economy than was the case of the top 50 in the earlier part of the century. For an interesting discussion of the issues related to industrial concentration, see M. A. Utton, *Industrial Concentration*, London, 1970. For a discussion of the changes in the composition of the Top 100 since 1948 see G. Whittington, 'Changes in the composition of the top 100 companies 1948–1968', *Journal of Industrial Economics, 1973*.

4 Principal sources used were: *Who's Who* and *Who Was Who; Who's Who in Finance; Dictionary of National Biography; Times* obituaries; *Leviathan Who's Who in Business; Directory of Directors; Burke's Peerage* and *Burke's Landed Gentry*.

5 R. V. Clements: *Managers, a Study of Their Careers in Industry*, 1958.

6 Results differ to some degree, of course, between different studies. For a brief conspectus, see Theo Nichols: *Ownership, Control and Ideology*, London, 1969. For an analysis of the social characteristics of the directors of the 'Top 100' industrial companies in 1966 see R. Heller, *op. cit.*

7 See R. Heller, *op. cit.*

8 We used a general classification as follows: 'working class' = manual labour; 'middle class' = white-collar administrative or professional workers; 'small businessmen' = small farmers, shopowners, self-employed

workers; 'upper class' = industrialists, land-owners, others who possess substantial property or wealth. The fairly high number of 'unknowns' reflect difficulties of categorisation on the basis of rather thin information. In a few instances, we have treated as 'upper class' those individuals who attended one of the nine Clarendon schools if the direct evidence on their social origins is inadequate; those who attended any other public school, where we have no direct information upon father's occupation, we have placed as 'middle class'.

9 Peter M. Blau and O. D. Duncan: *The American Occupational Structure.*

10 The remainder, as in the other instances quoted immediately following, are 'unknowns'.

11 These figures have to be treated with caution as an index of social recognition, since they do not include hereditary titles which are more commonly represented in certain sectors than in others.

12 This includes subsidiary firms as well as independent directorships.

13 For the continuing, and remarkable representation of Etonians in the City see Richard Whitley: 'The City and Industry: the directors of large companies, their characteristics and connections', chapter 5 in this volume.

14 This decline in the number of chairmen who were M.P.s does not mean that M.P.s as a whole have backed out of business involvement. As R. A. Johnson and Andrew Roth have demonstrated, recent Parliaments contain high proportions of M.P.s with business connections in the form of directorships or positions as consultants. It seems that as the stratification of industry has heightened with increasing industrial concentration, the Chairmen of large companies have devoted themselves almost entirely to an industrial career. R. W. Johnson, 'The British Political Elite 1955–72', in *E.J.S.* Spring 1973. Andrew Roth, *The Business Backgrounds of M.P.s 1972.*

15 For a study of family influence in the brewing industry see H. Beesley, 'The Family Ownership of Brewing Firms', unpublished Ph.D. thesis, University of Birmingham, 1952.

16 The number of brewers and distillers in the top 50 companies in 1905 was a remarkable 17. The figure for 1971 was 3.

17 These percentages are expressed as a proportion of the whole sample of the generation in question; however if these figures are expressed as a proportion of those on whom this particular information was successfully obtained then the figures are much higher.

Iron and Steel Leaders with upper class social origins (%)

	II	III	IV	V	VI
% of total sample	50	63	67	46	44
% of those on whom information obtained	100	83	89	86	80

18 See C. Erickson, *British Industrialists: Steel and Hosiery 1850–1950*, Cambridge, 1959. There is, in fact, another group of professionals of whom mention should be made. There were a number of engineering apprentices mainly in generations II, III and IV who have upper class and public school backgrounds. However, in a highly complex technological industry there are surprisingly few technical experts at the top, and they are always outnumbered by other professionals (barrister and accountant) or administrators with no technical or scientific qualifications.

19 For relevant discussions, see D. H. Aldcroft: 'The entrepreneur and the British economy, 1870–1914', *Economic History Review*, Vol. XVII, 1964; Donald N. McCloskey and Lars G. Sandberg: 'From damnation to

redemption: judgements on the late Victorian entrepreneur', *Explorations in Economic History*, Vol. IX, 1971. Roy Lewis and Rosemary Stewart, *The Boss*, London, 1958.

20 D. C. Coleman: 'Gentlemen and players', *Economic History Review*, Vol. XXVI, 1973.

21 *Ibid.*, p. 103.

22 One area in which a number of 'new' men have been prominent is that of property development. See O. Marriot, *The Property Boom*, London, 1969.

6. R. E. PAHL and J. T. WINKLER: **The economic elite: theory and practice**

1 Initially, we considered a scientifically correct sampling of companies. However, we anticipated that the intimate and unusual nature of the research we would be proposing would yield a very high rate of refusals in ordinary, unsponsored approaches, wasting effort and invalidating the very rigour the formal procedure would be designed to achieve. This anticipation proved correct. Even with personal introductions, we were refused access by about 85 % of the more than 130 companies we approached. By the end, however, we did manage to fill the boxes of the quota sample we adopted as a substitute. But one systematic bias in the sample emerged. Although some of the companies had had difficult recent histories and one subsequently went into receivership through failure to keep control of a very large project, all the firms were, at the time we studied them, very successful in terms of traditional business criteria, profitability and growth. The picture presented here may be that of successful company directors.

2 In addition to the more normal range of business activity, we witnessed four price-fixing rings, three strikes and the signing of a new wage agreement, the discovery of a senior manager who had been defrauding a public authority, a shareholder protest, the settlement of a threatened damage suit, a succession crisis, the sackings/demotions of directors in four companies and the recruitment of a new director from outside for another, two major reorganisations of subsidiaries and authority structures, the negotiation of a £100-million loan, an annual capital budget allocation, the decision point on a perennial loss-making operation, every stage of a take-over bid from the selection of the victim to the absorption of the acquired company, and three other academic social scientists conducting research on the same firms. One of us was the official witness to the sale of a company.

3 For a review of the various methods, see Geraint Parry, *Political Elites*, George Allen and Unwin, London, 1969, Ch. 4 and pp. 52–4.

4 See Robert Presthus, *Men at the Top*, Oxford University Press, New York, 1964. See also P. Bachrach and M. S. Baratz: 'Decisions and Non-Decisions: An Analytical Framework', *American Political Science Review*, 57 (1963), pp. 632–42.

5 For example, Mills defines elites as those in 'the command posts of the major institutional hierarchies', C. W. Mills, *The Power Elite*, O.U.P., New York, 1956, p. 4. In a scholarly exercise in conceptual integration and clarification, Giddens interprets the sociological tradition of elite theory as having what we here call a positional conception of elites and himself adopts such a conception, defining elites as 'those individuals who occupy formally defined positions of authority at the head of a social organisation or institution' (p. 348). Giddens is very aware of the two principal difficulties with the positional conception of elites – where the division between the elite and the non-elite is to be drawn and the relationship between formal authority and effective power. We will return to his suggested resolutions of these difficulties in Section II of this paper where we present

9-2

a critique of the positional conception and suggest an alternative. See Anthony Giddens, 'Elites in the British Class Structure', *Sociological Review*, chapter 1 in this volume.

6 P. M. Worsley, 'The Distribution of Power in Industrial Society', *Sociological Review Monograph*, No. 8, 1964. Reprinted in J. Urry and J. Wakeford (eds.), *Power in Britain*, pp. 247–61: the quotation is at p. 257 in the latter.

7 We are tempted to imagine what sociologists might have concluded if they had made similar assumptions about, say, the power of foremen as they commonly make about the power of directors, even with all the customary caveats – first-line supervisors pursuing their interests largely unconstrained by relations with their subordinates, sharing a common value system through similar education in secondary moderns, and forming an integrated 'Establishment of Foremen' through regular opportunities for contact in exclusive workingmen's clubs. Yet because they are less familiar with elites, sociologists have imputed a mystique to authority in the boardroom that they would never grant to authority on the shop floor. Apply the same assumptions in the realm of the known and they appear ludicrous.

8 For example, F. G. Bailey, *Stratagems and Spoils*, Blackwell, Oxford, 1969; P. M. Hall, 'A Symbolic Interactionist Analysis of Politics', *Sociological Inquiry*, 1972, 42 (3–4), pp. 35–75.

9 See J. M. Lee, *Social Leaders and Public Persons*, O.U.P., 1963; R. V. Clements, *Local Notables and the City Council*, Macmillan, 1969.

10 This point emerged strongly in the discussion on original presentation of chapters 9 and 10 at the Cambridge conference in 1973.

11 Bachrach and Baratz, *op. cit.*, and their earlier article, 'Two Faces of Power', *American Political Science Review*, 161, 56 (December, 1962), pp. 947–52. See also David Lockwood, 'Comment on P. M. Worsley's "The Distribution of Power in Industrial Society"', *Sociological Review Monograph*, No. 8, 1964. Reprinted in Urry and Wakeford, *op. cit.*, see p. 266.

12 Hall, 1972, *op. cit.*, p. 50.

13 This is the thrust of the argument by Myles Mace in *Directors: Myth and Reality*, Graduate School of Business Administration, Harvard University, Boston, 1971, by far the best single book on directors we have encountered. Mace, a Professor at Harvard Business School and himself a non-executive director on several boards, concentrates on the role of the non-executive in the United States and thus complements our own work, for our basic observational data concerns executive directors, although we also interviewed numerous non-executives. His conclusions on the irrelevance of boards as well as the irrelevance of non-executive directors, except in very limited and unusual circumstances, are congruent to the argument developed below.

14 See Michael Barratt Brown, 'The Controllers of British Industry', Ken Coates (ed.), *Can the Workers Run Industry?*, Sphere Books, London, 1968, in Urry and Wakeford, *op. cit.*, pp. 73–116 which is an updating of his much-quoted article 'The Controllers', *Universities and Left Review*, No. 5, 1959. He estimates that in 1966, of the 120 largest companies in Britain 38, or 32 %, were Tycoon or Family controlled. Cabals would, of course, be operative in his Managerial and Co-ordinator controlled companies as well.

15 Corroborative descriptions of board meetings may be found in Mace, *op. cit.*, Chap. 2, esp. p. 15, in C. Northcote Parkinson, *Parkinson's Law*, Houghton Mifflin, Boston, 1957, Ch. 3, and in Peter Brannen's as yet unpublished study of divisional boards in a nationalised industry. John Wakeford has suggested to us that the pre-empted placidity we observed may be a function of our sample. In studying only successful companies, we did not see a board confronted with a major crisis. In such a situation,

he suggests, previously quiescent directors (men we interpreted as being outside the cabal, non-elite directors) may stand and fight, and the board may become the forum for a conflict of interests. The split within the P & O board over the proposed merger with Bovis and the recent Lonrho affair are evidence for the point. We think they are remarkable for their rarity; it is not often a Conservative Prime Minister is moved to reflect on the 'unacceptable face of capitalism'. Nonetheless, the criticism is a reasonable one, on which our research does not provide any direct evidence. However, in the medium-sized crises we did observe (the succession fight, the sackings of directors, the embezzlement by a senior manager), our subjects retreated into even closer discussions with only most trusted colleagues, tighter information control, a clearer distinction between those who counted and those who didn't, and even less willingness to enter a public forum – in short, the pattern we had already observed only more so. Reports we have from major crises (the sacking of an inept executive, the company about to go bankrupt) suggest that this pattern also occurs in more serious matters. See the excellent report of the sacking of the United Air Lines chief executive in the U.S., Rush Loving jnr., 'How a hotelman got the red out of United Airlines', *Fortune*, March 1972. See also *Rolls Royce Ltd.*, H.M.S.O., 1973, the official report of the bankruptcy, and the many reports of the Penn Central collapse in the U.S. Clearly, men may respond to crises in different ways. But the limited evidence available on such situations does not require any change in the core point we are making here, that 'company director' is an inadequate operational definition of the economic elite.

16 After the single heated argument we witnessed in a board meeting, the chairman took us aside and effectively apologised for having let the meeting get out of control, negatively confirming the norm. Rarely in the business world does one see the 'fury of the man of moral absolutism aroused' in Gouldner's phrase. In other contexts, meetings may have more vigorous cut and thrust since there people may be more ready to fight for absolute principles. In business, survival is more precarious and boat-rocking for the sake of principle less likely. See A. W. Gouldner, *For Sociology*, Ch. 9, 'The Importance of Something for Nothing', Allen Lane, 1973.

17 The Wakefords suggest the same interpretation of university Senates. They also provide evidence for a distinction between allocative and operational control (see below) in the university world. However, see also footnote 15 above. See Frances and John Wakeford, 'Universities and the Study of Elites', chapter 10 in this volume.

18 We would entirely agree with Nichols' observation: 'Indeed, to ask "who controls?" may be to assume an over simplified interpretation of decision-making which leads one to equate the manifestation of power with power itself and to confuse power, authority, and influence'. Theo Nichols, *Ownership, Control and Ideology*, George Allen and Unwin, London, 1969, p. 147. See Bachrach and Baratz, *op. cit.*

19 The implications of manipulation for the scientific study of organisations are severe. Robert Dahl in his article 'A Critique of the Ruling Elite Model', *American Political Science Review*, Vol. LII, 1958, has articulated a classic scientific test of elite power and indeed of power relations in general. The test depends on there being a clear difference over a specific issue between protagonists whose preferences are known in advance, ending in a decision of some sort. But if subordinates' power depends on their being able to present their preferences as if they were their superior's, and this is recognised as everyday practice in organisations, then the classic scientific test is simply and totally inappropriate.

20 One of the more famous industrialists in the country – an odds-on elite number by any definition, passed much of the afternoon of the day we spent with him reading and approving subordinate-prepared policy papers. He

acknowledged his legitimator role wistfully, 'I'm a transmitting tool, not a thinking tool. It's very frustrating, especially in areas where you know you could make a contribution.' Our observations on directors would fit directly into Headey's typology of Cabinet Ministers as policy initiators, policy selectors, and policy legitimators. As the above remark indicates, some of our directors in large companies at least, were as aware of the limitations on their power as were Headey's Ministers. See Bruce Headey, *The job of Cabinet Minister*, Allen & Unwin, 1974. A further point is that given the unstable and undercapitalised state of many contemporary companies Directors have a short-term orientation focussed on the Annual Reports. Subordinates can take a longer view.

21 Again, there is no suggestion here that these subordinates' preferences are necessarily anything other than traditional business goals. Our concern here is with *who* makes the major economic decisions, not their content.

22 See Oliver E. Williamson, 'Managerial Discretion, Organization Form, and the Multi-division Hypothesis', in Robin Marris and Adrian Wood, *The Corporate Economy*, Macmillan, London, 1971, for a description of the emergence and importance of headquarters elite staffs. In Japanese companies the granting of substantial initiative to young men in the headquarters staff is apparently even more common and significant than in the West – personal communication from Keith Thurley.

23 Among the directors we interviewed were three well-known men with considerable reputations as company doctors, able to go into a loss-making company as a crisis chairman and turn it round to profitability. Their techniques were identical – call in the management consultants. One claimed he had used the same consultants in 15 such situations. In short, the consultants made the decisions, they legitimated the changes and acquired elite status as a result – at the time of interview each had at least seven directorships, at least two charimanships, was the head of at least one prominent, voluntary industrial body and was at least a Knight.

24 Occasionally, directors went out of their way to recall times when there had been 'genuine' discussion at board meetings. They would relate anecdotes of the form, 'I remember the occasion in 1967 when...'. Clearly, most discussion in most boards is not 'genuine' in the sense of being pertinent to the making of a decision.

25 This is the device businessmen have long recognised as the stab in the back, the final sanction in the what-have-you-done-for-me-lately ethic. It has recently been given a new name in the U.S., 'whistle blowing'. Exercised by people well down in organisational authority structures, including secretaries and office cleaners, such aggressive information control by subordinates has played a significant role in a succession of American scandals – ITT in Chile, My Lai, The Pentagon Papers, Cambodian bombings, and Watergate. See also Hall, *op. cit.*, 'Control of Information Flow', pp. 54–8.

26 See Alvin W. Gouldner, 'Reciprocity and Autonomy in Functional Theory', in N. J. Demerath III and Richard A. Peterson, *System, Change and Conflict*, The Free Press, New York, 1967. Without resurrecting the entire debate, there is no assumption here that the board totally represents the company collectively or 'the system'. Indeed, in the past few months the organisational sociologists' point about the tendentiousness of 'organisational goals' appears to have entered the public domain. A public debate involving the C.B.I., the Institute of Directors, the Industrial Participation Association, other employers' associations, and an informal group of leading industrialists/economic elites (see the discussion paper 'Worker Participation' available from the Publicity Dept., of Rio Tinto Zinc), culminated in the government's White Paper on Company Law (H.M.S.O., 1973, Command 5391), with the suggestion that directors be given a code of conduct spelling out their responsibilities to employees among others.

27 See Barratt Brown, *op. cit.*, for a recent example of a long tradition.

28 In her discussion comments at the Conference on Elites at Cambridge in April 1973, Jean Floud distinguished between *first order decisions*, governing the allocation of resources, and *second order decisions*, which are organisational decisions concerned with implementation. This is essentially the same distinction we are making here. We support her assessment of their relative importance as well.

29 Asset-stripping is nothing new, of course. In the 1950s, Charles Clore acquired control of the British shoe industry by buying a company and its retail shops, realising their capital value through sale-and-leaseback to institutional investors, then using the new capital to finance the next acquisition.

30 See B. W. Denning and M. E. Lehr, 'The Extent and Nature of Corporate Long Range Planning in the U.K.', *Journal of Management Studies*, Vol. viii (2), May, 1971. This probably underestimates the number relevant for our purposes because they adopt a rigorous definition of a planning department.

31 See R. Spiegelberg, *The City: Power Without Accountability*, Blond and Briggs, London, 1973, Ch. 2, on the power of institutional investment managers. Also, see Charles Raw, Godfrey Hodgson, and Bruce Page, '*Do You Sincerely want to Be Rich?*', Penguin Books, Harmondsworth, Middlesex, 1972, for the story of some manipulative allocative controllers, those of Investors Overseas Services.

32 See Kingsley Davis, 'Property', in *Human Society*, Macmillan, New York, 1948, pp. 452–70.

33 See Davis, *op. cit.*; also for a recent version of the same interpretation, see Gerald D. Newbould and Andrew S. Jackson, *The Receding Ideal*, Guthstead Ltd., Liverpool, 1972, pp. 228–9.

34 See Wayland Kennet, Larry Whitty and Stuart Holland, *Sovereignty and Multinational Companies*, Fabian Society, London, 1971.

35 See, for example, Spiegelberg, *op. cit.*, 'The years 1967 and 1968 saw an unprecedented build-up in company mergers and take-overs. No fewer than 2,500 companies, valued at £5,000 million, changed hands, and attempts were made to take over another £900 million worth of the corporate sector. An horrific ten per cent of all Britain's industrial, commercial and financial assets outside public ownership became take-over targets. Seventy per cent of the 100 biggest companies in the country were involved in one way or another and a quarter of all British firms with more than £10 million were taken over' (p. 174). A clear diagrammatic presentation appears as Chart I, Company Acquisition and Mergers: U.K. 1954–72 on p. 87 of *Mergers, Takeovers and the Structure of Industry*, IEA Readings, No. 10, London, 1973. In general see also Newbould and Jackson, *op. cit.*

36 This is one of the themes we hope to develop in our forthcoming book on *The British Director*.

37 See Nichols, *op. cit.*, p. 62, 'It follows from the absence of such empirical data as we mentioned above that, for the most part, *all* participants in the ownership-control controversy have been forced to rely on *inferences* drawn from industrial and social structure. This, of course, is not a fully satisfactory approach to the problem. But this situation will remain until a greater proportion of industrial sociologists turn their attention from aiding the operation of a given power structure to analysing that power structure itself and until corporations open, not only their shop floors but also their boardrooms, to the sociologist' (Nichols' emphasis).

38 This is the same conclusion, reached from a micro-analysis, that Brown arrived at through a study of the financial figures contained in company reports. The Managerial controlled companies were the most profitable of all his four types. See Brown, *op. cit.*

39 Personal communication from James Slater. See also for a different distinc-

tion between the ideal types, D. C. Coleman, 'Gentlemen and Players', *Economic History Review*, Second Series, Vol. XXVI, no. 1, February, 1973.

40 Other types of non-institutional allocative controllers are also left out, whom we have not dealt with. The most conventional are the privately wealthy with no significant corporate position. Less conventionally, it ignores the criminally rich who, if stories of the U.S. Mafia are to be believed, are now using their illegally accumulated capital to fund enterprises, as well as their more traditional activities. Still less conventionally, it ignores intellectuals (except those on secondment to governments). The case for recognising the influence Milton Friedman and other monetarists had on our contemporary capital allocations seems very strong, not to mention that of their economist predecessors Keynes, Adam Smith, and others.

41 Those using *The Times* '*1000*' as a sampling frame, which contains only the names of chairmen and managing directors are effectively drawing the line very high.

42 In at least four of our companies, perhaps more, it appeared that the younger directors were actively propping up a weak chairman. They appeared to be doing this because (*a*) it allowed them a free hand to do what they wished (preserved their autonomy); (*b*) they had not yet sorted out the order of succession among themselves; or (*c*) they were too young to be credible successors if they toppled the chairman immediately. Preserving a weak superior is not an unreasonable strategy for a subordinate.

43 See, for example, Suzanne Keller, *Beyond the Ruling Class*, Random House, New York, 1963, pp. 317ff. It should be made clear that elites-within-elites are an intellectual response only to the definitional problem, not to the more general issue of gradations in power mentioned earlier, that men have more or less of both sorts of control. Problems of gradation are commonly solved by drawing one or more arbitrary lines across continua. Elites-within-elites are a solution to the problems created by positional definitions.

44 See Giddens, *op. cit.*, p. 14. This is one of the resolutions mentioned earlier in footnote 5.

45 See Joan Woodward, *Industrial Organisation: Theory and Practice*, Oxford University Press, 1965.

46 Even financial directors, the *prima facie* candidates for our concept of allocative controllers, were not always such. Some concerned themselves more with the efficiency of the accounting systems than the allocation of capital. They were effectively operational controllers in the realm of money. One company we encountered had two finance directors, institutionalising the two different roles.

47 The limitations of a positional definition become clear when one considers the difficulty sociologists have in dealing with a concept like 'The Establishment', where an institutional framework is not provided in advance. Most avoid the issue: Parry at least makes the attempt. See his effort, *op. cit.*, pp. 86–9. The same limitations arise again, more complexly, in the difficulties sociologists have with some elite linkage concepts like ruling class.

48 Position is, after all, only an indirect attempt to isolate power in an age of large organisations. The chain of reasoning involved in the problem is:

Background Consensus: The elite are the powerful.
Macro Analysis: Power is institutional power.
New definition: Elites are holders of high institutional office.
Recognition: Office is not synonymous with control.
Problem: Relationship of formal authority and effective power.
Resolution: An elite within an elite.

See John Porter, *The Vertical Mosaic*, University of Toronto Press, 1965, for a good example of this development.

> (p. 25) Elites are 'Those who have the power to make the major decisions for the society.' But 'The hierarchical structure of the modern work world which has been created by occupational gradation and bureaucratic administration makes it difficult to draw the line between those in power and those excluded.'

> (p. 27) 'These institutional systems are, as suggested earlier, hierarchically organised and individuals or groups at the top of our institutions can be designated as elites.'

> (p. 207) 'People in power roles belong to an elite.'

> (p. 223) 'Power, it has been suggested, is a decision-making process that takes place at the top of bureaucratised institutions.'

This yields an operational definition:

> (p. 234) 'In total, a group of 985 men holding Directorships in 170 dominant corporations, the banks, insurance companies, and, as well, numerous other corporations, not classed as dominant, were designated as the economic elite.'

And a revised conception of the elite:

> (p. 264) 'The economic elite has been defined as those who occupy the major decision-making positions in the corporate institutions of Canadian society.'

49 This is Giddens' resolution of the other problem, referred to in footnote 5 earlier.

50 The prevalence of recruitment studies is perhaps indicative. The problems of positional definitions may have arisen in sociology as they did not in political science because sociologists frequently approach the study of elites through an interest in stratification and mobility, rather than power *per se*. In attempting to measure mobility, openness, access to elite status, they have had to delimit the category into which movement was taking place. Given the importance of occupational prestige measures in stratification studies, they may have been led to adopt a positional definition of elites.

51 Perhaps under cover of a footnote we may speculate on the possible direction of the error. Recruitment studies will, we suspect, have included too many operational controllers. One significant type of operational controller is the man with technical qualifications and/or experience who has worked his way up to the top of his speciality in a large organisation – a typical mobility route for men with working class and middle class backgrounds. By including too many of these, recruitment studies may have *under*estimated the continuing benefit of privileged backgrounds and *over*estimated openness.

52 John Goldthorpe in his discussion paper at the Cambridge Elites Conference.

53 The two-sided point we have been making in this paper – that the power of superiors may be limited and effective power may lie with their subordinates or advisors – is not just relevant to the context of elites. It points, we feel, to a major gap in the tools of the discipline. Sociology must develop a measure of power which is independent of incumbency in positions of authority. At issue are our very definitions of power and authority. The traditional Weberian definition of these concepts has seen authority as legitimated power. In other words, authority is a sub-class of power. He who has authority thus always has power, by definition. The Weberian definitions allow us to conceive of power without authority, but not authority without power. Yet this is precisely the situation of the irrelevant director. To cope with him we need a concept of *pro-forma authority*, that is, the situation of incumbents in formally defined positions of authority who do not have the capacity to realise their will against nominal subordinates' resistance, but whose theoretical right to expect obedience is

never overtly challenged. As indicated in the earlier discussion, one way such a situation is allowed to persist is that the men with pro-forma authority are never given any significant tasks to perform. The whole question of authority without power was obscured for years by the concepts of formal and informal organisation in industry. The conflict for power within a nominal hierarchy of authority was transmuted into two separate realms of social activity. What is needed, on the contrary, we feel, is a clear concept of *power from below*. See in this connection David Mechanic, 'The Sources of power of lower participants in complex organisations', *Administrative Science Quarterly*, 1962, Vol. VII, No. 3, pp. 349–64 and Michel Crozier, *The Bureaucratic Phenomenon*, Tavistock Publications, London, 1964.

7. C. D. HARBURY and P. C. M MAHON: **Intergenerational wealth transmission and the characteristics of top wealth leavers in Britain**

1 The collection of the data for the study was made possible by the award of two grants of financial assistance from the Houblon-Norman Fund to C. D. Harbury, who wishes to express his gratitude for it. Sincere thanks are also due to officials of the Probate Registry, the Estate Duty Office, the General Registry Office and Smee and Ford, the London Press Agents for assistance kindly provided for this inquiry, and to S. Gooders, D. Howell and E. P. Kyle for much of the hard labour of research assistance in the data collection. We are greatly indebted to A. C. McKay for computing advice and assistance. We are also grateful to A. B. Atkinson, C. F. Carter, S. J. Prais and W. D. Rubinstein for helpful comments on an earlier version of this paper.

2 C. D. Harbury, 'Inheritance and the Distribution of Personal Wealth in Britain', *Economic Journal*, December 1962, and J. Wedgwood, *The Economics of Inheritance* (Routledge, 1929), Ch. VI.

3 As has been estimated and published annually in the Reports of the Commissioners of Inland Revenue since 1961, and previously by such independent estimators as K. Langley (*Oxford Bulletin of Statistics*, 1954), G. W. Daniels and H. Campion, *The Distribution of the National Capital* (Manchester University Press, 1936), and J. Revell, 'Changes in the Social Distribution of Property in Britain during the Twentieth Century', Actes du Troisième Congrès International d'Histoire Economique, Vol. I, Munich, 1965).

4 C. T. Sandford discusses this apparent reduction in the inequality of personal wealth distribution in *Taxing Personal Wealth* (Allen and Unwin, 1971, pp. 28–9), and it is also the subject of comment by A. B. Atkinson in 'The Distribution of Wealth and the Individual Life Cycle' (*Oxford Economic Papers*, 1971), who gives some reasons for believing that recent estimates exclude certain important categories of personal wealth. See also his recent *Unequal Shares* (Allen Lane, The Penguin Press, 1972, Ch. 1). Interest currently developing in the United States in the promotion of research into the inter-generational transmission of personal wealth is shown in the impressive background paper on this topic by John A. Brittain at the Brookings Institution (mimeographed, December 1971).

5 Harbury, *op. cit.*

6 The reason for the exclusion of women is given below (footnote 12).

7 The extent of the bias is discussed by Harbury, *op. cit.*, pp. 857–8.

8 Given our later findings on the relevance of age at death, this might marginally bias downwards the proportion with inherited wealth.

9 This is the minimum success rate. It could have been as high as about 98 % had not a number of medium reliability predecessors been rejected.

10 Especially in *Burke's Peerage, Burke's Landed Gentry, Who's Who* and *Kelly's Handbook of the Titled, Landed and Official Classes.*

11 Except for the three illegitimate sons coming to light in this study.

12 The reason for restricting the original sample to men may now be explained as being due to the difficulty in tracing birth entries for married women, whose death certificates do not record their maiden names. This unfortunately means that no account is taken of the important role played by women, especially widows, in the chain of inter-generational wealth transfers.

13 Respondents included public librarians, churchyard superintendents and others. For example, Scotland Yard were helpful in one case where a father had been in the Police Force. On another occasion a family tomb in a local churchyard was inspected.

14 These were mainly very mild. An exception was a case where the letter to the widow of a deceased son inadvertently omitted to refer to her late husband by his title of Lt. Colonel (but was identical in all other respects to all other letters sent to relatives). The widow replied that '. . .if you require urgent information from persons of the upbringing and social status of my husband and his relatives your approach should be more civil' and asked for reasons why her late husband was a 'sample'. A most diplomatically worded letter was, of course, sent to her without eliciting any information. Nevertheless, further research led to the tracing of the father in this case, who turned out to have been a civil engineer, who had left an estate of some £12,000 in 1914. On the other hand, many relatives provided potted financial histories of their predecessors' fortunes, though these were not asked for. Several of these with foreign antecedents were included in the analysis as a result. One reply from an Executrix (who turned out, incidentally, to have been a research assistant to a colleague at Birmingham University), for example, was helpful in another way. The deceased had been articled to her own architect father, and in her view he had accumulated his fortune of £118,000 simply by a miserly mode of life – 'lived in squalor', 'possessed one suit', 'borrowed the landlady's newspaper', etc., etc.

15 Statistical tests used and described in Section III below indicate that inherited wealth was notably less important among those members of the sample traced by letter.

16 Corrections contained in J. Bateman, *The Great Landowners of Great Britain and Ireland* (London, Harrison, 1883) were incorporated where possible.

17 Settled land, moreover, is included in the Probate Calendars only since 1926.

18 The estimate was made with the assistance of the Estate Duty Office. Understandably the Office would not release information about individuals but they supplied figures of the amounts of settled property for *groups* of 6 named persons, which could be compared with probate valuations.

19 For a recent account of tax avoidance techniques, see *e.g.*, Sandford, *op.cit.*, pp. 78–90. The fact that life assurance policies generally have maturity values in excess of their surrender values during a person's lifetime, however, provides a modest counter to the general direction of bias here. Since large estates probably do not hold life assurance of sufficiently large value to offset tax avoidance devices, it is most unlikely that this influence will predominate.

20 C. T. Sandford and P. M. Wright's Property Price Index in 'Estate Duty: Inflation and Long Term Capital Gains', *The Banker*, March 1969, goes back only to 1949.

21 J. B. Jeffreys and D. Walters, 'National Income and Expenditure, 1870–1952', *International Association for Research in Income and Wealth*, Series V (Bowes and Bowes, 1956). For subsequent years the retail price index of the London and Cambridge Economic Service was used.

22 Readers who refer to the *Economic Journal*, 1962 (p. 854) will notice a slight difference in the percentages in two rows. It now appears that of the 530 estates, two were incorrectly classified previously when the sorting was done manually, whereas the present study used a high speed electronic computer and various devices to check on the accuracy of the data. The differences are negligible and in no way affect the earlier argument, however regrettable they may be.

23 If any evidence is needed, one relative wrote that his father (one of our 'sons') who had left £113,000 would have left £1 to £1½ million if he had not given most of it away during his lifetime.

24 This is a well-known problem discussed by, *inter alia*, L. Kish, 'Some Statistical Problems in Research Design' (pp. 391–406) in *Quantitative Analysis of Social Problems* (ed. E. R. Tufte, Addison Wesley, 1970).

25 This explains why the sample size for 1965 falls from 136 in Table I to 92 in Table II.

26 Note, however, the small sample sizes for 1965 in rows two and three.

27 Another possible influence is the rise in longevity which has occurred over the period. Reference is made to this below when age at death is considered. This is, perhaps, the place to add that the present study throws absolutely no light on the likelihood of the son of a wealthy father retaining his inheritance, since the sample of sons were all specifically top wealth leavers. Such a question can only be answered by taking a sample of fathers leaving substantial wealth and tracing the fortunes of their children. In fact, a sample has been drawn also of this kind and will appear as the substance of another article.

28 Harbury, *op. cit.*, pp. 862–5.

29 'The proportion of estates of females to the total passing in 1924–30 was about 40 per cent.' See G. W. Daniels and H. Campion, *op. cit.*, p. 9.

30 It may be noted that the price index used for revaluing all estates in constant 1956–7 prices rose by 42 % between 1915–16 and 1925–6. Hence the observed increase in the total number of estates of different sizes expressed in terms of current prices in the text, would be significantly less if expressed in real terms. This explanation of changes in the proportions of sons having fathers leaving relatively large estates between 1956–7 and 1965 is likely therefore to be of even smaller importance when expressed in real terms.

31 The analysis in the previous pages has deliberately avoided the use of sophisticated statistical methods. We are, of course, aware of the apparent relevance of Galtonian regression analysis to the relation between certain attributes of fathers and sons. However, the truncated nature of the sample data in the present case, the problems of tax avoidance and the fact that the sample was originally drawn of sons rather than of fathers, makes it difficult to obtain a reliable estimate of the required regression slope. However, we have some reason to hope that these difficulties may be mitigated after the collection of additional data: and in a future paper we hope to develop this approach. This did not appear to us to be a good reason for holding up presentation of our present results using rather more basic techniques.

32 The way in which the computer programme was written made this the most straightforward procedure, though it is, of course, true that comparisons between each sub-group and the remainder of the sample are statistically preferable. However, it was thought convenient to have a single universal bench mark for the purpose of the numerous comparisons, and in view of the large number of observations it was felt that the tests used would be justified. In fact, it should be mentioned for the benefit of those interested in paired comparisons that all tests were re-run using the stricter form of the 't' test for the differences in proportions, with the result that exactly the same cells were statistically significant as in the textual tables based on the simpler formula.

33 Baronets are here counted as Peers.

34 It is tempting to speculate, therefore, that Prime Ministers have not been disproportionately influenced in creating Knighthoods by the financial backgrounds of candidates.

35 An example may help to explain the procedure. One lawyer, banker (and politician) who was chairman and particularly associated with one company, in S.I.C. XV, but who was also a director of 5 other companies including a bank and a colliery, was classed in category XXV, while another person, styled as a financier, who was a director of a dozen companies, was put in S.I.C. XXI. Those about whose occupation the only record was 'of independent means' on their death certificate, were not included in this part of the study.

36 Of these industries the first three all exhibit the feature that the proportions of sons with fathers leaving more than £1,000 in every single size bracket are greater than for the population as a whole (*i.e.*, Pareto-type curves drawn of the distributions do not intersect in any place). In the case of distribution and the professions, this is true also if one ignores the small numbers of cases where fathers left more than £500,000. In the marginal case of textiles, there is one inconsistency.

37 Some confirmation of the tendency for those in finance to have less wealthy fathers was obtained by using the same analysis on the basis of number of company directorships held by each individual as indicated in the Directory of Directors, where the same conclusion tended to appear for those holding 6 or more directorships.

38 See, in this connection, W. D. Rubinstein, 'Occupations Among British Millionaires', 1957 to 1969 (*Review of Income and Wealth*, 1971).

39 Some judgment was exercised to include *e.g.*, licensed victualler and brewer, plumber and plumber's brass founder, draper and gown manufacturer, builder and estate agent, in a small number of cases where a clear occupational link existed. It may be added that we also examined the data on the basis of identical S.I.C.s. The results were virtually identical with those in Table V.

40 See A. B. Atkinson, 'The Distribution of Wealth and the Individual Life Cycle', *op. cit.*

41 Thereby not being caught in the estate duty statistics if outside the range of dutiable *inter vivos* gifts.

42 The difference between the sample size of 48 and 46 is accounted for by two fathers-in-law being found where no father had been traced.

43 They included mothers, maternal and paternal grandparents, uncles, aunts, cousins, etc.

44 The difference between 80 and 83 (and between 622 and 625) is accounted for by three predecessors other than fathers being found in cases where no father's estate had been traced.

8. W. RUBINSTEIN: **Men of property: some aspects of occupation, inheritance and power among top British wealthholders**

1 E.g., J. R. Revell, *The Wealth of the Nation* (Cambridge, 1967); C. T. Sandford, *Taxing Personal Wealth* (London, 1967); A. B. Atkinson, *Unequal Shares* (London, 1972).

2 As far as I am aware, the only previous research to make use of these sources are Josiah Wedgwood, *The Economics of Inheritance* (London, 1929); C. H. Harbury, 'Inheritance and the Distribution of Personal Wealth in Britain', *The Economic Journal*, 1962; and G. Z. Fijalkowski-Bereday, 'The Equalizing Effect of Death Duties', *Oxford Economic Papers*, 1950.

3 Net values are available separately, but not for the earliest valuations, from

the Probate Act sheet. The difference between net and gross, which represented personal debts and funeral expenses, was between 5 and 15 per cent of the gross value in approximately 90 per cent of the cases in which both values were known to me. Inventories left by Scotsmen may be inspected, and among those Scottish wealthholders of the nineteenth century I have seen, the difference invariably consisted of tradesmen's debts. Although the net value should certainly be used in calculations about national wealth, the gross value, it might well be argued, gives a more accurate representation of an individual's wealth level. Clearly personal debts, which are totalled for probate purposes, do not have to be repaid at one time.

4 The most common view of the state of death duties at the present time is that they are a 'voluntary tax' that few if any of the wealthy ever pay; hence, calculations from the probate valuations are practically useless. As Oliver Stutchbury put it, 'estate duty is now paid only by the misanthropic, the patriotic, the absent-minded, or the downright unlucky' (*The Case for the Capital Tax*, Fabian Pamphlet no. 388, p. 2). Those who make this point can surely never have seen the lists of large estates probated in recent years. In the past decade, the duke of Westminster, and Lords Marks, Rootes, Nuffield, Fraser of Allender, and Rank, to name only a bevy of wealthy peers, have left millionaire estates. Can an estimate of the level of tax avoidance among the very rich be made? Clearly not with certainty, but some light may have been shed by an article in the *Daily Express* of 31 March 1969, on Britain's living millionaires, in which it was claimed that millionaires 'probably number over 500', rather than the 100–200 estimated by the Inland Revenue. This is hardly the last word on the subject, but the paper had clearly done a good bit of research, as in the article 40 persons or families worth £5 million or more – including five estimated as worth over £100 million – were named. For the period 1967–71, the mean number of millionaires deceased annually, according to the *Annual Reports of the Inland Revenue*, was about fifteen. Assuming that one-twenty-fifth of the total number of millionaires are deceased annually (roughly the ratio of deaths among males aged 65–74), the number of living millionaires would be 250–300, indicating that about half the number of millionaires deceased annually actually appear as such. It might also be noted that there has been a substantial increase in the number of very large estates probated annually in recent years. In 1957–8, for example, the Somerset House calendars listed only 13 estates of £500,000 or over. In 1971–2 there were 72.

5 There would seem to be substantial differences between the Inland Revenue and the Somerset House valuations – the latter source listing only about 75 per cent of the total of the former (on this point see Harbury, *op. cit.*, p. 848). It may well be that the Inland Revenue counts large *estates* rather than *individuals* when, e.g., the real and personal portion of the estate are proven separately, as typically is the case. My suspicions on this score are aroused by the fact that for estates above £2 million, there seem to have been more proven in 1963–7 by the Somerset House figures than by the Inland Revenue's, while the difference at a slightly lower level is substantially in favour of the Inland Revenue figures. Insofar as this difference consists of settled personalty (rather than property situated abroad), it would affect my figures on social mobility – although this presumably would have been a factor since the series began. On the other hand, there are some good reasons for believing that the total *wealth picture* – and not just that part illumined by the probate valuations – is more dominated by 'self-made men' than the probate figures alone would indicate: (1) bankrupts are probably more likely to be engaged in speculative or novel fields, and therefore fewer bankrupts would come from those who inherit a fortune held in trust, or subject to regulations that would make investment in shares other than blue chips difficult. There is also a long line of

spectacular bankrupts, from 'Railway' Hudson to Cyril Lord, who were
new men, and very few – the duke of Buckingham is one – who were long-
established. (2) Persons with disproportionately high incomes in relation to
their wealth are more likely to be self-made, or, more precisely, those with
non-remunerative wealth (like Old Masters) or blue chips and bonds
yielding relatively little, as well as agricultural land, are likely to have
inherited their fortunes. (3) It may be that the newer types of business
activities are dominated by those younger than the average wealthholder,
and hence less likely to die. (But they would, presumably, eventually be
caught.) I have property development in mind here.

6 There is a risk of human error here. My wife and I therefore double-
checked a number of years that seemed to have suspiciously few wealthholders: we had invariably missed about 10 per cent of the final total of
those above £100,000. The early probate calendars are printed in a manner
that makes rapid, accurate scanning possible.

7 The acreage and yield properly refer to the figures in Bateman's *Great
Landowners* (1883), based on the return, but each of his estates was
mentioned in Morrison's will. Morrison's estate valuation is sworn at
'above £1 million' at Somerset House; the figure of £3 to 4 million is based
on contemporary estimates and on a personal inventory of his I have
examined.

8 Most of Beatty's estate was in Ireland. It is interesting to note that five of
these estates were left at a time when estate duties are supposed to be a
'voluntary tax'. Ellerman's son died recently leaving £53.2 million.

9 I mean no slight toward women here. In the entire nineteenth century,
there were fewer than a dozen women's estates worth £500,000 or more; in
1971–2 alone, there were 25. The increase in the number of women to
inherit property absolutely is arguably the most important single change in
Britain's wealth elite during this century. But it is far from easy to find
accurate data on these women, and there are bound to be ambiguities
about inheritance patterns. A 'foreigner' is a foreign national who leaves
a large estate in Britain, not an Englishman who earns his fortune abroad.

10 See my previous paper, 'Occupations Among British Millionaires, 1857–
1969', *The Review of Income and Wealth*, 1971. Those landowners who died
prior to 1926 and who are found as leaving very large estates at Somerset
House, left sufficiently large personal estates. Most of these had substantial
mineral, dock, or urban property interests.

11 See my article, 'The Decline of the Jewish Influence in Britain', *Jewish Social
Studies*, 1972. It may be that City men engage in estate duty avoidance to
a greater extent than other wealthy men: but is there any *a priori* reason to
believe that one group of wealthy men do this more than any other?

There are some indications that a previous secular change occurred in the
British wealth picture between 1800 and 1850. Many of the top wealthholders deceased in this period were government placemen or officeholders,
employed by the East India Company, in the military or Church, or had
West Indian plantation interests – the English ancien régime (or 'the
Thing') which some radicals and others believe, incorrectly, survives to the
present.

12 I have on occasion made the following assumptions in the above calculations: in cases where the 'sons' or 'children' were not named, I have
assumed that the testator had three sons or five children. In cases in which
the shares of a private company are disposed of, but not valued in the will,
I have assumed that it formed 60 per cent of the total portfolio. For
annuities, I have taken only *one* years' purchase. This will serve to increase
the share of the primary legatee. It should not be forgotten that, after
settling the debts and paying the probate duty and funeral expenses, the
residual legatee – who is generally the primary legatee – would receive that
much less.

13 Of course, this argument can at best be established here only as a probability: only an empirical reckoning of the actual careers of the wealth-holders in this study can actually prove it. It is interesting to note, however, how few descendants develop their inheritance into really vast fortunes.

14 The wills of wealthholders often specify that their estates be turned into stocks and securities of this sort, with the typical admonition 'but not Irish securities'. In many cases, personal companies may have been disposed of, at least at the discretion of the executors. This may have had an important effect on the British economy, but it is a matter of which nothing is known.

15 The difficulties are with the availability of the father's probate valuations before 1858, which would be scattered among the plethora of local probate courts, and with the impossibility of discovering even the father's name in many cases before birth certificates are available in 1837. It is often easier to trace a father's occupation than his date of death, especially so when there are no relatives living to come to the researcher's assistance. I do, however, plan to locate as many father's valuations as is possible in the future. There are, moreover, many questions concerning non-patrial inheritance that must not be ignored in this undertaking. Might there not in extreme cases be *inter vivos* gifts from the son to the father? The 75-year-old father of a 50-year-old self-made millionaire is not likely to die penniless.

16 There would seem to be confirmation of this from the *Daily Express* list of multi-millionaires cited above. About half of those whose origins are mentioned or known appear to have at least founded the businesses in which their fortunes were made.

Both Wedgwood and Harbury found that about 20 per cent were 'self-made' in the sense of having fathers who themselves left £3000 or less. My findings, for a much wealthier group, may indeed appear to be on the high side. It may be, paradoxically, that it is more common for a self-made man to make an immense fortune than a smaller one: a money-making genius who successfully breaks the initial class barriers may have found a niche in the economic structure, or a novel marketing or selling technique, that will bring him a vast fortune. It is interesting to note that three of the eleven wealthholders leaving £7 million or more, who were raised in Britain, were self-made men.

17 I seem to be at variance on this point with the conclusions of Professor Harbury and Dr McMahon. I can only suggest that the two- or three-year groups studied by them may not be representative: the mid-1950s, which provided the bulk of their examples, saw fewer wealthy deaths than any period since the First World War. It is possible, e.g., that at such times there are fewer self-made men than at other times, or that they are only to be found in certain fields.

18 On the other hand, it may be that such studies concentrate on heavy industry and finance, and ignore such fields as property-owning and retailing, as well as light industry, which might produce as many wealthy men as the better-known fields, but who might be of humbler origin. Certainly more comprehensive research needs to be done.

19 'The American Business Elite: A Collective Portrait', *Journal of Econ. Hist.*, 1945.

20 'American Millionaires and Multi-Millionaires', *The Journal of Social Forces*, Vol. III, p. 636.

21 *Ibid.*, p. 635.

22 *Ibid.*

23 'The Egalitarian Myth and American Social Reality: Wealth, Mobility, and Equality in the "Era of the Common Man"', *Amer. Hist. Rev.*, October 1971, p. 1012.

24 *Ibid.*, p. 1013. Pessen's findings may not, however, be useful as a generalization about America as a whole at that time. See R. Gallman, 'Trends in the Size Distribution of Wealth in the Nineteenth Century:

Some Speculations', in Lee Soltow, ed., *Six Papers on the Size Distribution of Wealth and Income*, New York, 1969, p. 28. Pessen's erroneous comments on British wealthholding in his period should also be noted, *op. cit.*, p. 1012.

25 'American Historians and the American Business Elite', in William Miller, ed., *Men In Business*, New York, 1952, p. 326.

26 Frances W. Gregory and Irene D. Neu, 'The American Industrial Elite in the 1870s', in *Men In Business, op. cit.*, p. 202.

27 Table 27, p. 116.

28 'The Fifty-Million Dollar Man', November, 1957; 'America's Centi-Millionaires', May, 1968.

29 R. J. Lampman, *The Share of Top Wealthholders in the National Wealth, 1922–1956*, Princeton, 1956, p. 84; Felix Lundberg, *The Rich and the Super-Rich*, New York, 1968, p. 10.

30 Party labels are from Dod's *Parliamentary Companion*, and may not echo other sources precisely. The sizeable portion of unknowns included a surprising number unlisted in *Who Was Who*, as well as those dying abroad, or leaving no property. Many members of the 1922 Parliament are still living, as is at least one member of the 1906 House of Commons.

31 According to Mr Andrew Roth, the journalist who specializes in the business backgrounds of M.P.s, and who was interviewed on the radio in September 1972, only about four members of the present House of Commons are millionaires, but probably 200 peers are.

32 'Borough of Hackney – Central Division – Conservative Association Minute Book', 1 May 1885. (Manuscript at the Shoreditch Public Library.) This situation was by no means unique.

33 P. L. Payne, 'The Emergence of the Large-Scale Company in Great Britain, 1870–1914', *Econ. Hist. Rev.*, 1967, pp. 539–40; list of largest units by profits in the *Sunday Times*, 21 May 1961.

10. F. and J. WAKEFORD: **Universities and the study of elites**

1 Carter, C., 'Universities for the 1970s: How to avoid a "Pecking Order"', *New Statesman*, 14 November 1969: see *T.H.E.S. c.* 20 April 1973.
A *purely mathematical* analysis of majority voting demonstrates the very high degree of control exercised by a small resolute group when the indifferent population is large. For instance three resolute voters among a committee of twenty-three will obtain the decision of their choice in seventy five per cent of the votings if the indifference of the rest leads them to vote in a random manner. (L. S. Penrose, 'Elementary Statistics of Majority Voting', *Journal of the Royal Statistical Society*, Vol. CLX, 1946.)

2 See Halsey, A. H. and Trow, Martin, *The British Academics*, London: Faber, 1971, pp. 72–5; Halsey, A. H., 'A pyramid of prestige', *Universities Quarterly*, September 1961; Halsey, A. H. and Crewe, I. M., *Social Survey of the Civil Service*, Vol. III (1) of *The Civil Service* (Fulton Committee), London, H.M.S.O. 1969, p. 402. See also Sampson, A., *The New Anatomy of Britain*, London: Hodder, 1971, pp. 158ff. and Green, V. H. H., *The Universities*, Harmondsworth: Penguin, 1969, Ch. 12, pp. 245–63.

3 For some recent remarks on this see *T.H.E.S.* 6 July 1973, p. 2.

4 Halsey, A. H. and Trow, M., *op. cit.*, pp. 75–83.

5 See for instance Ashby, E. and Anderson, M., *The Rise of the Student Estate in Britain*, London: Macmillan, 1970, p. 152, and Ashby, E., 'Hands off the universities?', *Minerva*, VI (1967–8), pp. 244–56.

6 Trow, Martin, 'Reflections on the transition from Mass to Universal Higher Education', *Daedalus*, Vol. IC, No. 1, 1970. The dichotomy proposed by Trow, between the 'autonomous' and the 'popular' functions of contemporary universities is particularly relevant here. The 'autonomous' functions involve a commitment to a broad liberal education and

the transmission of civilised elite values and particular character traits, the belief in the creation, maintenance and preservation of knowledge through pure scholarship and scientific research and a concern with selection for and preparation of candidates for membership of elite groups, together with a process of certification. In contrast the 'popular' functions involve, first, a commitment to provide higher education for as many students as want it, not as a privilege but as of right, and, second, the provision of useful knowledge and other services to such groups and institutions that request them. The contemporary dilemma, it is suggested, lies in heightened tension between the two.

7　W. L. Guttsman, *The British Political Elite*, London: MacGibbon and Kee, 1963, pp. 359ff.; Tom Lupton and C. S. Wilson, 'The Social Background and Connections of "Top Decision Makers"', *The Manchester School*, Vol. XXVIII, No. 1, January 1959. See also T. J. H. Bishop and R. Wilkinson, *Winchester and the Public School Elite*, London: Faber, 1967; Kelsall, R. K., *Higher Civil Servants in Britain*, London: Routledge and Kegan Paul, 1955; W. L. Guttsman (ed.), *The English Ruling Class*, London: Weidenfeld and Nicholson, 1969. The conceptual and methodological assumptions of the current Cambridge study are contained in Anthony Giddens, 'Elites in the British Class Structure', contained in this volume, and Anthony Giddens, 'Elites', *New Society*, Vol. XXII, No. 528, 16 November 1973.

8　For a discussion of the use of directory inclusions as an elite index see E. D. Baltzell, '"Who's Who in America" and "The Social Register"' Elite and Upper Class Indexes in Metropolitan America', in R. Bendix and S. M. Lipset, *Class, Status and Power*, New York: Collier Macmillan, 1966, and the contribution by Colin Bell in Crewe, I. (ed.), *The Sociology of Politics Year Book*, London: Croom Helm, 1974.

9　See J. N. Morgan and J. A. Sonquist, 'Problems in the Analysis of Survey Data, and a Proposal', *American Statistical Association Journal*, June 1963.

10　John and Frances Wakeford and Douglas Benson, 'A research note on a "k-means" cluster analysis of some social and educational characteristics of selected elite groups in contemporary Britain', in Ivor Crewe, *op. cit.*

11　The vagueness and variety of conceptual definition of the notion of elite evident in classical elite theory persists in contemporary terminological wrangles. We decided to use Bottomore's definition. See Bottomore, T. B., *Elites and Society*, Harmondsworth: Penguin, 1966, p. 14.

12　Collison, P. and Millen, J., 'University Chancellors, Vice Chancellors and College Principals: A Social Profile', *Sociology*, Vol. III, No. 1, January 1969, p. 106.

13　Collison, P. and Millen, J., *op. cit.*, p. 106.

14　Collison, P. and Millen, J., *op. cit.*, p. 79.

15　Council is particularly important. Its functions may include in addition to the control of the university's finances, also the role of employer of academic and administrative staff and the responsibility for good order. For an analysis of the composition of the Council of Warwick University see Thompson, E. P., *Warwick University Limited*, Harmondsworth: Penguin, 1970, pp. 28ff. Otherwise evidence of links with various 'elite' groups only comes to light accidently. Thompson quotes a letter from the Warwick files: 'I regard the association between Barclays Bank and the University of Warwick as especially close. Not only are we Bankers to the University and the only bank represented on the site, but we have endowed a Chair, the Chairman of our Local Board serves on the Finance Committee, and our Chairman and the Vice Chancellor are friends of long standing who, during their time, have been jointly involved in the problems of University finance, i.e., the University of Oxford. I cannot think, therefore, that any university could have a claim on the Bank's favourable consideration of a need stronger than that of the University of Warwick.' Thompson, E. P., *op. cit.*, p. 38. Another such disclosure was made by a student newspaper at the University of Lancaster in 1970. It reproduced the details of correspondence between the industrialist, pro-chancellor of the University, Lord Derby, and the Vice Chancellor, which had been circulated by the latter to members of the Senate. An extract from one of Lord Derby's letters said: 'At a meeting of the Parliamentary Committee of the County Council very strong views were expressed about student behaviour and the fact that unless the universities took disciplinary action Local Authorities could do nothing about grants. The only thing they have got left is to withdraw their donations, and this they will not hesitate to do if there is further trouble. If this does happen there is no doubt that the lay members will hold the Senate fully responsible.

'I was interested when driving Ted Heath back here from Bury on Friday to hear an infinitely more alarming report on student behaviour at other universities than you had reported at our meeting. To quote one instance, I gather the "anarchists" have virtually taken over Balliol College. There is a feeling that the authorities have completely lost control of discipline and if this continues there will be an ever-increasing hardening of public opinion.' (*Spark*, 21 April 1970, pp. 5–6.) In 1972 the University attempted to make the distribution of grants dependent on students' willingness to sign a promise to abide by university rules.

16 Beck, H. P., *Men who Control our Universities*, New York: Kings Crown Press, 1947, pp. 74ff. and Hartnett, R. T., 'College and University Trustees: Their Backgrounds, Roles, and Educational Attitudes', in J. Skolnick and Currie (eds.), *Crisis in American Institutions*, Boston: Little, Brown and Co., 1970, pp. 266–80.

17 Hoffman, D. R., 'The Power Elite of Chicago'. Paper presented to the annual meeting of the American Sociological Association, Denver, Colorado 1971. See also Domhoff, G. W., *The Higher Circles*, New York: Random House, 1970, pp. 34ff.

18 See Young, M. F. D., 'Curricula as Socially Organized Knowledge', in Young, M. F. D. (ed.), *Knowledge and Control: New Directions in the Sociology of Education*, London: Collier Macmillan, 1971, p. 43, n. 33, and Newman, J. H., *On the Scope and Nature of University Education*, London: Dent, Everyman, ed., (First published 1852), 1949, pp. 137–9, 154.

19 Bernstein, B., 'On the Classification and Framing of Educational Knowledge', Ch. 2 in Young, M. F. D. (ed.), *op. cit.* We have little systematic data as yet into the substantive *content* of education within either school or university.

20 See Blume, S., 'Research Support in British Universities', *Minerva*, Vol. VII, no. 4, Summer 1969. Applications for research funds from the research councils are already considered by the councils with reference to comments made by the relevant government department, and the Government Green and White Papers of 1971 and 1972 support a further diminution of university powers. In Lord Rothschild's view the academic should become a 'contractor' working for his 'customer', the government department. *The Framework of Government Research and Development*, H.M.S.O., 1971, Cmnd. 4814.

21 For instance the Institute of Chartered Accountants spent £100,000 for the establishment and support of a Chair of Accounting at the London Graduate School of Business in 1973. Similarly the Finance Houses Association has endowed a Chair of Credit Law at Queen Mary College, London. University prospectuses often list a number of such posts, but in many, perhaps the majority of cases sponsored posts are not listed as such.

22 *UGC* Letter to University Vice Chancellors, 15 January 1973.

23 Reynolds, P. R., 'Lancaster 1972–1977', *Lancaster Comment*, No. 28, 1 March 1973, p. 6. Proposals from Lancaster for schools of law, medicine and architecture were among those which were viewed with disfavour by the UGC and subsequently dropped.

24 Sanderson, M., *The Universities and British Industry, 1850–1970*, London: Routledge and Kegan Paul, 1972, p. 391.

25 The Robbins Report. *Committee on Higher Education Report*, Cmnd. 2154, H.M.S.O., 1963, pp. 134–6.

26 Characteristics in the university's history, from 1891 to the present, are evident in the formulation of the 'Objects of the University' in the Charter of the University of Aston: 'The Objects of the University shall be to advance disseminate and apply learning and knowledge by teaching and research for the benefit of industry and commerce and of the community generally and to enable students to obtain the advantage of a university education and such teaching and research may include periods outside the University in industry or commerce or whatever the University considers proper for the best advancement of its objects.'

27 Perkin, H. J., *New Universities of the United Kingdom*, O.E.C.D., 1969, p. 217. Thompson, E. P. (ed.), *op. cit.*, pp. 23ff.

28 Sloman, A. E., *A University in the Making*, BBC, 1964. Subsequently the electrical engineering department at Essex was started by a chief scientist from Plessey-UK, the GPO gave the University £100,000 for a chair of Telecommunications, and close contacts developed with several other major firms in the communication business. The Institute of Marketing endowed a chair of marketing at Lancaster, where ICI also funded the establishment of a department of Systems Engineering and Wolfson a department of Financial Control. In May 1971 Lancaster University further announced the support of the 'Rank Group Charity' for the foundation of a major 'International Centre for Research in Accounting': 'The financial viability of the new International Centre is now secure as a result of a most generous contribution from the J. Arthur Rank Group Charity, who have agreed to donate an annual sum of £10,000 for the next ten years. Further contributions in support of the activities of the International Centre are expected, along with the active co-operation of professional bodies, public accounting firms, British industrialists and commercial organisations, Government, and individuals and institutions overseas...A strong Board of Trustees has been formed under the Chairmanship of Sir Ronald Leech. The Board will have charge of the finances of the International Centre and will provide important liaison between the officers of the Centre and the world at large, assisting the Director and his staff in establishing research priorities and in advancing the purposes of the Centre.' Of the seventeen Trustees in charge of the finances of the Centre and who would 'provide important liaison between the officers of the Centre and the world at large...', at least six are top industrialists, including Lord Kearton, Sir Frederick Catherwood and Sir Basil Smallpiece. Warwick University, with Lord Rootes as its first chancellor, who claimed to have raised over £1 million for the Appeal through personal contacts, similarly developed a close relationship with prominent industrialists, with many senior appointments made from and sponsored by, major industrial and commercial organisations, including the Institute of Directors, Pressed Steel Fisher, Volkswagen and Barclays Bank. The Docksey Report is quoted in M. Sanderson, *op. cit.*, p. 387.

29 See R. Miliband, *op. cit.*, p. 250. The letter to local businessmen announcing the establishment of an 'Advisory Panel for Local Organisations' at Lancaster to offer advice in the solution of their problems epitomises this ideal: 'The University is well aware of its continuing obligation to provide a service to the community in a diversity of ways. In fact our motto "Truth lies open to all" makes this obligation quite clear, and our success in developing links with outside organisations has established Lancaster as a University which is able to "keep its feet on the ground" whilst at the same time developing academically.' (Press Release, 1972.) This attitude is not by any means limited to the new universities. For instance Queen Mary College established an 'Energy Research Unit' in 1972, financed by British

Petroleum and staffed by British Petroleum personnel on secondment. With the discovery of North Sea oil Heriot-Watt University is to add a Chair of Underwater Technology, an Institute of Offshore Engineering and (within the Department of Brewing and Biological Sciences, largely financed by grants from the brewing industry), a new degree course in Marine Biology. Aberdeen University is concentrating on geology with particular reference to oil exploitation, with a new postgraduate course in Petroleum Technology backed by Total and Conoco and taught by staff previously employed by oil companies.

30 This is also common in the technological universities where such activities are considered equivalent to academic research. The particulars of new posts in certain departments at Lancaster indicate that new staff will be 'encouraged to participate' in the activities of one of four 'subsidiary companies' through which consulting contracts and short courses for industrialists are organised. Much of the subsequent income is used to finance research students who are thereby committed to work on problems referred to them often in confidence by industrial firms or other organisations as part of their postgraduate work. See also Halsey, A. M., 'Social Scientists and Governments', *T.L.S.*, 5 March 1970, pp. 249, 251.

31 See Becker, H. A. and Horowitz, I. R., 'Radical Politics and Sociological Research: Observations in Methodology and Ideology', in Anderson, C. A. *et al.*, *Varieties of Political Expression in Sociology*, Chicago: Chicago U.P., 1972, pp. 48–66.

32 See Becker, H. S. and Horowitz, I. R., *op. cit.*, and Miliband, R., *op. cit.*, p. 251. Halsey, A. H., *op. cit.*, 1970. This is a particular problem where the renewal of covenants coincides with a period of unrest. At Lancaster the Vice Chancellor wrote to Heads of Departments quoting a letter from a 'generous donor', 'typical' of letters received during 1972: 'We are... most disturbed to read the reports on the unsavoury happenings at the university and until these occurrences are eliminated we would not be prepared to make further donations to the university.' *Lancashire Evening Post*, 2 June 1972. The events of 12 October 1972 are reported to have cost Stirling over £1 million in lost donations alone. *T.H.E.S.* 17 November 1972.

33 However, it was estimated some years ago now that industry contributes at least £1.8 million annually to university funds in the form of grants and contracts for research, and the direct or indirect support of postgraduate and 'sandwich course' students, in addition to gifts and endowments in response to appeals and the not inconsiderable sums presumably paid to individuals for advice, consultancy and guest lectures. See Blume, S., 'Research support in British universities: the shifting balance of multiple and unitary sources', *Minerva*, Vol. VII, No. 4, Summer 1969. There are also considerable differences between universities, and the contribution of industry to some of the smaller new universities has at times been substantial. For instance, in one in 1970–1 the consultancy and project income of three departments together was equivalent to about ten per cent of the size of the whole recurrent grant and contributed more than 6 per cent of the total university income.

34 The Robbins Report, *op. cit.*, p. 215. For one instance of the effect such funding can have on the development of one university, see Thompson, E. P., *op. cit.*, pp. 78ff.

35 Dahl, R. A., *A Preface to Democratic Theory*, Chicago: Chicago U.P., 1965, pp. 137–8.

36 Undoubtedly the government plays by far the greatest role in financing universities but the 'need' for resources has been so pressing that the new universities in particular have had to make numerous appeals for funds; obviously a quicker start will be made where more money is available than the Treasury and Local Authorities can provide. It is pointed out in

'Fund Raising: A helping hand for the new universities', *Financial Times*, 19 January 1967, that industry's policies vary: 'Ford, for example, gave £200,000 to Essex but nothing to any other new university; while ICI and Unilever often given £25,000 to new university appeals. On the whole, the size of donations are fairly standard: in the region of £5,000 from the Bank of England, £2,500 from the joint stock banks, £5–£10,000 from middle-range industry, and so on.'

There is keen competition in this search for endowment, many Oxford and Cambridge colleges have made large appeals. University College, Cambridge, for instance, has been renamed 'Wolfson College' in recognition of a gift of £2 million for improving facilities at the College which has specifically concentrated on promoting contacts and work with industry and is to house the archives of the Confederation of British Industry. Cf. the search for endowments in contemporary American higher education: 'Universities: Anxiety Behind the Facade', *Time*, 23 June 1967, pp. 52–7.

37 Roszak, T., *The Dissenting Academy*, New York: Pantheon, 1968, pp. 10–11; Kerr, Clark., *The Uses of the University*, Cambridge, Mass.: Harvard U.P., 1963.
38 Wolff, R. P., *The Ideal of the University*, Boston: Beacon Press, 1969, p. 40.
39 Shils, E., 'The Intellectuals. I. Great Britain', *Encounter*, April 1955.
40 Perkin, H. J., *op. cit.*, p. 342.
41 Dahrendorf, R., 'Recent Changes in the Class Structure of European Societies', *Daedalus*, Vol. VIIC, No. 1, 1964, p. 225.

11. K. THOMPSON: Church of England bishops as an elite

1 Cf. Anthony Giddens, 'Elites in the British Class Structure', chapter 1, in this volume for a discussion of these three dimensions.
2 Paul Ferris, *The Church of England*, Harmondsworth, Penguin, 1964, p. 85; also quoted in D. H. J. Morgan, 'The Social and Educational Background of Anglican Bishops – Continuities and Changes', in *British Journal of Sociology*, Vol. XX, No. 3, September 1969, pp. 295–310.
3 *The Times*, 1 March 1973.
4 These figures relate to the average age when first made a diocesan bishop for all the English diocesan bishops at five dates. See D. H. J. Morgan, 'The Social and Educational Backgrounds of English Diocesan Bishops in the Church of England 1860–1960', University of Hull, unpublished M.A. thesis, part 3, chapter 2, p. 4.
5 Leslie Paul, *The Deployment and Payment of the Clergy*, London, Church Information Office, 1964, pp. 97–8.
6 The document which reversed previous qualification policies was the Report of a Committee of the Central Advisory Council for the Training of the Ministry, *The Training of Non-Matriculated and Non-Graduate Candidates*, confidentially circulated in 1952. (Cf. Paul, *The Deployment and Payment of the Clergy*, p. 98.)
7 *Social Trends*, London, H.M.S.O., 1970, p. 133.
8 Cf. Morgan, 'The Social and Educational Background of Anglican Bishops – Continuities and Changes', p. 299.
9 Morgan, 'The Social and Educational Background of Anglican Bishops – Continuities and Changes', p. 297.
10 Cf. Paul, *The Deployment and Payment of the Clergy*, p. 277; and Morgan, 'The Social and Educational Background of Anglican Bishops – Continuities and Changes', p. 298. It is worth mentioning, furthermore, that from 1900 to 1960, the percentage of bishops who had attended a public school had been steadily increasing. In the latter half of the nineteenth century it had remained fairly stable, abound 61 % of the schooling of

bishops had been public schools – the rest was probably accounted for by private tuition. The number of bishops who attended schools run by local authorities had been tiny: possibly 2 in the period of 1940–59 and one in the year 1960. (Cf. Morgan, 'The Social and Educational Backgrounds of English Diocesan Bishops in the Church of England 1860–1960', part 2, chapter 2, p. 21.)

11 This calculation is based on figures from Anthony Coxon's *Ordinands' Survey*, as quoted in Paul, *The Deployment and Payment of the Clergy*, pp. 280–2.
12 Giddens, 'Elites in the British Class Structure'.
13 A. M. Ramsey, Article in *The York Quarterly*, February, 1958.
14 Cf. Kenneth A. Thompson, *Bureaucracy and Church Reform*, Oxford, Oxford University Press, 1970.
15 We will turn to the question of different types of authority and power in the final section. Cf. also Thompson, *Bureaucracy and Church Reform*.
16 Cf. Thompson, *Bureaucracy and Church Reform*, chapter 7.
17 Leslie S. Hunter (ed.), *The English Church: A New Look*, Harmondsworth, Penguin, 1966, p. 81.
18 Hunter, *The English Church: A New Look*, p. 76.
19 *The Times*, 3 March 1973.
20 Thompson, *Bureaucracy and Church Reform*, p. 243.

12. J. REX: **Capitalism, elites and the ruling class**

1 Anthony Giddens: 'Elites in the British class structure', chapter 1 in this volume.
2 Idem: 'Elites', *New Society*, Vol. XXII, No. 528, 16 November 1972, pp. 389–92.
3 *Ibid.*, p. 392.
4 Christopher J. Hewitt: 'Elites and the distribution of power in Britain'.
5 R. E. Pahl and J. T. Winkler: 'The economic elite: theory and practice'.
6 C. Wright Mills: *The Power Elite*, New York, 1959.
7 Ralf Dahrendorf: *Class and Class Conflict in Industrial Society*, London, 1961.
8 Especially in the school of Louis Althusser. See Louis Althusser: *For Marx*, London, 1971. The same problem is raised in a wider frame of reference in David Lockwood: 'Social integration and system integration' in George Zollschan and Walter Hirsch: *Explorations in Social Change*, London, 1964.
9 We speak throughout this paper of 'elite educational institutions' as a matter of convenience. In so doing we do not, however, wish to beg the question and simply assume that elites emanate only or primarily from these institutions.
10 Philip Stanworth and Anthony Giddens: 'An economic elite: a demographic profile of company chairmen', chapter 5 in this volume.
11 Max Weber: *Economy and Society*, Vol. II, Chapter, 9, New York, 1968.
12 Michalina Vaughan and Margaret Scotford Archer: *Social Conflict and Educational Change in England and France, 1789–1848*, Cambridge, 1971.
13 See Joseph Marie de Maistre: *Considerations on France* (*1796*), *Essays on the Generative Principle of Political Constitutions* (1814).
14 Anthony Crosland: *The Future of Socialism*, London, 1953.
15 Sir Michael Swann's intervention to apologise to M.P.s who were insulted by their studio audience during a televised discussion, without reference to the producers, showed a remarkable failure to understand the necessity of ruling with the consent and aid of those in the middle levels of power.

Index